The
1994-95
HOCKEY
ANNUAL

BOB McKENZIE & MURRAY TOWNSEND

The 1994-95 HOCKEY ANNUAL

Warwick Publishing Inc.
Toronto   Los Angeles

© 1994 Warwick Publishing

Published by the Warwick Publishing Group
Warwick Publishing, Inc., 24 Mercer Street, Toronto, Ontario M5V 1H3
Warwick Publishing Inc. 1300 N. Alexandria, Los Angeles, California 90027

Front cover photograph: Bruce Bennett
Cover design: Nick Pitt
Text design: Jacqueline Lealess

ISBN 1-895629-34-9

Distributed in the United States and Canada by:
Firefly Books Ltd.
250 Sparks Avenue
Willowdale, Ontario
M2H 2S4

Printed and bound in Canada by Webcom

Publisher's Note

What an insane amount of work this book is. The space between the NHL draft in late June and our press date in early August is about five weeks. In that time everything comes together — the entire manuscript plus all design. Compounding this tight schedule is the fact that the NHL has no rest over the summer; the trading doesn't take two weeks off for our typesetter.

Last year Bob McKenzie compiled the entire manuscript himself — a Herculean task that dealt his summer a fatal blow. As a well-known hockey analyst, Bob's time from mid-September until someone kisses the Cup nine months later is constrained to say the least — he could be in Pittsburgh or Dallas tomorrow — meaning that his summer off takes on an increased importance. Adding this book to the mix proved too much to accomplish two years running.

At Bob's suggestion, we brought a second author aboard. His choice was Murray Townsend, who, as the back cover suggests, is a freelance sports writer who contributes frequently to the Toronto Sun and the Financial Post.

What the bio doesn't mention is that Murray is one of the best stat-crunchers in the business. The hockey world is increasingly looking at statistical analysis to offer meaningful insight into a team's or a player's performance. Murray's dexterous handling of such numbers puts him on the leading edge of this search.

The result is a book filled with the sort of dead-on McKenzie analysis of draft selections and bottom-line performance expectations that you've come to expect from last year's edition of *The Hockey Annual*, plus an increased emphasis on fascinating, quick-reference numbers.

This book is fast-paced and, at times, brutally honest — just what we need in this anything-goes age of parity in the NHL.

So, keep it near the TV or radio as the best, fastest and most accurate handbook for the season — and enjoy!

Contents

Introduction

Welcome to the cut-throat NHL.

Now that parity has arrived in a big way, so too has a mercenary spirit.

So many teams believe they are so close to being able to win the Stanley Cup, that they are doing anything and everything possible to make it happen.

That, along with the increasing economic pressures of pro sports in the '90s, accounts for an unusually large number of big names switching teams, and perhaps the balance of power, too.

Al MacInnis is a Blue. Phil Housley a Flame. Mats Sundin a Leaf. Wendel Clark a Nordique. Wendel a Nordique? Believe it. Bob Probert a Blackhawk. Maybe...On and on it goes.

The upheaval even extends to the front office. Mike Keenan perpetrated one of the boldest moves ever when he declared himself a free agent and bolted the New York Rangers for the Blues.

In today's NHL, all protestations to the contrary, everyone is looking out for himself.

That said, last season was one of the league's best, on and off the ice. The thrilling playoff run that culminated with the Rangers knocking off the Vancouver Canucks in seven games took the game to a new level in the hearts and minds of fans and non-fans alike and the NHL got some long overdue recognition from the U.S. non-hockey media and public.

The success the league enjoyed in the sun belt — Miami, Tampa, Dallas, Anaheim and San Jose — bodes well for the game's future. And as clichéd as it may sound, any one of a dozen or more clubs do have legitimate shots to win it all.

If nothing else, the NHL has momentum going for it. It should pick right up where it left off — unless, of course, the nasty business of negotiating a new collective bargaining agreement intrudes.

With no contract in place, the possibility of a strike or a lockout must be considered as real, although both sides have a lot to lose by calling one or the other.

If it should happen that labor strife does intrude upon the game — again — it will come as no surprise.

It's the cut-throat NHL, after all.

—Bob McKenzie
August 1994

The Top 10 NHL Players by Position

GOALTENDERS

1. PATRICK ROY, Montreal Canadiens

Roy didn't make the first or second all-star team this year. That's because two other goalies came through with phenomenal seasons. That's okay, because every season is a great one for Roy.

He's been a first team all-star on three occasions and made the second team two other times. He's also won the Vezina Trophy three times and the Conn Smythe Trophy as the most valuable player in the playoffs, twice.

Year in, year out, there's nobody better. And nobody that you'd want in your net more if the playoffs were starting tomorrow.

Roy has already punched his ticket to the Hockey Hall of Fame. Whatever he does from now on is just gravy.

2. DOMINIK HASEK, Buffalo Sabres

Based on last season's play, there was no better goalie in the league. He won the Vezina Trophy, was voted a first team all-star and was second in the Hart most valuable player voting.

The 29-year-old with the lightning-quick reflexes was the first netminder since Bernie Parent in 1973-74 to earn a goals against average under 2.00. Along with his 1.95 GAA, he had a save percentage of .930, which also led the league.

The strange thing about Hasek is that he was never supposed to be a number one goalie. He was a backup in Chicago to Belfour and was inked in as the relief man for Fuhr in Buffalo. All he needed was a chance to show his stuff and with Fuhr down with injuries he got it.

3. JOHN VANBIESBROUCK, Florida Panthers

It's scary to think where the expansion Florida Panthers would have been without him. His goals against average of 2.53 was fourth best last year and his save percentage of .924 was second.

His motivation last year stemmed from the fact that the Rangers chose to keep Mike Richter over him. They knew they'd lose one of them in the expansion draft, so Vanbiesbrouck was shipped to Vancouver, whose interest was in protecting the two goalies they already had.

You can't say the Rangers were wrong in letting him go because Richter had a great year, but still it's not much fun to get tossed around like yesterday's newspaper.

Vanbiesbrouck showed them all.

4. BILL RANFORD, Edmonton Oilers

At various stages of his career, Ranford has been called one of the best two or three goalies in the world.

It's pretty tough to measure his effectiveness on a team that doesn't provide any protection, but put him on a decent squad and you'd probably have a perennial first or second all-star.

5. FELIX POTVIN, Toronto Maple Leafs

Expectations are so high for Potvin that anything below unbelievable is considered a disappointment. Last year he had some off-times where his concentration didn't appear to be at its highest. He started giving up some easy goals and didn't stand on his head every game.

Big deal. He's still only 23 years old, he's allowed a little down time. When he's on, watch out because nothing gets

by him that wouldn't get by any of the other best goalies in the league.

6. CURTIS JOSEPH, St. Louis Blues

The cheese stands alone. Just like Curtis Joseph in the St. Louis nets last season.

He faced an average of 35 shots per 60 minutes in the nightly shooting gallery and still came out a winner. His record in the nets was 36-23-11. Otherwise it was just 4-10.

His .911 save percentage was more than just a call for help. It was one of the best in the league, even more impressive because on poor defensive teams the quality of the shots opponents are allowed is better.

With Mike Keenan running things now, Joseph will get some help. Don't be surprised if he's a first team all-star.

7. ED BELFOUR, Chicago Blackhawks

For the third straight season, Belfour was either tied or leading the league in shutouts. He's had 19 over the three seasons.

Belfour is always among the league leaders in everything. And he has his share of rough times. But those are balanced out by stretches where he is unbeatable.

The knock against him is that he's not a playoff goalie. That's the same rap on every veteran who hasn't won a Stanley Cup.

In other words, it doesn't have much merit.

8. KIRK MCLEAN, Vancouver Canucks

You'd probably expect him to be ranked higher if you were just using last year's playoffs as a guide. And he would be too, if that were the only criteria.

But, he didn't have a great regular season. In fact, he had a losing record and his goals against average was only 20th among qualifying goaltenders.

9. ARTURS IRBE, San Jose Sharks

The Sharks probably wouldn't have even made the playoffs last year if it weren't for Irbe.

His forays outside of the net were humourous at times, but that's partly the result of learning the game on the big European ice surface, where they don't have to handle the puck very often.

Last season, it was hard not to wonder when the magic was going to end. He couldn't possibly keep up that type of hot goaltending over an entire season.

He did, and into the playoffs as well.

10. MIKE RICHTER, NY Rangers

It was Richter's first crack at being the undisputed number one goalie and he responded well, finishing fifth overall in goals against average and piling up a 42-12-6 record, one of the best winning percentages in the history of the NHL. When he wasn't the goalie of record, the team was just 10-12.

It always helps a goalie to play on a Mike Keenan coached team because there's more defensive help. Some criticize Keenan's quick hook, saying it hurts goaltenders' confidence, but there's no evidence to suggest it hurts their effectiveness.

DEFENCEMEN

1. RAY BOURQUE, Boston Bruins

The most amazing thing about Bourque is that he's been in the league 15 years and has been a first or second all-star every single one of them. Nobody else in the history of the NHL can claim such an accomplishment.

Only Gordie Howe, with 21, has more overall all-star selections.

Bourque also collected his fifth Norris Trophy last season and moved up to eighth place among all-time career assist earners.

The 11th Commandment states: Thou shalt not compare anyone to Bobby Orr.

Bourque tempts us a lot of us into being sinners.

2. SCOTT STEVENS, New Jersey Devils

He's the whole package: offence, defence, and physical play. Stevens was a first team all-star for the second time last season and missed by a very narrow margin beating out Bourque for the Norris Trophy.

The second half of last season was especially good for Stevens. After scoring 29 points in the first half, he cranked it up and scored 49 in the second.

3. BRIAN LEETCH, NY Rangers

The Conn Smythe winner and second team all-star can be counted on mostly for his offence, but he can contribute defensively as well.

The former Norris trophy winner led all playoff scorers last season with 34 points after earning 79 during the regular season.

His prowess on the power play is especially notable. He earned 53 points with the man-advantage during the regular season, second only to Wayne Gretzky.

4. AL MACINNIS, St. Louis Blues

With MacInnis playing the point, it makes a team's power play strategy simple: just find a way to get him the puck.

MacInnis possesses the hardest shot in the NHL (give or take an Iafrate) and scored 28 goals last season, the sixth time he's passed the 20 goal mark.

It will be a big change for the 31 year old after spending all of his career in Calgary. He was a free agent with compensation last season and tested the market, finding the money suitable in St. Louis. Technically, he was traded there, with the two teams working out a deal to avoid compensation proceedings.

Opposing goalies won't have much fun next year with both him and Hull (unless he's traded) firing at them on the power play.

5. CHRIS CHELIOS, Chicago Blackhawks

Some call him the dirtiest player in the NHL, but on three occasions he's also been called the best defenseman in the league.

He'll hurt you with his offence, his defence, and yes, sometimes with his stick. A guy everbody hates unless he's on their team. Then they love him.

6. PAUL COFFEY, Detroit Red Wings

The NHL's all-time defenseman leader will be 33 years old when he starts the season. You wouldn't be able to tell it from his skating, though. He's still one of the smoothest and fastest ever to play the game.

So, he's no prize on defense. Neither is Wayne Gretzky. A sure Hall-of-Famer.

7. ROB BLAKE, Los Angeles Kings

Blake's main contribution is with his offense where he scored a career-high 68 points last season. But, the 6-3, 215 pounder also knows how to use his size to advantage.

Some have predicted a Norris Trophy for Blake. It could happen. Maybe sooner than later.

8. SERGEI ZUBOV, NY Rangers

Although it's questionable whether or not he's really a defenseman, you can't ignore 89 points, leading the Stanley Cup winning Rangers during the regular season.

Sure, he's all over the ice, and isn't good defensively, but, when you're in the other team's end most of the game and you can handle the puck like him, it more than makes up for it.

9. AL IAFRATE, Boston Bruins

Iafrate is one of the most talented players in the NHL. He has all the tools - great shot, great skater, good toughness, great puck carrier.

His only problem is that he's not all of those things every night. If the Wild Thing ever does manage to do them all over an entire season, you can inscribe his name on the Norris Trophy.

10. DEFENSIVE DEFENSEMEN

These guys don't get the recognition they deserve often enough, because we can't measure their contribution with statistics. Most of the time, only the people that play with them, or against them, know their true value. Some of those type players are Sylvain Lefebvre, Craig Muni, Bobby Dollas, Craig Ludwig, Kjell Samuelsson, Ulf Samuelsson, and Joe Reekie, just to name a few.

CENTRE

1. MARIO LEMIEUX, Pittsburgh Penguins

When he's healthy there's no debate, he's the best in the game. There's no need to go into any explanation and don't even bother arguing.

Unfortunately, the health part is the big problem. As of this writing, he was considering sitting out the season.

2. SERGEI FEDOROV, Detroit Red Wings

Fedorov finished only 10 points behind Gretzky in the scoring race and 73 goals ahead in the plus/minus stat.

There's not much more a forward can do than Fedorov accomplished last season: his 120 points were second behind Gretzky; he won the Hart Trophy as the league's most valuable player; and took home the Selke Trophy as the best defensive forward.

3. WAYNE GRETZKY, Los Angeles Kings

Gretzky won the scoring title for about the zillionth time last season, earned a spot on the second all-star team behind Fedorov, and set the all-time goal scoring record.

Everybody keeps waiting for signs that the 33-year-old is nearing the end of the road. While he's not the dominant player he was in his prime, no dead-end sign has been posted yet.

The chances aren't good that we'll ever see a major dive in Gretzky efficiency, like we do with many of the superstars in all sports. If he thinks it's going, he'll be gone. The best centre in the history of the game, and perhaps the best player period, has nothing left to prove.

4. ERIC LINDROS, Philadelphia Flyers

This year or next, Lindros is going to lead the league in scoring and become the dominant player that was predicted of him since he could spell his name. If you project his totals over the games played in his first two years he's already had two 100 point seasons.

If he can stay injury-free, nobody is going to be anywhere near him. This year's scoring champ.

5. DOUG GILMOUR, Toronto Maple Leafs

If these rankings were for the best all-round player, you could put Gilmour right up there at the top along with Fedorov.

Gilmour is Mr. Everything to the Toronto Maple Leafs. He comes to play every single game. Every one of them. And probably means more to his team than any other player in the league.

Gilmour was fourth in Hart Trophy voting last season and second in Selke Trophy balloting.

An amazing thing about Gilmour is that despite how well he plays during the regular season, he gets even better in the playoffs. Last year, despite the fact that Toronto were knocked out in

the conference finals, his 28 points were fourth best in the post-season.

6. JEREMY ROENICK, Chicago Blackhawks

Another player who means everything to his team. He's had three 100 point plus seasons in a row, two 50 goals seasons, two 40 goal campaigns, and he's still only 24 years old.

Roenick is a guy you can depend on to show up every night, physically as well as mentally. He hasn't missed a game in three seasons, and in five full years in the league, he's missed just three.

7. STEVE YZERMAN, Detroit Red Wings

Yzerman only played 58 games last season due to injury. He still earned 82 points. That projects to a total of 119, which would have been good enough for third best in the league.

In fact, Yzerman outscored Fedorov in the second half of the season, 58 to 46, and was fourth overall in the league.

But, Fedorov is now the number one centre in Detroit, so there have been trade rumours swirling around Yzerman. Any team in the league would be delighted to get him.

In the six seasons prior to last year he averaged 122 points. Over his career he has 1,122 points. He's still only 29 years old, so give him a couple more years and he will probably move up to the all-time top ten in scoring.

8. MARK MESSIER, New York Rangers

Messier moved into ninth place on the all-time scoring list last year and strengthened his hold as the number two all-time playoff scorer.

Throw in heart, determination, leadership and everthing else that goes along with being a winner and you come out with one of the all-time greats.

Oh yeah, and he has six Stanley Cup rings. Not bad.

9. ADAM OATES, Boston Bruins

If you combined everybody's scoring over the past two seasons, Oates would be the leader with 257.

The 32 year old has scored at least 100 points in each of his last five seasons except for one. That year he got 99.

Oates is mostly a playmaker, but he can also score goals himself. He doesn't need anybody special on the wings; whomever it is, he makes them special.

10. RON FRANCIS, Pittsburgh Penguins

After Fedorov and Gilmour, Francis is the most complete player of the bunch. A fine defensive type, he's also called up often to handle the number one centre role on the Penguins with Lemieux injured so often.

In fact, he seems to thrive under the responsibility, coming up with two of his best seasons the last two years. Ninety-three points last year, and 100 the season before.

LEFT WINGERS

1. BRENDAN SHANAHAN, St. Louis Blues

For many years, the right side has been the glamour wing in the NHL. Most of the big scorers that weren't playing in the middle were right wingers.

On left wing was Luc Robitaille and Kevin Stevens. Things have changed. Left wingers have come into their own in a big way. It's almost as if it's become the power forward position. Big, physical guys who can put the puck in the net.

Nobody exemplifies that better than Shanahan - 52 goals, 102 points, 211 penalty minutes.

2. ADAM GRAVES, New York Rangers

When Adam Graves was scoring seven goals for Edmonton just a couple years ago, he was still a valuable defensive type.

Now that he's scoring over 50 goals, that defensive ability just makes him that much more valuable. And a second team all-star selection.

His 52 goals last season were twice as many as any other Ranger.

3. GARY ROBERTS, Calgary Flames

Yet another power forward left winger. He can score, he can check, play defense, hit, and fight. That just about says it all.

Roberts doesn't shoot as often as some, but when he does there's a one in five chance it's going in the net. He had the best shooting percentage (20.3%) of anybody in the league with at least 200 shots.

4. KEVIN STEVENS, Pittsburgh Penguins

Hey, guess what? Another power forward left-winger. It was an off year for Stevens coming back from a serious injury. But, if an off-year is 41 goals and 88 points, it's still better than most.

For the first time in four years, Stevens didn't make the first or second all-star team. Don't be surprised if he's back this year.

5. DAVE ANDREYCHUK, Toronto Maple Leafs

Andreychuk has always been a good scorer but he didn't become a great one until he got to Toronto. Two years ago, when went over from Buffalo, he scored 54 goals and 99 points. Last year, his first full season in a Maple Leaf uniform, he had 53 goals and had 99 points again.

His two best NHL seasons at the ages of 29 and 30. Pretty unusual.

Another thing about Andreychuk is that he performs disappearing acts at times. But, when he's hot, he more than makes up for the absences, often carrying the team for weeks.

6. VINCENT DAMPHOUSSE, Montreal Canadiens

Damphousse sometimes gets off to a slow start and may go through prolonged slumps, but by the end of the year his point production is always up there.

After eight NHL seasons, the 26 year old has passed the 600 mark in career points, has led three different teams in scoring and is still only 26 years old.

Last season, he set a career high with 40 goals and went over the 90 point plateau for the third time.

Much of his career has been spent at center and he does still play there at times. He's also played every game in six of his eight seasons.

7. LUC ROBITAILLE, Pittsburgh Penguins

Robitaille's stock dropped rapidly last year and for the first time in his eight year career he failed to make the all-star team. It's tough to follow-up a season when you score 63 goals. He still potted 43, a more characteristic year for him. He's scored in the forties four times during his career and still was selected an all-star.

The trade to Pittsburgh during the summer was a curious one in that the Kings received a battered and bruised Rick Tocchet in return. Not much for someone with Robitaille's credentials.

8. ROD BRIND'AMOUR, Philadelphia Flyers

He just keeps getting better. Still only 25, he's averaged 87 points in three seasons in Philadelphia after falling out of favor in St. Louis.

Brind'Amour is also a centre, and he may spend more time at this position this year.

9. KEITH TKACHUK, Winnipeg Jets

When almost everybody else on the Jets had crashed and burned, Tkachuk came through with an outstanding season.

Forty-one goals, 40 assists and 255 penalty minutes. Sound familiar? Yup, another power forward.

The big left-winger also played some centre last season, but seems better suited to left wing where he can crash and burn opposing right-wingers.

10. WENDEL CLARK, Quebec Nordiques

If only he could stay healthy. Then, quite possibly he'd be the premier power forward in the bunch.

Last year, he set career highs with 46 goals and 76 points in just 64 games.

The thing is, he's never going to be healthy all the time. so as much as you can get is a bonus.

RIGHT WINGERS

1. PAVEL BURE, Vancouver Canucks

On the excitement scale, the Russian Rocket rates a 10. He's simply the most exciting player in the game today. When he picks up the puck and starts to go, don't blink or you'll miss something. A burst of that unbelievable speed and it's all over.

Bure scored 60 goals last season to lead the league and earned his initial first all-star team selection. It won't be the last.

2. CAM NEELY, Boston Bruins

Neely only played 49 games last season but he scored 50 goals. Projected over 84 games, the goal total works out to 86, not far away from the all-time record of 92 set by Gretzky.

Not many 49 game players get selected to any all-star teams, but Neely earned a second team berth last season. Neely's knees, of course, are his worst enemy. Over the last three seasons, he's only played a total of 71 games.

3. MARK RECCHI, Philadelphia Flyers

There's always a shadow cast on Recchi's abilities because he's played with great players. First, Lemieux in Pittsburgh and now Lindros in Philadelphia.

Forget it, he doesn't need those guys, he's a great scorer in his own right. He just hasn't had a chance to prove it, except when the big guns have been injured. In those situations he not only still holds his own, he plays better to compensate for their loss. Last year, for instance, in the 19 games Lindros didn't play, Recchi had 32 points. Pro-rated over 84 games, it gives him 141 points. That would have led the league scoring race.

But, he's still a good compliment to Lindros now and Lemieux in the past because he's not just a playmaker out on the ice. He can score goals himself with the best of them.

Maybe the most under-rated player in the game today.

4. JAROMIR JAGR, Pittsburgh Penguins

Jagr is still only 22 years old, but he's already had two 90 plus seasons. Each year he's been in the NHL his point production has increased. Last season, he scored 99 points. This year he should go over the century mark.

5. ALEXANDER MOGILNY, Buffalo Sabres

Not a great year for Mogilny, scoring only 32 goals after leading the league with 76 the year before. But, he was coming back from a broken leg and had other problems, only playing 66 games.

Look for a return to form this year, especially with Pat LaFontaine by his side again for the full season.

6. BRETT HULL, St. Louis Blues

Hull has averaged 68 goals over the past five season. The last two years he scored 54 and 57 goals. Funny how that's considered a disappointment. But, when somebody has scored 70, 86 and 70 goals, 50 doesn't seem so wonderful.

But, it is, of course. Hull, who is 30 years old may have slowed down some, but 50 goals is still a major accomplishment.

Hull was still with St. Louis as of this writing, but additional writing on the wall suggested he would be traded. His laid-back style doesn't mesh with new coach Mike Keenan. He admits it himself and would like a trade, preferably to Los Angeles so he could play with Gretzky.

7. TREVOR LINDEN, Vancouver Canucks

Linden is also a center and may in fact be more suited to that position without another dominant pivot in Vancouver.

In six NHL seasons, the 24 year old has scored 30, 21, 33, 31, 33 and 32 goals. That's consistency. But, he brings much more to the party than just goals. He's rugged, tenacious, and gives the Stanley Cup finalists good leadership.

Maybe Linden hasn't scored as often as people predicted when he was the second choice overall in the 1988 draft, but don't be shocked if pots 50 one of these days.

8. THEOREN FLEURY, Calgary Flames

This little guy just keeps on going and going.... The 5-6, 160 pounder makes up for his lack of size with great determination and feistiness. He earned 186 penalty minutes last season to go along with 40 goals and 85 points. The 26 year old has a 50 goal season to his credit and has had two 100 point years.

9. TEEMU SELANNE, Winnipeg Jets

Seventy-six goals and 132 points is no accident. Selanne went through the sophomore jinx last season and also had some injury problems, slumping to 25 goals and 54 points in 51 games. He'll be back.

10. RAY SHEPPARD, Detroit Red Wings

Don't expect anything fancy, but who cares when you score 50 goals. After a great 38 goal rookie season, Sheppard's value dropped steadily over the next couple years to the point where he was a free agent without demand. The Red Wings took a chance and have never regretted it.

EASTERN
CONFERENCE

EASTERN CONFERENCE
PREDICTED ORDER OF FINISH

1. NEW JERSEY
2. NEW YORK RANGERS
3. QUEBEC
4. PITTSBURGH
5. MONTREAL
6. BUFFALO
7. BOSTON
8. WASHINGTON
9. PHILADELPHIA
10. FLORIDA
11. NEW YORK ISLANDERS
12. HARTFORD
13. TAMPA BAY
14. OTTAWA

Boston Bruins

There are two things Boston fans can count on every season. One is that some defenseman, somewhere, will be compared to their very own Bobby Orr. The other is that the Bruins will make the playoffs.

Twenty-seven consecutive seasons in the post-season, the longest streak in NHL history. Remarkable.

The bad news, of course, is that the Bruins haven't won a Stanley Cup since 1972. Then again, neither have 18 other NHL teams.

By design, there's no such thing as a rebuilding year in Boston. They just have all sorts of little works-in-progress. Eventually, they're added to the main frame or else sent to the scrap yard, and new projects are started.

Harry Sinden likes to bring up young players at the end of the season, give them a little taste of NHL action, and then throw them into the heat of the playoffs.

The Bruins regularly have the most, or near the most, rookies in their playoff lineup.

Last year, for example, Mariusz Czerkawski and Fred Knipscheer both had more playoff games than regular season contests. The year before, Bryan Smolinski followed a few regular season games with a full playoff slate. The year before that, it was the same thing with Joe Juneau, Ted Donato, Glen Murray, Gord Hynes and Stephen Heinze.

The individuals respond to this sort of treatment. But does the team?

It would be hard to imagine it helping out team unity and cohesiveness when players who have toughed it out over the long regular season suddenly see their jobs disappear a few games before the playoffs. Those who remain might question whether or not the new player lining up beside them has earned the opportunity to be there, all the while knowing his buddy up in the press box most certainly had.

Then again, maybe we should wait until Sinden has had a losing season (22 years as GM) before we start telling him what he's doing wrong.

1993-94 REGULAR SEASON AT A GLANCE

RECORD: 42-29-13, 97 points

FINISH: 2nd in Northeast, 4th in Eastern Conference

HOME: 20-14-8 (11th)

AWAY: 22-15-5 (2nd)

OVERTIME: 2-2-13 (13th-t)

VS OWN DIVISION: 14-13-4

VS OTHER DIVISIONS: 28-16-9

VS OWN CONFERENCE: 31-20-9

VS OTHER CONFERENCE: 11-9-4

FIRST HALF RECORD: 19-15-8

SECOND HALF RECORD: 23-14-5

GOALS FOR: 289 (8th)

GOALS AGAINST: 252 (10th)

TEAM PLUS/MINUS: +11 (11th)

POWER PLAY: 21.7% (3rd)

PENALTY KILLING: 84.7% (1st)

PENALTY MINUTES: 17.2/game (2nd)

1993-94 REGULAR SEASON LEADERS

GOALS: 50, Cam Neely

ASSISTS: 80, Adam Oates

POINTS: 112, Adam Oates

POWER PLAY GOALS: 20, Cam Neely

SHORTHANDED GOALS: 3, Ray Bourque, Bryan Smolinski

PLUS-MINUS: +29, Don Sweeney

SHOTS: 386, Ray Bourque

PENALTY MINUTES: 152, Glen Featherstone

1993-94 PLAYOFFS AT A GLANCE

RESULTS: Conference Quarterfinals — beat Montreal 4-3 **Conference Semifinals** — lost to New Jersey 4-2

RECORD: 6-7

HOME: 2-5

AWAY: 4-2 Goals for: 3.0/game

OVERTIME: 3.2/game

POWER PLAY: 18.5% (5th)

PENALTY KILLING: 78.4% (12th)

PENALTY MINUTES: 12.9/game (1st)

1993-94 PLAYOFF LEADERS

GOALS: 5, Smolinski

ASSISTS: 9, Oates

POINTS: 12, Oates

POWER PLAY GOALS: 2, Smolinski, Oates, Donato

SHORTHANDED GOALS: 1, Dave Reid

OVERTIME GOALS: None

GAME-WINNING GOALS: 1, Brent Hughes, Al Iafrate, David Shaw

PENALTY MINUTES: 27, Hughes

PLUS-MINUS: +6, Hughes

SHOTS: 64, Bourque

A LOOK AHEAD TO 1994-95

GOAL: It's not often that a goalie who has a 30-15-9 regular season record, a 2.87 GAA, four shutouts, and a 2.92 playoff GAA is offered a termination contract. But that's exactly what happened to Jon Casey.

So, what was the problem? For starters, he only faced an average of 24 shots per game and his save percentage of .881 was one of the worst among regular goalies in the league.

Let's put that into perspective. Let's say his save percentage was up there, but not quite as good as the leaders, Dominik Hasek and John Vanbiesbrouck. A .920 save percentage with the number of shots he faced would have given him a GAA of 1.94, best in the league, and almost a full goal less than than the GAA he actually recorded. Even an average save percentage of .900 would have cut half a goal a game off his average.

Maybe more than that, it was his inconsistency and the lack of confidence he inspired that sealed his fate. In his first four starts in April, he was pulled from three of them.

Casey signed with St. Louis, where he will backup Curtis Joseph.

The Bruins want more than capable. They're looking for THE goalie.

It isn't John Blue, who also lost Brownie points and visited the minors, and it isn't Vincent Riendeau, who could probably handle the back-up role quite nicely. There seems to be some hope for Joakim Persson, who came over from Sweden at the end of his season and played 24 scoreless minutes with Providence, but he'll need more North American experience.

Right now, the Bruins don't have a number one goalie, a situation that should be rectified in training camp. They signed free agent Blaine Lacher from Lake Superior State and used their first round draft selection to take Yevgeni Ryabchikov from Russia.

DEFENCE: Easily the best defence in the NHL with the puck, and probably one of the best without it.

Nobody can compare with the Bruins top four — Ray Bourque, Al Iafrate, Glen Wesley and Don Sweeney. Between them, they earned 228 points last season, an average of 57 each. Fifteen NHL teams didn't even have one defenseman with that many points.

The battle is on for the remaining two regular spots. There is dependable David Shaw, Paul Stanton, the ageless Gordie Roberts and Glen Featherstone who gives the group some muscle. Thirty-four year old free agent Alexei Kasatonov was also signed as insurance.

Waiting in the wings is John Gruden, who provides yet more scoring promise. He signed with the team after a successful collegiate career at Ferris State. He led CCHA defensemen in scoring (11-25-36 in 38 games), was named the league's top defenseman and was second in the most valuable player voting.

FORWARD: If Cam Neely had played 84 games last season, his pro-rated total would have been 86 goals. Cam Neely is never going to play 84 games, however, so they'll take what they can get from one of the best right wingers in the business. Fifty goals in 49 games will do just fine.

Adam Oates is one of the best playmakers in the league, and at 34 years of age, is coming off his best two NHL seasons. Bryan Smolinski had an excellent rookie year, and Ted Donato a good sophomore season.

After that, we have potential, question marks, inconsistency, and curiosity.

Most of the younger players had their problems last year:ë Glen Murray, the heir apparent to Neely on right wing, scored 18 goals, but none in the first 18 games; Cam Stewart had a 26 game pointless streak and was dispatched to the minors; Josef Stumpel didn't make an impact and was sent to Providence, only to be recalled later, where he did show something; Stephen Heinze was pointless in his first 18 games; Kvartalnov was...well, Kvartalnov; Sergei Zholtok, Andrew McKim and Grigori Panteleev all had their chances but couldn't find the net. The Bruins, were, however, doing backflips over flambuoyant Polish product, RW Mariusz Czerkawski (pronounced cher-KOFF-skee). He joined the Bruins late in the season after playing in Sweden and had three points in four games. In the playoffs, he had six points in 13 games.

The Bruins love Europeans. Any Europeans. They've failed miserably in this area, but still they keep on trying. Vladimir Ruzicka, Kvartalnov, and others have proven that their offensive only style isn't suited to the Bruins or Boston Garden.

The latest signee is Mikko Makela, who's already an established dud in the NHL. After a 36 goal season with the Islanders in 1987-88, he had years of 17, 9, and 15, before returning to Finland in 1991.

Well, when he doesn't work out, there's always Vladimir Krutov.

SPECIAL TEAMS: Cam Neely on the power play is about as good as it gets. Even when he's not around, though, top-of-the-line point men like Bourque, Iafrate and Wesley can move the puck around with the best of them. Bourque had 52 power play points, one behind Brian Leetch of the Rangers among defensemen. The Bruins ranked third in the league with the man advantage last season

The penalty killing was also excellent, somewhat of a Bruin tradition. They ranked first last season, and have ranked in the top eight in 21 of the last 25 years. Could have something to do with the small rink in Boston and knowing how to use it.

Besides allowing only 58 goals on the power play (tied with Buffalo) the Bruins also scored 17, for a net of just 41. Not bad for a full season's work.

COACHING: If Brian Sutter makes it through the season it will be an accomplishment. Not because he isn't a good coach, but because coaches don't last long in Boston. That's another Bruin tradition under Harry Sinden.

MANAGEMENT: Somehow, the Bruins always come up smelling like roses. Sinden sees, he assesses, he makes the deals he needs to, he develops young players, and the team makes the playoffs. Simple, eh?

Sixty-two year old Sinden needed a new assistant and possible successor after Mike Milbury left to coach Boston College. Curiously, though, Milbury quit that job almost as soon as he got it. Mike O'Connell, who played 13 NHL seasons, moves up in the organization to take the job.

TEAM NEEDS: Youth on the forward lines to come through, and a number one goalie to come through.

POTENTIAL NEW FACES: Most new players get an audition the previous season. That means players like Fred Knipscheer, Mariusz Czercawski, and John Gruden could be regulars this season. Others: G Yevgeni Ryabchikov (Russia), G Blaine Lacher, Lake Superior State.

McKENZIE'S BOTTOM LINE: This is supposed to be Harry Sinden's last year as GM of the Bruins. If so, his swan song could end on a sour note.

This Bruin team looks like an accident waiting to happen.

Start with goaltending. It's impossible to imagine the Bruins starting the year with a No. 1 goaltender of Russian Evgeny Ryabchikov or collegian Blaine Lacher or veteran retread Vincent Riendeau. Unless there's a trade for an established netminder (Glenn Healy, Grant Fuhr etc.), though, that's a possibility.

The Bruins had bad goaltending last season. It could be worse this year.

On defence, Ray Bourque shows no signs of slowing up despite his advancing years. He is truly a marvel, a physical specimen. Heaven help the Bruins if Bourque wakes up one morning and realizes how many miles are on his chassis. As long as Al Iafrate has his head screwed on, or at least

reasonably fastened to his body, the Bruins have some decent insurance there, although in the big picture they lack depth.

Up front, the B's still rely too heavily on a couple of players — centre Adam Oates and right winger Cam Neely. The latter, though, is coming off yet more knee surgery and it remains to be seen what level he can get back to. The emergence of Bryan Smolinski as a credible NHL centre helps, but the Boston offence will miss Joey Juneau.

One could argue these worries are nothing new, that the Bruins always look as though they're not long for this world. And then they go out and make the playoffs going away with a better than .500 record. And that will probably happen again this year, too, but it says here it might not.

And with each passing day toward Sinden's retirement, the Bruins seem one step closer to an eventual disaster — a sub. 500 season and/or missing the playoffs.

DRAFT PICKS

Of all the choices made on draft day 1994, perhaps none was more shocking than the Boston Bruins' first-round selection of Russian goaltender Evgeny Ryabchikov.

The 20-year-old was the third of four goalies chosen in the first round, being taken after Jamie Storr (L.A.) and Eric Fichaud (Toronto) but before highly-touted Dan Cloutier (N.Y. Rangers). The Bruins fervently believe they got the best goaltender in the draft, though they admitted they based much of their decision the goalie's efforts at the 1994 world junior championships in the Czech Republic. In fact, GM Harry Sinden's only exposure to Ryabchikov was via videotape.

Unlike the vast majority of North American goaltenders, who play the patented Patrick Roy butterfly style, or flop a la Ed Belfour, Ryabchikov is a strict stand-up style goalie. Whether that translates into immediate NHL success, which is another reason the Bruins took a 20-year-old goalie, remains to be seen. Consider it a huge gamble, especially when you consider the Bruins' lack of depth and experience at the position.

The Bruins picked up a decent power winger prospect in the second round with Laval's Daniel Goneau, who in time may be able to bang in the NHL and score a few goals, too.

1993-94 KEYS

KEY DEALS:

* Obtained Al Iafrate from Washington for Joe Juneau.

* Obtained Vincent Riendeau from Detroit for a provisional 5th round 1995 draft pick.

KEY INJURIES: Joe Juneau, broken jaw before traded; Cam Neely (32 games), Steve Leach (42 games), David Shaw (27 games).

KEY STAT:

Most consecutive seasons in the playoffs - NHL history

Team	Years	Seasons
Boston Bruins	1968 - 1994	27 *
Chicago Blackhawks	1970 - 1994	25 *
Montreal Canadiens	1971 - 1994	24 *
Montreal Canadiens	1949 - 1969	21
Detroit Red Wings	1939 - 1958	20
Philadelphia Flyers	1973 - 1989	17
Atlanta-Calgary Flames	1976 - 1991	16
St. Louis Blues	1980 - 1994	15 *
Toronto Maple Leafs	1931 - 1945	15
NY Islanders	1975 - 1988	14
Edmonton Oilers	1980 - 1992	13

* streak is current

Buffalo Sabres

The Buffalo Sabres 1993-94 season was a disaster. For, oh, about the first nine games.

As the odds against them improving got longer and longer, the team just got better and better.

The Sabres started off with a 1-7-1 record, and in their first six games at home had the same winning percentage as the Buffalo Bills in the Super Bowl.

It didn't help that Alexander Mogilny was out of the lineup still recovering from the broken ankle he suffered the previous season. But, the real culprit was a weak defence, and get this, inconsistent goaltending. After those first nine games, only four teams had worse goals against averages.

By the end of the season, 25 teams were below them in the goaltending department.

Buffalo was 42-25-8 after the bad start, and at home were 25-9-2 after losing their first six.

There were two big factors in the Sabre turnaround. One, of course, was the emergence of Dominik Hasek as perhaps the league's premier goaltender, and the other was the introduction of a new style of play as dictated by coach/GM John Muckler.

All this was accomplished with a potentially devestating number of injuries to key players. The worst was to Pat LaFontaine. He tore the anterior cruciate ligament in his right knee, and was gone for the season after just 16 games. Craig Simpson missed 61 games with back problems, Petr Svoboda, Mogilny, Grant Fuhr, Yuri Khmylev, Wayne Presley, and Bob Sweeney all missed more than a dozen games with injuries.

Buffalo could have folded up the tent and gone home, and no one would have blamed them. That the Sabres could play as well as they did is some kind of minor miracle.

Oddly enough, it is quite possible that all the injuries served to make the team better. Without their superstar, LaFontaine, a new defensive style was devised, and the result was that they played more like a team. They couldn't wait for the big gun to go off so they had to fire themselves.

With Mogilny also missing extensive time, there wasn't much point trying to shoot the lights out in the other teams' ends, so they took care of things in the neutral and defensive zones. And it worked very well.

1993-94 REGULAR SEASON AT A GLANCE

RECORD: 43-32-9

FINISH: 4th in Northeast Division, 6th in Eastern Conference, 10th overall.

HOME: 22-17-3 (13th)

AWAY: 21-15-6 (4th)

OVERTIME: 0-4-9 (26th)

VS OWN DIVISION: 19-9-3

VS OTHER DIVISIONS: 24-23-6

VS OWN CONFERENCE: 28-26-6

VS OTHER CONFERENCE: 15-6-3

FIRST HALF RECORD: 20-18-4

SECOND HALF RECORD: 23-14-5

GOALS FOR: 282 (11th)

GOALS AGAINST: 218 (1st)

TEAM PLUS/MINUS: +26 (5th)

POWER PLAY: 22.6% (2nd)

PENALTY KILLING: 84.7% (2nd)

PENALTY MINUTES: 21.0/game (13th)

1993-94 REGULAR SEASON LEADERS

GOALS: 35, Dale Hawerchuk

ASSISTS: 51, Hawerchuk

POINTS: 86, Hawerchuk

POWER PLAY GOALS: 17, Alexander Mogilny

SHORTHANDED GOALS: 5, Wayne Presley

GAME WINNING GOALS: 7, Mogilny, Hawerchuk

PLUS-MINUS: +31, Craig Muni

SHOTS: 258, Mogilny

PENALTY MINUTES: 274, Rob Ray

1993-94 PLAYOFFS AT A GLANCE

RESULTS: Conference Quarterfinals — lost to New Jersey 4-3

RECORD: 3-4

HOME: 2-1

AWAY: 1-3

GOALS FOR: 2.0/game

GOALS AGAINST: 2.0/game

OVERTIME: 0-1

POWER PLAY: 10.5% (13th)

PENALTY KILLING: 81.3% (10th)

PENALTY MINUTES: 22.4/game (13th)

1993-94 PLAYOFF LEADERS

GOALS: 4, Mogilny

ASSISTS: 7, Hawerchuk

POINTS: 7, Hawerchuk

POWER PLAY GOALS: 1, Mogilny, Presley, Boucher

SHORTHANDED GOALS: None

OVERTIME GOALS: 1, Hannan

GAME-WINNING GOALS: 1, Hannan, Simon, Presley

PENALTY MINUTES: 43, Ray

PLUS-MINUS: five players tied at +2

SHOTS: 22, Mogilny, Yuri Khmylev

A LOOK AHEAD TO 1994-95

GOAL: Dominik Hasek was traded to the Sabres from Chicago in the summer of 1992 for Stephane Beauregard, a goaltender who was traded four times in four months that summer.

Obviously, not particularly highly regarded, Hasek appeared destined for backup duty over the rest of his NHL playing days.

When Wally Pipper, Grant Fuhr, after starting 16 of the Sabres first 21 games, was forced out of the lineup with a knee injury, Hasek stepped in and started the next 29 games in a row.

A star was born. In those 29 games, he earned six shutouts, allowed only one goal in five of the games, and just two in 10 others. Even though he wasn't selected to play in the all-star game, he won the Jennings Trophy (with Fuhr), the Vezina, and was second in Hart Trophy voting for the most valuable player.

His 1.95 GAA marked the first time a netminder had gone under 2.00 since Bernie Parent did it with Philadelphia in the 1973-74 season.

Fuhr was hampered by a knee injury all year long, and his 3.68 GAA was 40th among the 43 goaltenders with enough minutes played to qualify.

Fuhr still considers himself a number one goalie, but his days are numbered. There were some teams, including Detroit, who were interested in acquiring his services at the trading deadline hoping to capitalize on his playoff reputation, but the Sabres weren't biting.

That could have been a mistake, passing on a chance to get something of value for an insurance policy that wasn't needed. Hasek played every minute of the playoffs and will get the bulk of the playing time this year as well.

DEFENCE: It was obvious that the Buffalo defence was in dire need of some old blood at the start of the last season. With injuries to a couple regulars, the youngsters proved they weren't ready for prime time.

Muckler had the answer to their problems in a player he knew well from his years with Edmonton. He traded a young prospect, Keith Carney, to Chicago for Craig Muni. Muni provided experience, and more importantly, a presence in their own end, especially in front of the net. He finished with a plus 31, tops on the team.

Randy Moller, whose career was supposedly finished, showed dedication and committment to rehabilitate himself from a back injury suffered the year before. He played in 78 games.

Ken Sutton has quietly developed into a full time NHL defenseman and Richard Smehlik surprised with consistency at both ends of the ice. Smehlik had the added dimension of being able to score while shorthanded. He scored three goals and added three assists when the team was down a man.

Doug Bodger provides a point man on the power play when he's not injured and Petr Svoboda rounds out the top six. Svoboda, however, is better friends with his doctors than some of his teammates. Three times in the last five years he has played exactly 60 games.

Rookies Denis Tsygurov and Phillipe Boucher spent some time with the big club, most of it in the press box.

Boucher is considered an up and coming talent, but the Sabres have had so many young, offensive defenseman who just haven't worked out. Who knows why.

If the defence plays within itself like they did last season they should be okay for another season. But, they're not getting any younger.

FORWARD: With LaFontaine and Craig Simpson back from missing almost all of last season, the Sabres have a good mix of scoring, defence, toughness and youth on the forward lines. Expect Mogilny to rebound with a vengeance after an injury-plagued season. He scored 76 goals and 127 points two years ago, but fell to 32 and 79. With LaFontaine around, it should make the comeback considerably easier.

Dale Hawerchuk, who is 31 years old, has yet to show his age. He led the team in points with 86. More impressively, he took up a lot of the goal scoring slack, improving from 16 goals to 35, to lead the team.

He wasn't the only one to improve their goal scoring totals. Audette, Khymylev, May, Wood, Presley, and Hannan also scored more goals than the previous season. And that with a predominantly defensive style.

Brad May and Rob Ray provide the toughness with Matthew Barnaby also mixing things up when he was in the lineup.

Lots of good defensive forwards with Hannan, Wood, Presley and Sweeney.

The youth comes in the form of centre Derek Plante who had 56 points in his first NHL season. He exhibited a committment to the cause when he decided not to join the U.S. Olympic team in favor of the Sabres who desperately needed him at the time. His contract allowed for him to go, and there's little doubt that he would have liked to enjoy the once in a lifetime experience, but he put his own desires aside. That will work out for him in the long run. See...already he has the reputation of being an unselfish player.

The bad news for him, however, is that he isn't likely to improve upon the 56 points he tallied last season. Twenty-six of his points came on the power play, just three less than he had at even strength. With LaFontaine back, that power play time will be reduced.

Other good young forwards include winger Jason Dawe, a prolific junior scorer with Peterborough, who impressed the Sabres immediately. Matthew Barnaby, with his robust style; and Todd Simon, the leading scorer at Rochester, who got some playoff time with the Sabres, all look to have a future with the team.

SPECIAL TEAMS: Don't look for improvement in this area of the Sabres game.

That's because it couldn't get much better than last year. Second on the power play, second in penalty killing, the second most short-handed goals. All those seconds added up to a first for special team play.

LaFontaine had 20 power play goals two years ago, while Mogilny had 27. No one else had more than eight.

Who would pick up the slack? How about everybody. Mogilny had 17 to lead the team, but Audette (16), Hawerchuk (13), Khymylev (11) and Derek Plante (8) also contributed.

LaFontaine and Mogilny should still score the bulk of the man-advantage markers, but it's nice to know there's lots of help in reserve.

The Sabres didn't just kill penalties, they killed the opposition with goals of their own. They allowed only 58 goals, tied with Boston for the fewest in the league, and then scored 21 of their own, for a net of 37 shorthanded goals allowed, tops in the league.

Dave Hannan, an underated defensive player, led the shorthanded scoring parade with eight points, on three goals and five assists. He only had 13 points at even strength. Wayne Presley (5-2-7) Smehlik (3-3-6), Sweeney (3-2-5), Wood (2-2-4) were next in the team shorthanded race.

COACHING/MANAGEMENT:
Muckler was third in the Adams Trophy balloting, but if they had a combined Coach/GM award he would have won hands down. It was a stroke of coaching/management genius what he was able to pull off last season.

He recognizes problems quickly and fixes them quickly. They needed some help in their own end, he went out and got it; they didn't have the scoring potential with their injuries, he made them into a defensive team.

Muckler also has the respect of his players. Maybe the smartest thing he did last season was charter a plane for the team, along with their family and friends, and fly them down to Florida for a mini-vacation over the all-star break. People, not just players, respond to that type of thing.

If there are problems on the Sabres this year they won't linger. Muckler will fix them one way or another. And quickly.

TEAM NEEDS: A defenceman who can understudy the role of Craig Muni, a backup goalie to Hasek after Fuhr's gone, and a defenseman to step up and handle one of the power play points with Bodger.

POTENTIAL NEW FACES: LW Jason Dawe (6-7-13 in 32 games with the Sabres, 22-14-36 in 48 games with Rochester), C Todd Simon (33¬52-85 in Rochester), LW Matthew Barnaby (2-4-6 in 38 games for Buffalo, 10-32-42 in 42 games at Rochester, LW Doug MacDonald (25-19-44 in 63 Rochester games), D Denis Tsurgov (1-10-11 in 24 Rochester games.)

McKENZIE'S BOTTOM LINE: If the Sabres without Pat LaFontaine were trouble last season, what are they going to be with their No. 1 centre back and healthy?

How about better?

GM-coach John Muckler did a masterful job last season of holding together a team that had every reason to fall apart. Instead of collapsing when LaFontaine went down with a season-ending knee injury, the Sabres rallied and altered their style dramatically to become one of the NHL's best defensive teams.

Netminder Dominik Hasek was a key part of that, winning the Vezina Trophy as the top goaltender. We all kept waiting for the flopping Czech to fizzle, but he never did. No one is quite sure how Hasek stops the puck, but the bottom line is he does.

Still, in an era where goaltenders have a tough time putting together years of excellence, all eyes will be on the Sabre stopper to see if he can duplicate last season's heroics. His work in the playoffs against New Jersey would suggest the answer is affirmative.

Muckler will also have to be careful to not significantly alter the club's mindset. Just because LaFontaine, a legitimate game-breaker, is back in the lineup is no reason to abandon the defence-first approach that resulted in so much success.

Still, there's something fishy about these Sabres.

The defence isn't particularly big or strong.

The offence relies heavily on aging players such as Dale Hawerchuk.

It's not as if there's a huge infusion of young talent on the way.

So why would anybody suggest the Sabres will be better this season than they were a year ago? Simply because of LaFontaine and Muckler's ability to duplicate one of the most inexplicable success stories of last season.

DRAFT PICKS

Wayne Primeau won't address the Buffalo Sabres' immediate need to get bigger and stronger up front. But in time, he may.

The Owen Sound Plater pivot, younger brother of Detroit Red Wing forward Keith Primeau, was the Sabres' first-round pick. At 6-foot-3 and 193 pounds, he has yet to begin to fill out. Like his brother, Wayne has offensive potential, but it's his eventual size and strength that makes him most attractive as a first-rounder. He, is, however a project that will require some work. GM-coach John Muckler has no illusion about that and intends to give Primeau as much development time as is required.

The Sabres' most pressing need, though, is getting some depth on the back end. That's why, after taking another centre, Curtis Brown of Moose Jaw, in the second round, the Sabres took four defencemen and a goaltender with their next five picks. In fact, seven of their 12 draftees were D-men. The one with the best chance of one day cracking the Sabre lineup is Nigerian-born Rumun Ndur, a big, strong physical stay-at-home type who played for Guelph of the OHL. The third rounder will need to work on his mobility, but his defence-first physical approach is exactly what a Sabre defence corps that is neither big nor strong requires.

1993-94 KEYS

KEY DEALS:

* Obtained Craig Muni and futures from Chicago for Keith Carney

KEY INJURIES: LaFontaine (68 games), Simpson (61), Svoboda (24), Fuhr (24), Sweeney (21), Presley (18), Mogilny (17), Khmylev (12).

KEY STAT: If the Sabres continue their fine special teams play, opposing clubs might want to think about declining penalties. The accompanying table shows the net number of goals Buffalo allowed when shorthanded. That means goals allowed minus shorthanded goals scored.

NET POWER PLAY GOALS ALLOWED (power play goals allowed minus shorthanded goals scored).

Team	Goals Allowed	Goals Scored	Net allowed
TOP FIVE			
1. Buffalo	58	21	37
2. Boston	58	17	41
3. NY Rangers	67	20	47
4. Tampa Bay	58	7	51
4. Dallas	68	8	60
5. Montreal	68	8	60
BOTTOM FIVE			
26. Ottawa	110	9	101
25. Hartford	88	8	80
24. Winnipeg	91	13	78
23. Quebec	87	10	77
22. Edmonton	78	2	76

Florida Panthers

The Florida Panthers went beyond respectability in their inaugural NHL season. Teams were afraid of them, and not just because of that ferocious looking Panther on their logo.

In a script that was even more unbelievable than that of The Mighty Ducks, the Panthers weren't good just for an expansion team. They were just good.

Two more points. That's all they needed to make the playoffs and meet the Rangers in the first round. They would have given them a run for their money, much more so than the Islanders did. After all, Vanbiesbrouck, the ex-Ranger, lived to play his ex¬mates. During the regular season, the Panthers beat them two out of five times, losing two by just one goal.

With nine games remaining, the Panthers had a five point lead on the Islanders for the final playoff position. But, an injury to captain Brian Skrudland and an 0-4-4 spell, combined with a 4-0-4 hot streak by the Islanders, and it was all over. They finished with 83 points, one behind the Islanders.

Nevertheless, it was some kind of season. First and foremost, John Vanbiesbrouck was some kind of hero in the net. Secondly, coach Roger Neilson was some kind of genius behind the bench. Thirdly, Bob Clarke was some kind of wizard in the front office.

Check out these Panther accomplishments:

* One game away from becoming the first expansion team in any North American sport to have a .500 record.

* Set NHL expansion team records for most points (83), longest unbeaten streak (9 games), and tied Anaheim for most wins (33).

* Their longest losing streak was five games, and in four of those games they lost by only one goal.

* They were above .500 on the road (18-16-8), good enough for the ninth best road record in the league.

* Thirty-six of their games were decided by one goal (16-20).

* Goaltender John Vanbiesbrouck was second in Vezina voting and third in the Hart Trophy balloting. Vanbiesbrouck earned a second team all-star selection.

* Brian Skrudland was third in Selke Trophy voting.

* During the regular season, they swept Vancouver (2-0), the NY Islanders (5-0), and Anaheim (2-0).

* They were undefeated against Tampa Bay (3-0-2), Ottawa (3-0-1), Los Angeles (1-0-1), Edmonton (1-0-1), and perhaps most impressively of all, they had a 3-0-1 mark against the Montreal Canadiens.

1993-94 SEASON AT A GLANCE

RECORD: 33-34-17, 83 points

FINISH: 5th in Atlantic Division, 9th in Eastern Conference, 16th overall

HOME: 15-18-9 (20th)

AWAY: 18-16-8 (9th)

OVERTIME: 2-5-17 (21st)

VS OWN DIVISION: 13-11-6

VS OTHER DIVISIONS: 20-23-11

VS OWN CONFERENCE: 24-23-11

VS OTHER CONFERENCE: 9-11-6

FIRST HALF RECORD: 17-17-8

SECOND HALF RECORD: 16-17-9

GOALS FOR: 233 (22nd)

GOALS AGAINST: 233 (4th)

TEAM PLUS/MINUS: +4 (15-t)

POWER PLAY: 15.9% (21st)

PENALTY KILLING: 82.6% (9th)

PENALTY MINUTES: 19.3/game (6th)

1993-94 REGULAR SEASON LEADERS (with Florida only)

GOALS: 30, Scott Mellanby (Kudelski had 40 overall)

ASSISTS: 33, Jesse Belanger

POINTS: 60, Mellanby (Kudelski had 70 overall)

POWER PLAY GOALS: 17, Mellanby

SHORTHANDED GOALS: 3, Tom Fitzgerald

GAME WINNING GOALS: 5, Jody Hull

PLUS-MINUS: +13, Brian Skrudland

SHOTS: 204, Mellanby (Kudelski, 251 overall)

PENALTY MINUTES: 156, Brent Severyn

A LOOK AHEAD TO 1994-95

GOAL: It doesn't get much better than this, expansion team or otherwise. Vanbiesbrouck was fourth in the league with a 2.53 goals against average, and second in save percentage at .924 (behind Hasek).

It's impossible to say just how many games he won for the Panthers on his own, but suffice to say it was more than a few.

He was an inspired goaltender last year. He had something to prove when after 10 seasons with the Rangers, they opted for Mike Richter, knowing they would lose one or the other in the expansion draft. The Rangers made a deal with Vancouver who were only interested in Vanbiesbrouck so they could leave him open in the expansion draft and not lose one of their top two netminders.

Can Vanbiesbrouck be inspired again this year? No reason to think otherwise. He did slump late in the season after cutting open his hand, but no big deal.

When he's not available or needs a rest, Mark Fitzpatrick can handle things just fine. His GAA was 2.73, 11th best in the league and his save percentage of .914 was fifth best overall.

Obviously, not a worry position for the Panthers.

DEFENCE: There's a good mix of size, toughness, and experience. Depth and youth, however, doesn't enter into the equation. At least not yet. Ed Jovanovski, the first player taken in the draft this year, could change that. He has everything: size at 6-2, 205; toughness with 221 penalty minutes for Windsor in the OHL; scoring ability with 50 points in 62 games as a 17 year old; and maybe most importantly, a good attitude.

He may need to polish his skills, however, and there's some question whether it will be at the NHL level right away. It was an unbelievable rise up the ladder for Jovanovski. Get this, he didn't start playing hockey until he was 11 years old.

If he does make the team, he automatically takes one of the points on the power play. Gord Murphy was the only rearguard who produced there. He had nine power play goals, which was sixth best among NHL defensemen.

Brian Benning manned the other point much of the time last year but he

struggled at times and the Panthers would like a replacement, maybe Jovanovski.

Keith Brown, who will be 34 this year, is the most experienced of the defensemen, but that aspect is not a big issue. There aren't a bunch of kids running around back there that need the stabilizing influence of a veteran like Brown.

Murphy (27), Benning (28), Joe Cirella (31), Brent Severyn (28), and Peter Andersson (29) all have a big dose of professional experience. Geoff Smith at 25 and tough guy Paul Laus at 24, round out the defence corps.

FORWARD: The key to expansion success on the forward front?

Start with an outstanding checking line, centered by Selke Trophy candidate Brian Skrudland. Mike Hough played the left side and Jody Hull manned right wing.

Then throw in sometime sniper Bob Kudelski, top draft pick Rob Niedermayer, who led the team with 19 points in his first 20 games before separating his shoulder, and dependable right winger Scott Mellanby.

The rest is easy. Just pick out a bunch of guys whose teams didn't have room or time for them to show their talents, and stick them into the fire.

It worked for center Stu Barnes who couldn't find a spot on the misguided Winnipeg team. He came through with flying colors, going 18-20-38 in 59 games. He still has room for improvement, and at only 23, lots of time.

And it worked for another center, Jesse Belanger, selected from the

Montreal organization in the expansion draft. His 33 assists led the team despite missing 14 games, 12 because of a broken bone in his hand. He too will get better.

Center is the strongest Panther position on the forward lines with Skrudland, Barnes, Belanger and Niedermayer. With the exception of Skrudland, all are young.

It gets a little shakier on the wings. On the left side, there's dependability, but little in the way of scoring. Mike Hough and Dave Lowry are veterans who have been around and know what it takes to play in the NHL. Bill Lindsay hasn't scored much, but might yet. He has some good junior and minor league scoring totals, and he tied for the scoring lead with four goals and one assist for the United States team at the world championships this past season. Another defensive specialist, Jeff Daniels can help out there as well.

Right wing has Bob Kudelski, whose scoring slowed down considerably in the second half after the Panthers obtained him from Ottawa; Scott Mellanby, who fits the definition of power forward and who can score with the man advantage. Andre Lomakin, Jody Hull, and Tom Fitzgerald also patrol the area.

There's not much toughness up front, which hurts them. No scrappers to speak of except for maybe Mellanby.

Some more scoring wouldn't hurt, either, but in the Roger Neilson scheme of things you take care of your own end first.

SPECIAL TEAMS: Mellanby and Kudelski each scored 17 goals on the power play (Pavel Bure led the league with 25) last year, so they can put the puck in the net if someone can get it to them or get the shots on goal so they can pick up the garbage.

Gord Murphy, who set a career high with 43 points, does some of that from the point, and rookie center Jesse Belanger showed some playmaking ability up front, leading the team in assists, and finishing third among rookies with 23 power play points (Alexei Yashin was first with 27). He missed 14 games, so it's likely he could have led all rookies in that category had he not been injured.

Even if the Panthers do get a first unit that performs decently, they won't move up too much in the league rankings (from 21st), because other teams have second units that can also contribute and backup players should someone from their top unit be injured or fall into a slump.

Florida has no such luxury.

The penalty killing is led by Brian Skrudland, one of the best defensive players in the game. There are plenty of other forwards around too who can handle the short-handed duties well. Assistant coach Craig Ramsay is in charge of penalty killing for the Panthers, and he was one of the best at that when he was with Buffalo, so they're in very good hands. They finished a very respectable ninth last season and should continue to be solid.

COACHING: Roger Neilson may be the best coach in the history of the game at getting the most out of the least. He's also the most innovative, one of the smartest, one of the most travelled, and one of the most often fired.

The latter is because he often gets so much out of players when he first arrives, that improvement is difficult. Coaches are often judged on how much the team improves from the previous season.

When he was between coaching jobs, Neilson had a tenure as a TSN (The Sports Network) analyst, telling us (with video, of course) just exactly what was going on in the game we were watching. Nobody has done it better before or since in the history of televised hockey.

Neilson is also one of the few coaches who truly understands statistics. Many coaches are mostly interested in what they can see and don't attempt, or don't know how, to get inside numbers that often reveal much more than what is evident on the surface. Neilson can do that.

Hard to belive he turned 60 years old this year. Doesn't look it.

MANAGEMENT: Bob Clarke will be sorely missed by the Panthers. He had a knack of picking out the right players to help the club. He signed 13 free agents before the start of the season and was one of the most active traders in the league, disproving the theory that you have to have something to get something. Most of the trades worked out very well.

But, Clarke wanted to go back to his first love, Philadelphia, and when he got the opportunity it was hard to turn

down. There were also some rumours about a strained relationship with Bill Torrey.

Torrey is on his own for the time being, which isn't a problem in the least, but look for someone to be hired before the start of the season.

He has mentioned former Detroit GM Bryan Murray as a possibility along with ex-Philadelphia boss Russ Farwell.

NEEDS: Scoring and depth at every position. A quarterback on the power play.

POTENTIAL NEW FACES: D Ed Jovanovski, 25-40-75 in 50 games for Windsor (OHL); D Chris Armstrong, 12-55-67, Moose Jaw (WHL).

McKENZIE'S BOTTOM LINE: Coach Roger Neilson's team came oh so close last spring to making the playoffs, but it's probably best they didn't.

As it was, the Panthers' effort was considered heroic. If they'd made the playoffs and been dismissed in the first round by the eventual Cup champion New York Rangers, they couldn't have added any lustre to a near perfect first-year season.

But they could have skewed the expectation level for their fans and everyone else. If they'd made the playoffs last spring, everyone would have expected — no, make that demanded — another playoff appearance this season.

It's the kind of pressure a second-year NHL club just doesn't need.

Neilson's formula last year was simple and straightforward —

outstanding netminding from Hart Trophy finalist John Vanbiesbrouck and Mark Fitzpatrick, plus diligent defence at the expense of anything offensive.

It worked. If the Panthers got an early lead, and they did so often, they were tough to come back on. Neilson's boys virtually perfected the neutral zone trap.

That said, the Panthers won't do quite as well this season. They won't fall off the face of the earth, but they may not be as close to the playoff race as they'd like.

First, they have lost the element of surprise. For the better part of last season, Florida capitalized on other team's overconfidence. Second, it's hard to imagine Vanbiesbrouck played every bit as well this season as he did a year ago. And third, as any expansion team personnel will tell you, things tend to become just a little bit flatter in the second year of a team's existence.

Barring a lot of trades, the Panthers' lineup will be remarkably similar to last season's roster. Their draft picks from this year simply aren't ready to play and for shame on the Panthers if they even try to forcefeed their kids.

Florida will be competitive, make no mistake. But don't be surprised if things don't go quite as smoothly this time around. The Panthers have a shot at a playoff spot, but it's not necessarily a good one.

DRAFT PICKS

In the end, the Panthers decided they would rather draft than trade. So Florida ended up with the highest concentration of top picks, selecting four players amongst the first 36 chosen, including No. 1 overall Ed Jovanovski.

The selection of the big Windsor Spitfire defenceman came as little surprise, even though many NHL teams had Las Vegas centre Radek Bonk as the No. 1 rated player. Florida's reasons for taking the bruising blueliner with offensive potential is that he's most likely to become the best player in the class of '94. He's not that now and it would be a mistake to think Mr. Ed is ready to walk in and assume a spot on Roger Neilson's blueline. His game needs a lot of polish and defence is the most difficult position to master in the NHL. The Panthers intend to be patient with him.

In time, though, they should be rewarded. Still, it is not a pick without risk. The easy way out would have been to take Bonk, who's NHL ready now and would perhaps do wonders to bolster a sagging Panther offence. That's why the Panthers used two of their three second-round picks on offensive players.

The first of the second-round trio was Rhett Warrener of Saskatoon, a big, tough banging defenceman. The second was Spokane's gifted but sometimes troubled centre Jason Podollan, whose commitment and sense of team hasn't equalled his natural flair for playing the game. If the Panthers can adjust his attitude, his skill level suggests he's a second-round steal. The third was Thunder Bay's Ryan Johnson, younger brother of Detroit Red Wing centre Greg Johnson. He's headed to the University of North Dakota, where he'll incubate for at least a year or two.

Notable is that the Panthers chose not to select a goaltender, having taken two (Kevin Weekes and Todd MacDonald) last year to go with their already strong starting unit of John Vanbiesbrouck and Mark Fitzpatrick.

1993-94 KEYS
KEY DEALS:
* Obtained Keith Brown from Chicago for Darin Kimble
* Obtained Brent Severyn from Winnipeg for Milan Tichy.
* Obtained Mike Foligno from Toronto for future considerations
* Obtained Stu Barnes from Winnipeg for Randy Gilhen
* Obtained Greg Hawgood from Philadelphia for future considerations
* Obtained Geoff Smith from Edmonton with draft choices for draft choices
* Obtained Bob Kudelski from Ottawa for Scott Levins, Yvgeny Davydov and draft picks
* Obtained Jeff Daniels from Pittsburgh for Greg Hawgood
* Obtained Peter Andersson from NY Rangers for 9th round draft pick

KEY INJURIES: Keith Brown (32 games), Rob Niedermayer (17), Jesse Belanger (14).

KEY STAT:
FLORIDA FIRSTS
GAME: 4-4 at Chicago
GOAL: Scott Mellanby at 12:31 of first period
ASSISTS: Rob Niedermayer and Evgeny Davydov
SHOT: Brian Skrudland at 1:07 of first period
PENALTY: Bill Lindsay (1:44 of first period for hooking)
WIN: 2-0 at Tampa Bay (third game)
SHUTOUT: John Vanbiesbrouck (2-0 over Tampa Bay in third game)
GOAL AGAINST: Chris Chelio at 13:17 of first period
STARTING LINEUP: G: John Vanbiesbrouck D: Joe Cirella D: Keith Brown LW: Dave Lowry C: Brian Skrudland RW: Scott Mellanby

Hartford Whalers

A new broom sweeps clean. True. But, the proud new owners of the Hartford Whalers will need an industrial size mop to clean up the mess they inherited.

The Compuware group from Detroit, now known as KTR Hockey Ltd, Partnership, will attempt to bring a new era of stability to Hartford.

They have the money, and they have the smarts. The only thing they don't have yet is a winning team on the ice, but that will come.

Gone is coach Pierre McGuire, despised by the players. Returning to bench duty is ousted GM Paul Holmgren.

Former NHL goaltender Jim Rutherford, Executive of the Year in the OHL last season, takes over as general manager, chief operating officer and president. He also has a 10% share in the team.

Rutherford will attempt to make the Whalers more newsworthy on the ice than off it.

Last year's fiasco began with the incident in Buffalo where five players - Pat Verbeek, Geoff Sanderson, Chris Pronger, Mark Janssens, Todd Harkins — and assistant coach Kevin McCarthy, were arrested after a brawl outside a nightclub.

The team owner at the time, Richard Gordon, immediately suspended the players, including underage drinker Pronger. But, Gary Bettman stepped in and rescinded the order pending a review by the league. Subsequently they were fined, but no suspension. The principles were also sentenced to community service in Buffalo.

GM at the time, Paul Holmgren was later arrested on drunk driving charges, his second such incident in two years.

Next was Bryan Marchment, also with impaired driving charges.

All of the above happened over just a three week span. Not long after, Pronger was charged with driving under the influence and sentenced to three days in jail (alcohol awareness program) and a $483 fine.

The new owners, who have their roots in youth hockey in Detroit, will try to project a better image for the team. That won't be hard because it couldn't get much worse.

It'll take some time, but it should be fun for Whaler fans to watch their team improve over the coming years.

1993-94 REGULAR SEASON AT A GLANCE

RECORD: 27-48-9

FINISH: 5th in Northeast Division, 13th in Eastern Conference, 24th in league.

HOME: 14-22-6 (23rd)

AWAY: 13-26-3 (22nd)

OVERTIME: 4-1-9 (1st)

VS OWN DIVISION: 9-18-3

VS OTHER DIVISIONS: 18-30-6

VS OWN CONFERENCE: 21-32-5

VS OTHER CONFERENCE: 6-16-4

FIRST HALF RECORD: 17-22-3

SECOND HALF RECORD: 10-26-6

GOALS FOR: 227 (24th)

GOALS AGAINST: 288 (20th)

TEAM PLUS/MINUS: -34 (23rd)

POWER PLAY: 15.0 (23rd)

PENALTY KILLING: 78.8 (24th)

PENALTY MINUTES: 21.5/game (17th)

1993-94 REGULAR SEASON LEADERS

GOALS: 41, Geoff Sanderson

ASSISTS: 42, Andrew Cassels

POINTS: 75, Pat Verbeek

POWER PLAY GOALS: 15, Verbeek, Sanderson

SHORTHANDED GOALS: 1, Cassels, Robert Kron

GAME WINNING GOALS: 6, Sanderson

PLUS-MINUS: +8 Alexander Godynyuk

SHOTS: 266, Sanderson

PENALTY MINUTES: 272, Marc Potvin

A LOOK AHEAD TO 1994-95

GOAL: The Whalers are in good hands with Sean Burke between the pipes. We'd probably hear more about the 6-foot-4 goalie giant were he playing for a good team, maybe even when all-star selections were announced.

As it was, he was voted MVP for the Whalers last season. His goals against average of 2.99 was excellent and his save percentage of .906 was up among league leaders.

You can't really compare save percentage from team to team because a big consideration is the quality of shots allowed. Against strong teams a lot of shots come from the perimeter, outside the danger area. On weak teams, the shots usually come from in closer.

If, however, a goalie on a weak team has a good save percentage, it is significant.

Injuries cut into some of Burke's playing time last season, but look for him to handle the bulk of goaltending duties this season, upwards of 60 games if he's healthy.

Frank Pietrangelo didn't do the job as backup last year so he was offered a termination contract.

Jeff Reese will handle those duties full-time this season and will do more than a capable job.

DEFENCE: Chris Pronger was a huge disappointment to the Whalers last season after the huge contract they laid out. He struggled offensively and defensively, mentally and physically, on the ice and off the ice.

That's a lot of double negatives. Eventually they'll all even out to a positive, and it could be this season.

The Whalers traded away most of their defensemen with offensive capabilities, so it will be up to Pronger to step to the forefront. And he will. Sooner or later.

Elsewhere, there's Bryan Marchment to take care of the toughness on the blueline. He's the kind of guy who irritates the heck out of other teams but somebody they'd love if they had him on their side.

Jeff Chychrun, a free agent signee, who played in the Edmonton farm system last year, is another big guy who likes the rough stuff.

Other regulars include Adam Burt, who has his ups and downs; Alexander Godynyuk, who has his ups and downs; and Frantisek Kucera, who has his ups and downs.

This isn't exactly a Stanley Cup contending defence, or even a playoff contending defence.

Expect big changes before the Whalers play their first game. Or at least before their 10th game.

FORWARD: It's not often you can call 41 goals a disappointing year, but in Geoff Sanderson's case it fits. That's mostly because bigger things were expected of him. His goal total only dropped from 46 to 41, but his assists went from 43 to 26.

It's probably not all his fault. And after all, he's only 22 years old. Maybe he felt too much pressure to score because there were few others on the team with that capability.

Pat Verbeek is one of them. He had 37 goals, the sixth time he has reached the 35 goal plateau. He also plays a rugged game, making him a valuable commodity even though he's on the smallish side.

Andrew Cassels was another disappointment. The center looked to be on the fast track when he earned 85 points two years ago, but he fell to just 58.

Robert Kron had a decent 50 points and then there's a major drop on the scoring list, all the way down to 30 for Pronger.

Obviously, this team needs an offensive kick in the butt. They only scored 227 goals last season, third lowest in the league and the worst in their history.

If Cassels and Sanderson can return to form they make a decent number one line along with Verbeek, but even so, there's little else to back them up.

The team is fairly deep at center, at least in terms of numbers. Behind Cassels are Darren Turcotte, who has a couple 30 goal seasons under his belt but only four last year in 32 games; Ted Drury, a six goal scorer obtained from Calgary, who led the ECAC in scoring for Harvard two years ago; Robert Petrovicky, Hartford's first pick and ninth overall in 1992, who has done nothing to justify such a high selection; and Andrei Nikolishin, who played with Moscow Dynamo last year and is expected to sign.

Better yet, the number five selection in the draft, Jeff O'Neill may step in right away. He's considered a Doug Gilmour type without the same day-to-day intensity. With the Guelph Storm in the OHL he had 126 points in 66 games.

The problem is there's nobody there you can hang your hat on. It's all up in the air. Maybe a couple of them will start proving their NHL existence, or return to form, but you wouldn't want to bet on who or when.

The left side is pretty decent, defensively at least. Behind Sanderson are pleasant surprise Jim Storm, a good two way player whom they signed off the U.S. Olympic team; Joceyln Lemieux, who also plays right wing is a handy guy to have around but won't turn on the red light too often; and Paul Ranheim.

Ranheim only had 27 points but he'll improve on that. An excellent skater, there just wasn't room for him in Calgary to play much offensively, so he got stuck in a defensive role. He only had three points in 15 games after being obtained from the Flames but give him a chance. He was a proven 40-50 point scorer before last season.

Six-foot-two, 217 pound Kevin Smyth will also get a look¬see there. On the right side, after Verbeek, is Kron, Jocelyn Lemieux, when he's not playing left wing, and defensive specialist Jim Sandlak.

Here's how it plays out. If all the forwards have great seasons they might make the playoffs. Pretty tough to get excited over such an improbability.

COACHING: Paul Holmgren started the season as coach and GM but gave up the bench job to assistant GM Pierre McGuire. He said it frustrated him too much when players didn't make the most of their talent.

McGuire got rave reviews early and then became one of the league's most hated coaches. He didn't think so, but the players didn't respect him, and didn't want to play for him, especially after the brawl in Buffalo. Pat Verbeek was very outspoken on the matter, suggesting that McGuire should have stuck up for his players rather than try to save his own skin.

When the Compuware people came in, Jim Rutherford took over as GM and Holmgren was kicked back behind the bench, a place he already admitted wasn't his favorite place.

He mentioned something about not knowing how much you like something until you don't have it anymore, but what do you expect him to say.

Not to worry, chances are he won't last there long anyway. Look for Holmgren to be the first coach fired this year.

MANAGEMENT: The old regime made a lot of their trades just to save money. That won't be the case with the new owners. The Compuware people have money, but they'll likely put a long term plan into affect and stick with it, which could very well turn the Whalers into winners in the future.

NEEDS: A miracle. In the meantime, proven scorers up front, or somebody to emerge, and more depth at every position except centre.

POTENTIAL NEW FACES: C Jeff O'Neill, 45-81-126, Guelph (OHL); C Andrei Nikolishin, 9-12-21 in 32 games for Moscow Dynamo; LW Kevin Smyth 22-27-49 in 42 games for Springfield; G Manny Legace, Canadian Olympic Team.

McKENZIE'S BOTTOM LINE: An ownership change — from Richard Gordon to the Compuware group out of Detroit — will benefit the Whalers in a couple of ways.

First, there'll be no day-to-day speculation about the club leaving Hartford for sunnier climes since the deal guarantees another three or four years in the Insurance City.

Second, the general lack of leadership that led directly to the Whalers' celebrated problems with embarrassing alcohol-related incidents has been replaced by a much firmer hand.

GM and part owner Jim Rutherford, the ex-NHL goalie, simply will not tolerate it. Some might suggest he demonstrated an odd way of showing it by hiring Paul Holmgren as the coach.

Holmgren, who checked into the Betty Ford Clinic for treatment of alcohol abuse last spring, was the GM when the Whalers were experiencing bar fights and the like. But Rutherford saw Holmgren for what he was — a good coach who is liked and respected by the Whaler players.

Holmgren knows the team better than anyone else. Bringing in an outsider would have meant starting over in some respects and this is a team that isn't as far away from the playoffs as some think.

The one advantage the Whalers have over some of the other playoff fringe teams is good goaltending. Veteran Sean Burke looks as though he's overcome the problems that led to his departure from New Jersey and is prepared to be a bona fide No. 1 man in the NHL.

Towering Chris Pronger is only going to get better on a defensive unit that can be quietly proficient with guys like Adam Burt and Bryan Marchment providing a physical element back there.

Up front, the Whalers are a little weak up the middle, but have good scoring from the wings with Geoff Sanderson and Pat Verbeek.

The entire team will benefit from the greater sense of direction the new owners will provide. While it may be a reach to suggest the Whalers are playoff bound, this is a team on its way up.

DRAFT PICKS

The Whalers had only one pick in the first three rounds, but it was a good one. They used the fifth overall selection to take Guelph's Jeff O'Neill, a talented two-way centre who may not be too far off playing in the Whaler lineup. O'Neill has the speed and smarts to play the pro game now. He must develop consistency of intensity and show he's capable of steering his modest frame through heavy, pro-style traffic. Certainly, O'Neill will help to fill a big void at centre for the Whalers, if not this season and then certainly next year.

After taking O'Neill, the Whaler scouts went on vacation until the fourth round. But they took an intriguing prospect in Kamloops Blazer centre-winger Hnat Domenichelli, a late-blooming talent with a better than average skill level. And in the fifth round, the Whalers took O'Neill's teammate, Ryan Risidore, a big, strong, physical stay-at-home type. Nothing fancy about him, but he's the type of mid-round pick who has a chance to play a role.

In the later rounds, it wasn't difficult to detect the influence of new GM Jim Rutherford, who was the GM of the Detroit Jr. Red Wings last season. Hartford took two OHLers — Matt Ball of Detroit and Steve Nimigon of Niagara Falls — who played little last season because of inexeperience and injury, respectively. Both are the type of youngsters who could still yet develop into top junior players and perhaps one day Whalers.

1993-94 KEYS

KEY DEALS:

* obtained Bryan Marchment and Steve Larmer from Chicago for Eric Weinrich and Patrick Poulin

* obtained James Patrick and Darren Turcotte from the NY Rangers for Steve Larmer, Nick Kypreos, Barry Richter and a 1994 draft

* obtained Jeff Reese from Calgary for Dan Keczmer

* obtained Alexander Godynyuk from Florida for Jim McKenzie

* obtained Gary Suter, Paul Ranheim and Ted Drury from Calgary for Zarley Zalapski, James Patrick and Michael Nylander

* obtained Frantisek Kucera and Jocelyn Lemieux from Chicago for Gary Suter, Randy Cunneyworth and 1995 third round draft pick

KEY INJURIES: Darren Turcotte missed 52 games with the Rangers and Hartford; Jim Sandlak (57).

KEY STAT: The Whalers had high expectations for Chris Pronger last season. Too high. Defense is the toughest position to learn on the job in the NHL.

It takes time. Offensive types in their first season are sometimes overwhelmed by the defensive responsibilities and can't contribute with the puck as much as they'd like.

Here's how six of the top offensive defensemen in NHL history performed in their first NHL season. None exactly shot the lights out.

		Year	G-A-Pts
Ray Bourque	Bos.	79-80	17-48-65
Paul Coffey	Edm.	80-81	9-23-32
Larry Robinson (33 games)	Mtl	72-73	2-4-6
Bobby Orr	Bos.	66-67	13-28-41
Denis Potvin	NYI	73-74	17-37-54
Brad Park	NYR	68-69	3-23-26
Chris Pronger	Hfd.	93-94	5-25-30

Montreal Canadiens

Hey, what do you want? A Stanley Cup every year? It's not like you don't already have more than your share.

Relax.

Not in Montreal. It's all or nothing, baby. A first round playoff loss, such as last year to Boston, isn't a common occurence for them. The last time it happened was in 1982-83.

The team never played as well as expected, especially during the regular season, despite the fact they earned just six fewer points than in their Stanley Cup year.

Of course, those expectations were pretty high. It's not easy to have a record of 84-0.

Jacques Demers couldn't seem to light a fire under the troops. Not for lack of trying. He was always benching, or threatening to bench players in the hopes of getting them going. Sometimes it worked, sometimes it didn't.

When you win the Stanley Cup you have to have everything going for you in the playoffs, including a little luck. When the Canadiens won, they had an incredible 10 overtime victories, easily breaking the all-time record.

That kind of thing doesn't happen every year. Maybe every other year if you're Montreal.

Another post-Stanley occurence is that after the pressure¬packed excitement of the previous playoffs, it's difficult to get up for games against weak teams the following season. Ho hum. We already proved we're the best, we don't need to do much to beat an expansion team.

So they didn't. Didn't quite work out though. In five games against Florida they won none of them. They lost to Ottawa three times and twice to Tampa Bay.

They forgot that they made it as far as they did because of hard work. It's unlikely they'll need to be reminded this year.

1993-94 REGULAR SEASON AT A GLANCE

RECORD: 41-29-14

FINISH: 3rd in Northeast Division, 6th in Eastern Conference, 9th overall

HOME: 26-12-4 (4th)

AWAY: 15-17-10 (15th)

OVERTIME: 3-2-14 (11th)

VS OWN DIVISION: 17-10-4

VS OTHER DIVISIONS: 24-19-10

VS OWN CONFERENCE: 25-25-10

VS OTHER CONFERENCE: 16-4-4

FIRST HALF RECORD: 20-15-7

SECOND HALF RECORD: 21-14-7

GOALS FOR: 283 (10th)

GOALS AGAINST: 248 (7th)

TEAM PLUS/MINUS: +25 (6th)

POWER PLAY: 20.1% (10th)

PENALTY KILLING: 82.6% (8th)

PENALTY MINUTES: 18.1/game (4th)

1993-94 REGULAR SEASON LEADERS

Goals: 40, Vincent Damphousse

Assists: 51, Damphousse

Points: 91, Damphousse

Power Play Goals: 13, Damphousse, Brian Bellows

Shorthanded Goals: 3, Benoit Brunet

Game Winning Goals: 10, Damphousse

Plus-Minus: +17, John LeClair

Shots: 274, Damphousse

Penalty Minutes: 276, Lyle Odelein

1993-94 PLAYOFFS AT A GLANCE

RESULTS: Conference Quarterfinals - Lost in seven to Boston Record: 3-4

HOME: 1-2

AWAY: 2-2

GOALS FOR: 20, 2.9/game

GOALS AGAINST: 22, 3.1/game

OVERTIME: 1-0

POWER PLAY: 21.4% (2nd)

PENALTY KILLING: 77.4% (13th)

PENALTY MINUTES: 15.1/game (3rd)

1993-94 PLAYOFF LEADERS

GOALS: 6, Kirk Muller

ASSISTS: 4, Brunet, Paul DiPietro, Patrice Brisebois

POINTS: 8, Muller

POWER PLAY GOALS: 3, Muller

SHORTHANDED GOALS: none

OVERTIME GOALS: 1, Muller

GAME-WINNING GOALS: 2, Muller

PENALTY MINUTES: 19, Kevin Haller

PLUS-MINUS: +4, Guy Carbonneau

SHOTS: 16, Muller and Brian Bellows

A LOOK AHEAD TO 1994-95

GOAL: The hockey world was stunned last year when one of the best playoff goaltenders in history was felled by appendicitis. They were stunned even further when he only missed one game, and looked like he was never hurt in the first place.

That was even suggested by some. But, pay no attention, he had the pesky appendix removed after the season.

Whatever the story behind the playoff story, Roy is not only one of the best all-time in the playoffs, but also during the regular season. Last year, he finished third in GAA, fourth in wins, third in save percentage, and tied for first with seven shutouts.

Roy is a Hall of Famer even if he never plays another game. The only problem in Montreal has been finding a capable backup. Andre "Red Light" Racicot was doomed by reputation, and with no one else ready, the Habs traded for Ron Tugnutt, a capable backup, even if he didn't show it in a limited audition last season.

DEFENCE: They're not big, and they're not very physical, but there's a lot of talent and a fair amount of depth.

Still, few escaped the wrath of Demers at some time or another last season. In the playoffs, he had Patrice Brisbois and Kevin Haller stay in the dressing room after the first period of Game Four against Boston to atone for their defensive mistakes.

Haller was traded after the season to Philadelphia for Yves Racine.

Racine is a power play specialist who should line up with Matthieu Schnieder on the point with the man-advantage. Both had 52 points last season.

Unfortunately, for Lyle Odelein, tough guy turned prolific scorer, that should limit his power play duties to the second unit.

Odelein was an amazing story. In 214 games prior to last season, he had a total of three goals and 28 points. He broke out with a bang, scoring 11 goals and 29 assists, second only to Schneider among defensemen on the team.

Odelein had five assists in one game, a 9-2 defeat of Hartford, and in a another game against St. Louis, scored a hattrick, the first Hab defenseman since Larry Robinson in 1985 to do so.

Eric Desjardins is probably the team's most reliable defenseman. He's playing his sixth NHL season but still is only 25 years old.

Others include J.J. Daigneault, who's on the smallish side for a defenseman at 5-11, 185 and Peter Popovic, who at 6-5, 224, is on the biggish side for any position. He needs to use his size to better advantage, however, before he can carry a full-time job in the NHL.

Bryan Fogarty is also in the mix. The former first round Quebec pick was once considered a great prospect, but drinking problems wore out the patience of his previous teams. He claims to be dry, but still has a ways to go to earn a regular NHL spot.

Finally, there's Patrice Brisebois, another high scoring junior defenseman. He will have to show more intensity in his own end before Demers will be happy with him.

It's a very mobile unit, most with the capability to contribute offensively. It's exactly the type of defense that was supposed to sweep the league in the nineties. It appears things have changed already, however, and teams are looking for more size, toughness and defensive ability from their rearguards.

FORWARD: It's pretty safe to say that few if any of the Montreal forwards lived up to expectations from coach Demers.

Even Damphousse, who led the team in goals, assists, and points, was issued an ultimatum during the season: two games to produce or else. The left-winger responded with four points in the second one, and then went on to another 90 plus season.

Damphousse has often been a streaky player, so there shouldn't have been cause for panic. The rest of the team must have forgotten what took them to the Stanley Cup win the year before — hard work and discipline.

Demers tried everything to get them going, but instead all he got was a bunch of disgruntled players who weren't scoring.

Tentatively scheduled at left wing, behind Damphousse, is Gilbert Dionne, another player who saw the bench from time to time. He asked to be traded, suggesting he couldn't score from the bench, press box or fourth line. After a promising start as a rookie in 1991-92, when he scored 21 goals in 39 games, his goal production dropped to 20 and then 19 last season.

Benoit Brunet and Pierre Sevigny also patrolled the left wing with little scoring prowess, although injuries had a hand in that.

Bigger things are expected out of both of them.

Mario Roberge stuck around for his toughness, but didn't play very often.

Donald Brashear is another tough guy who excited the Forum faithful. At Fredericton, he showed some ability to score, as well as fight, so he could get more of an opportunity to stick.

At center, Kirk Muller had an off year, hampered by injuries. There's no reason to expect that he won't rebound this season.

John LeClair moved over from left wing and gave the Canadiens some size in the middle, and did a good job. He's a restricted free agent, but there's little chance he'll go anywhere.

Paul DiPietro has apparently decided he will only play well in the playoffs, where for the second year in a row he came through offensively after a mediocre season. In Demers' doghouse much of the year, he will have to show something to make it to the post season, especially since he's another one of the many small forwards in the lineup.

Guy Carbonneau had an outstanding comeback season, but he can't last much longer at the age of 34. He still thinks he can play two more years, but Montreal management may not be willing to pay what Carbonneau wants to let him prove it.

There are some interesting prospects on the way up. Two Olympians, Brian Savage from Canada, and Jim Campbell, from the U.S. team tore up the AHL when they joined Fredericton late in the season. Savage got the call to Montreal for the playoffs, so he could stick.

Brian Bellows heads up right wing, along with Mike Keane, Oleg Petrov and Ed Ronan.

Bellows turns 30 before the start of the season and while he can be counted on for 30 plus goals, who knows how much longer. Ronan is a defensive type player who doesn't score, Keane is a small forward who doesn't score much either, and Petrov is really small at 5'9" and will have to score more than he's capable of to justify his existence in the NHL.

On the horizon is Valeri Bure, a talented junior player, but yet another one on the small side.

The Habs showed a couple years ago that they could compensate for their lack of size in other ways. Last year, they couldn't, so expect them to get bigger and grittier, or at least start playing bigger again.

SPECIAL TEAMS: A good power play starts with people who can move the puck around from the points. Montreal has that in abundance, especially since trading for Racine. He joins Schneider, Odelein, Desjardins and Brisbois as capable point men on the power play.

Damphousse, Bellows and a healthy Muller can handle things up front just fine. After them, however, there aren't many talented scorers who should be on the ice with the man advantage.

The Canadiens also have many of the elements necessary for good penalty killing — good defensive forwards, and defensemen who can get to the puck and clear it out. It should be above average as well, although a little more size from the defense could better keep the front of the net clear.

COACHING: Jacques Demers has always been considered a master motivator. It just didn't work out last season. Or maybe it did and would have been a lot worse otherwise.

Who knows. But coaches are always judged on the team's performance in relation to expectations. That's why the coach of the year award usually goes to someone who improved the most over the previous season, and why they hardly ever win it twice in a row.

Ironically, Demers is the only coach to ever win the Adams Trophy in consecutive seasons.

If you're a motivator and the players aren't motivated, a coaching change can't be too far behind.

MANAGEMENT: Savard took over the GM reigns in 1983. Since then, he's guided them to four first place division finishes, three 100 point seasons and two Stanley Cups.

Apparently, he does his job quite well.

NEEDS: Size, on the wings and on defense. Traditionally one of the least penalized clubs in the league, they're going to have to keep pace with other teams that seem to be going for size more and more.

POTENTIAL NEW FACES: D Yves Racine (obtained from Philadelphia), C Brian Savage, Canadian Olympic Team; RW Valeri Bure, 40-62-102, Spokane (WHL); C Jim Campbell, U.S. Olympic team; LW Donald Brashear, Fredericton.

McKENZIE'S BOTTOM LINE: Any team with Patrick Roy in net can't be discounted. And so it is for the Habs, who enter this season with no baggage connected with their Cup victory of two years ago.

If there's a hangover this year, it's as a result of last spring's first-round exit at the hands of the arch-rival Boston Bruins.

Roy's appendix is gone and there's no reason to believe he won't supply all-star calibre goaltending.

As for the rest of the team, GM Serge Savard indicated major changes would be made. Since none were made well into the summer, one suspects the Hab team that starts the season will not resemble the Hab team that finishes it.

Savard is putting an emphasis on getting bigger and stronger. Certainly, the Hab defence could use some added muscle and picking up Yves Racine from Philadelphia for Kevin Haller ins't exactly what the doctor ordered.

Up front, the Habs will continue to rely on Kirk Muller and Vincent Damphousse. Players such as Brian Bellows and Gilbert Dionne, well, that's another matter. Both names popped up frequently in off-season trade talk. So, too, did John LeClair, a sleeping giant who must frustrate Habs' management to no end.

Montreal is looking to increase its physical presence and it has, in LeClair, one of the pre-eminent power players in the NHL. But he so rarely uses his size to advantage and when he does, it comes in inconsistent bursts.

In the Habs' Cup run, LeClair looked as though he was ready to take off and become one of the league's elite at his craft. That didn't happen last year and if the Habs are to get it back on track, LeClair is a key man for them. If he's traded, it shows just how exasperated the Canadiens are with their big man.

Last spring's first-round exit notwithstanding, the Canadiens have enough talent, experience and goaltending to be in the thick of any race.

DRAFT PICKS

The Canadiens have never shied away from drafting big, physical specimens — witness Brent Bilodeau and Turner Stevenson. But they also have taken their share of little speedsters — witness Valeri Bure and Saku Koivu.

But after bowing out in the first round of the playoffs against Boston last spring, Habs' GM Serge Savard suggested the team would have to start placing a greater emphasis on size and strength.

And their 1994 draftees reflect that attitude.

Montreal took North Bay's Brad Brown, all 6-foot-3, 218 pounds of him, in the first round. The Newfoundland-born bruiser has already played three seasons in the OHL, so some might suggest he's close to making the NHL grade. Not in Montreal.

Traditionally, the Habs let their prospects develop to the max in junior and then nurture them with at least a year in the minors. It should surprise no one if Brown follows that route, although he's liable to get a little stale after four or five years of junior hockey.

Montreal has made no secret of their desire to start grooming a young talent behind veteran superstar Patrick Roy and took a step in the right direction with the drafting of Jose Theodore of the St. Jean Lynx in the second round. Theodore was the fifth goalie taken and the No. 2 man out of the Quebec League (next to Toronto's Eric Fichaud), although there are a limited number of scouts who think there's not much to choose between Theodore and Fichaud.

After addressing that need, the Habs

went back to the toughness angle in the third round, taking junior veteran Chris Murray from the Kamloops Blazers. Murray engaged in one of hockey's most spirited fights last season, when he slugged it out toe-to-toe with North Bay's Steve McLaren (drafted by Chicago) at the Memorial Cup in Laval, Que. In all, the Habs had three third-round picks, taking Finnish defenceman Marko Kiprusoff and homegrown talent Martin Belanger of Granby with the others.

1993-94 KEYS

KEY DEALS:

In-Season

* Obtained Ron Tugnutt from Anaheim for Stephan Lebeau

Post-Season:

* obtained Yves Racine from Philadelphia for Kevin Haller

KEY INJURIES: None

KEY STAT: The Montreal Canadiens are the most successful major professional sports team in North America. The numbers speak for themselves.

MAJOR NORTH AMERICAN CHAMPIONSHIPS

Montreal Canadiens	NHL	23
New York Yankees	MLB	22
Boston Celtics	NBA	16
Toronto Maple Leafs	NHL	13
Green Bay Packers	NFL	10
Los Angeles Lakers	NBA	10
St. Louis Cardinals	MLB	9
Oakland A's	MLB	9

* wins also include those from previous franchise locations

New Jersey Devils

The New Jersey Devils started the season off by winning their first seven games.

But, their winning ways started somewhat earlier with the hiring of Jacques Lemaire.

Lemaire, who last coached in the NHL for Montreal in the 1984-85 season, thought he had something to offer again and was obviously right. It didn't hurt either having Larry Robinson as his assistant. Two winners who get respect.

It translated into a coach of the year award for Lemaire and an outstanding season for the Devils.

With very few personnel changes on the ice from the previous season, Lemaire transformed the team into a group that was strong everywhere. Offensively? They had the second most goals in the league. Defensively? They gave up the second fewest goals in the league.

Okay, that's fine during the long, mostly meaningless regular season, but what about these guys in the playoffs. Some pundits — okay, this pundit — figured they were too "soft" on the forward line to go anywhere. It was time for the Stephane Richer's of the world, and some of the Europeans, to fold the tent and go home.

Not a chance. They beat out Buffalo (95 regular season points) and Boston (97), and took the Rangers to double overtime in gave seven of the conference finals before Stephane Matteau scored to end a very successful season.

1993-94 SEASON AT A GLANCE

RECORD: 47-25-12

FINISH: 2nd in Atlantic Division, 2nd in Eastern Conference, 2nd overall

HOME: 29-11-2 (2nd)

AWAY: 18-14-10 (6th)

OVERTIME: 1-1-12 (13th-t)

VS OWN DIVISION: 17-11-3

VS OTHER DIVISIONS: 30-14-9

VS OWN CONFERENCE: 34-19-7

VS OTHER CONFERENCE: 13-6-5

FIRST HALF RECORD: 24-14-4

SECOND HALF RECORD: 23-11-8

GOALS FOR: 306 (2nd)

GOALS AGAINST: 220 (2nd)

TEAM PLUS/MINUS: +149 (1st)

POWER PLAY: 18.3% (17th)

PENALTY KILLING: 81.1% (16th)

PENALTY MINUTES: 20.6/game (13th)

1993-94 REGULAR SEASON LEADERS

GOALS: 37, John MacLean

ASSISTS: 60, Scott Stevens

POINTS: 78, Stevens

POWER PLAY GOALS: 8, MacLean, Valeri Zelepukin

SHORTHANDED GOALS: 3, Stephane Richer

GAME WINNING GOALS: 9, Richer

PLUS-MINUS: +53, Stevens

SHOTS: 277, MacLean

PENALTY MINUTES: 244, McKay

1993-94 PLAYOFFS AT A GLANCE

RESULTS: Conference Quarterfinals - defeated Buffalo 4-3 Conference Semifinals - defeated Boston 4-2 Conference Finals - lost to NY Rangers 4-3

RECORD: 11-9

HOME: 5-5

AWAY: 6-4

GOALS FOR: 2.6/game

GOALS AGAINST: 2.5/game

OVERTIME: 2-4

POWER PLAY: 17.3% (6th)

PENALTY KILLING: 87.1% (4th)

PENALTY MINUTES: 21.1/game (12th)

1993-94 PLAYOFF LEADERS

GOALS: 7, Claude Lemieux, Richer

ASSISTS: 11, Lemieux

POINTS: 18, Lemieux

POWER PLAY GOALS: 3, Richer

SHORTHANDED GOALS: 1, Nicholls

OVERTIME GOALS: 2, Richer

GAME-WINNING GOALS: 2, Richer, Lemieux

PENALTY MINUTES: 64, Mike Peluso

PLUS-MINUS: +5, Tommy Albelin

SHOTS: 72, Richer

A LOOK AHEAD TO 1994-95

Goal: Martin Brodeur and Chris Terreri provided the Devils with the best goaltending duo in hockey. Nobody else split the netminding chores so evenly (on purpose) or did as good a job. Three percentage points is all that separated them from the lead league in GAA, and the Jennings trophy.

Brodeur, who won the rookie of the year award, wasn't even penciled in as the Devil backup. That was supposed to go to Peter Sidorkiewicz, but an injury gave Brodeur all the opportunity he needed.

In the playoffs, the rookie was handed the number one job. He didn't disappoint with a 1.95 GAA, second only to Dominik Hasek.

Terreri was kind of pushed to the back of the net, only appearing in four the 20 playoff games. He didn't do anything that warranted it, but in the playoffs, teams aren't likely to do much rotating. You go with one guy and stick with him until he falters.

Because Brodeur came up so big last season, there has been trade talk involving Terreri. If Brodeur is to get the bulk of the work, Terreri is expendable and one of Peter Sidorkiewicz or U.S. Olympic goalie Mike Dunham can step in as the backup.

DEFENCE: There was no way the Devils were going to let Scott Stevens go. The Blues, who signed him as a free agent, could have given him the arch in the St. Louis, and the Devils would have still matched the offer.

It all worked out fine for Stevens. Curiously, he said the only place he ever felt he had been treated properly was in St. Louis and was overjoyed to sign with them. But, when New Jersey matched the offer, he said he couldn't be happier.

What's up with that? Who cares, say the Devils. They're even happier than he is.

Stevens is Mr. Everything. When you add up all the components — offense, defense and the physical game — he was the best in the league.

There is some other talent on the New Jersey defense. Ken Daneyko for example, is an excellent defensive defenseman who has toughness and durability. He broke off the longest

current consecutive games played streak at 388 last season when he suffered a separated shoulder.

Scott Niedermayer struggled at times last season and wasn't a force in the playoffs, but he's still very young, and will eventually become one of the more productive point getters in the league. It all depends on the amount of time he spends on the power play point.

Bruce Driver has held down one of those positions, along with Stevens, for many years. He's getting on, however, at 32. Tommy Albelin is still useful in an offensive capacity and had a good playoff.

With Viacheslav Fetisov gone, more responsiblity will fall to younger players like Jason Smith, who has a very promising future, and Jaroslav Modry, who was up and down last season and didn't see any playoff action.

FORWARD: The Devils disproved the theory last year that you need strength down the middle to be successful.

At times, Bernie Nicholls was reduced to spot duty, as was Corey Millen, who lost his job by the playoffs. Alexander Semak did a Houdini act and completely disappeared. He went from 79 points to 29. Bobby Carpenter, however, a former 50 goal scorer, was a pleasant surprise. Even though he only scored eight last year, he was outstanding defensively.

Nicholls, a free agent, signed with Chicago, but the Devils have a couple diamonds in the rough. Jim Dowd, a New Jersey native came up at the end of the season and earned 15 points in 15 games, centering Valeri Zelepukin and

Bill Guerin. He also performed well in the playoffs. The other is Brian Rolston, who was the best player on the U.S. Olympic team. He is expected to be a big scorer at some time, and will likely get his first shot at it this season.

The left wing position is okay with Stephane Richer (also right wing), Zelepukin, Tom Chorske, and Bobby Holik (also center), with Mike Peluso adding the toughness.

Richer seems a likely candidate for trade. He didn't always see eye-to-eye with Lemaire on his style of play and even sat out a couple games during the season.

The biggest enigma in the group is Holik. Hartford's first round pick in 1989 (10th overall) hasn't developed as expected. Instead of improving offensively, he's been getting worse. This will be his fifth NHL season, but he's still only 23, so it's not time yet to throw in the towel.

Right wing is probably their strongest position. They have sniper John MacLean, rugged Claude Lemieux, up-and-comer Bill Guerin, and scrappy Randy McKay. David Emma and Ben Hankinson can fill in there when the need arises.

It was an off year for Lemieux, who was besieged with personal problems stemming from his marriage. He was even granted a week's leave of absence from the team. His playoff performance, leading the team with 18 points in 20 games, shows he's already putting his troubles behind him.

The Devils don't have a dominating type scoring forward. For a team that was second in the league in scoring, their top point-getter, Richer, only had a very low 72.

That's not usually considered a positive, but maybe it is in their case, because it meant the offensive responsibility was split among more people. With one guy, he needs to come through every game, and opponents can key on him. But, more players scoring consistency at a lower level means more overall balance and little drop in efficiency if one player slumps or becomes injured.

As long as the Devil forwards continue to play at both ends of the rink, the need for one individual to step up and handle the bulk of the scoring doesn't seem necessary.

SPECIAL TEAMS: Nothing at all special here last year, which is surprising. The Devils broke yet another hockey stereotype, showing a team can be successful without a dominant power play or penalty killing unit.

The power play was only 17th in the league, and they were the only team without an individual reaching double figures in power play goals. You almost wonder if they weren't also playing their defensive style with the man advantage. Perhaps this goes back to the reality of not having one dominant sniper type.

The penalty killing percentage was only 16th best, again curious for such a good team.

Expect an improvement for both units this year. Lemaire will find a way for both to move up at least into the top third of the league.

COACHING: Jacques Lemaire did an outstanding coaching job last season and earned the Adams Trophy as coach of the year.

That's the good news. The bad is that teams that show a big improvement one year often suffer a backlash the next.

It's easier for a coach to make a big difference in his first season with a team. It's a little more difficult in the second year.

Most of the players had nothing but great things to say about Lemaire and assistant Robinson. Around playoff time, however, there were a couple disgruntled players who felt they should be on the ice.

Lemaire said he was going to play his best in the playoffs and that's what he did. That helps send a message to next year's team. Play hard all the time, or else.

There's no reason, other than that nasty backlash trend, to think it won't be another successful year for Lemaire and Robinson, who reportedly was being considered for other coaching jobs but chose to stay.

MANAGEMENT: If it ain't broke don't fix it. That appeared to be GM Lou Lamiorello's philosophy last season.

There was never any great pressure to make deals because the team kept on winning. Until April, their longest losing streak was two games.

That made the Devils the least active NHL trading partner last season. Some might suggest the fewer trades the better anyway considering past performance in that area.

But give Lamiorello credit. He finally hired the right coach and let him do his stuff.

If a player fell out of favor with Lemaire, like Millen and Semak, the replacements came from within the organization rather than a wholesale disruption of a winning team.

POTENTIAL NEW FACES: C Tom Rolston, U.S. Olympic Team; C Jim Dowd, Albany

NEEDS: Most would say they need more scoring up front. But, if you're one of the best teams as you stand, how does that translate to a need? Besides, they scored the second most often last year anyway.

McKENZIE'S BOTTOM LINE: The Devils are the top Eastern Conference team from last season that has undergone the least amount of off-season trauma and, therefore, should be able to build on coach Jacques Lemaire's outstanding first year behind the New Jersey bench.

That's as long as Devils' GM Lou Lamoriello bites the financial bullet and keeps defenceman Scott Stevens, as opposed to trading him because of his $4 million a year deal. If economics dictate that Stevens has to be traded, all bets are off for the Devils. The rock-hard blueliner is such an integral part of Devil success, especially under the Lemaire-Larry Robinson scheme of things, that his departure would create an unfillable void.

The Devils must find a replacement for useful veteran Bernie Nicholls, who has gone to the Chicago Blackhawks, but youngster Brian Rolston could fill that role nicely. The only other major concern would be a sophomore jinx for netminder Martin Brodeur, last season's rookie of the year. If that were to happen, the Devs might slip a little but it would hardly be a free fall. Veteran Chris Terreri is good insurance in that area.

As long as Stevens remains in the picture and comes close to duplicating his career year of last season, there's no reason to think the Devils won't be a rock-solid defensive team with the best balanced scoring in the NHL.

Now, if only the fans in Jersey cared.

DRAFT PICKS

The Devils have never been hesitant to jump into the European talent pool and proved it at the '94 draft.

Their first two picks were from across the pond — Russian right winger Vadim Sharifjanov in the first round and Czech winger Patrik Elias in the second.

Having said that, Sharifjanov is hardly a stereotypical European. He's been described by some as a Russian grinder, a potential power forward perhaps in the mold of another fine young (American) Devil, Bill Guerin. A year ago, Sharifjanov was being touted as a possible No. 1 overall selection. But being scouted in his draft year resulted in greater scrutiny than being watched in the season beforew his draft year. It turned out his skill level wasn't perhaps as high as some thought, but he's still a

solid NHL prospect and an excellent choice, given the fact the Devils were drafting in the second last position of the first round.

New Jersey obviously had a strong interest in drafting Tri-City American defenceman Sheldon Souray because they gave the Calgary Flames three picks (a third, fourth and fifth) to move up six spots in the third round. Of course, it's a deal the Devils could afford to make because they had an extra pick in each of the fourth and fifth rounds.

1993-94 KEYS

KEY DEALS: None

KEY INJURIES: Alexander Semak (17), Bruce Driver (14)

KEY STAT: All things being equal, like man-power for instance, there was no better team in the NHL last season. In fact, no one else was even close. The top ten are listed below.

OVERALL PLUS/MINUS RANKINGS

1.	New Jersey	+96
2.	Detroit	+69
3.	Calgary	+49
4.	NY Rangers	+39
5.	Buffalo	+26
6.	Montreal	+25
7t.	NY Islanders	+23
7t.	Toronto	+23
9t.	Washington	+18
9t.	Chicago	+18

New York Islanders

Mediocrity is forgiveable when it's backed up by a strong playoff performance. That way, at least there's some hope for next year.

Few teams in the history of the NHL have suffered as humiliating a defeat as did the Islanders in their first round series against the Rangers last season.

They bowed out in four straight, which is bad enough, but check out the scores: 6-0, 6-0, 5-1, and 5-2.

Outscored 22-3. One less goal and they would have tied the all-time mark for the fewest in a four game series.

Thanks for coming out fellows; see ya around. So much for upset predictions. And there were a few. After all, the Islanders had reached the conference finals a year earlier, also coming off an average regular season record. Both years they had to play well at the end of the year just to make the playoffs. And, most importantly, they had a history of playing well against their crosstown rivals.

At least it wasn't difficult to figure out what went wrong. Everything.

We shouldn't get too carried away because they did finish with a .500 record. It wasn't exactly a total disaster, at least during the regular season.

But there were problems. Coach Al Arbour was clearly unhappy. Not normally given to speaking out in public on such matters he suggested the team had no chemistry.

GM Don Maloney stated after the season that they lacked character and leadership.

Injuries, of course, were also a problem; goaltending was inconsistent, and just plain awful in the playoffs; and finally, they were bullied and pushed around with little resistance.

These things can be fixed and you can bet that the latter point at least, won't happen again.

1993-94 REGULAR SEASON AT A GLANCE

RECORD: 36-36-12

FINISH: 4th in Atlantic Division, 8th in Eastern Conference, 15th overall

HOME: 23-15-4 (10th)

AWAY: 13-21-8 (20th)

OVERTIME: 5-2-12 (5th)

VS OWN DIVISION: 14-13-3

VS OTHER DIVISIONS: 22-23-9

VS OWN CONFERENCE: 27-25-8

VS OTHER CONFERENCE: 9-11-4

FIRST HALF RECORD: 17-20-5

SECOND HALF RECORD: 19-16-7

GOALS FOR: 282 (11th-t)

GOALS AGAINST: 264 (13th)

TEAM PLUS/MINUS: +23 (7th-t)

POWER PLAY: 20.1% (9th)

PENALTY KILLING: 81.1% (15th)

PENALTY MINUTES: 21.3/game (16th)

1993-94 REGULAR SEASON LEADERS

GOALS: 42, Steve Thomas

ASSISTS: 56, Pierre Turgeon

POINTS: 94, Turgeon

POWER PLAY GOALS: 17, Thomas

SHORTHANDED GOALS: 5, Benoit Hogue, Marty McInnis

GAME WINNING GOALS: 7, Derek King

PLUS-MINUS: +31, McInnis

SHOTS: 254, Turgeon

PENALTY MINUTES: 237, Mick Vukota

1993-94 PLAYOFFS AT A GLANCE

RESULTS: Conference Quarterfinals - lost to NY Rangers 4-0

RECORD: 0-4

HOME: 0-2

AWAY: 0-2

GOALS FOR: 0.8/game

GOALS AGAINST: 5.5/game

OVERTIME: none

POWER PLAY: 5.9% (16th)

PENALTY KILLING: 70.4% (16th)

PENALTY MINUTES: 20.8/game (10th-t)

1993-94 PLAYOFF LEADERS

GOALS: 1, Ferraro, Thomas, Dan Plante

ASSISTS: 1, six players tied

POINTS: 1, nine players tied

POWER PLAY GOALS: 1, Thomas

SHORTHANDED GOALS: None

OVERTIME GOALS: None

GAME-WINNING GOALS: None

PENALTY MINUTES: 17, Vukota

PLUS-MINUS: 0, five players tied.

SHOTS: 9, Thomas

A LOOK AHEAD TO 1994-95

GOAL: Ron Hextall was a dud in the playoffs, but he's back as number one and as usual will play sixty plus games. He's no longer considered one of the best in the league, but he's still one of the toughest, and still capable of carrying a team when he's hot.

Last season, his goals against average was 3.08, good for 23rd in the league. He also earned five shutouts, one more than his previous career total in seven NHL seasons.

Jamie McLennan, who had no NHL experience before last season, handled the backup chores quite nicely, with a 2.84 GAA in 22 games.

Also vying for a job will be Tommy Salo, the netminder for the gold medal winning Swedish team at the Olympics.

DEFENCE: The Islander will ice a very young and inexperienced defense this year.

Gone are veterans Uwe Krupp and Tom Kurvers, which allows some of the youngsters to get more valuable playing time. There is only one proven offensive type, however, in Vladimir Malakhov. He earned 57 points and was a mainstay on the power play point, along with Kurvers. At times, he looked like the best defenseman in the league. Other times, he looked more like the worst. He's one of the elder statesmen at 26 years old.

The search is on for someone to play the other point on the powerplay. Darius Kasparaitis (21 years old) and Scott Lachance (21) have shown some ability in that area, but not enough, and certainly not last season.

Kasparaitis adds spark to the team with his feistiness, or whatever you want to call it. One player called him the dirtiest player in the league.

Both contribute to a fairly decent defensive group that includes the steady Dennis Vaske (26) and Richard Pilon (26), both of whom missed much of last season with injuries. Dean Chynoweth (25), a first round pick in 1987 could also find regular NHL employment for the first time.

If they have to go out and get a power play point guy it won't be difficult. They're among the most traded of defensmen because they're often on the weak side defensively. Like

Kurvers for instance.

If the Islanders don't dig one up from somewhere else, it probably won't be a big problem anyway. All some players need is a chance. Case in point: Lyle Odelein with Montreal last season, a proven non-scorer previously. With Malakhov as the quarterback, they won't be expected to do as much.

There's a lot of toughness on defense which helps make up for some of the lack of experience. Still, they'll be looking for seasoned veterans before the season gets too far along.

FORWARD: The Islanders were worried about their size and toughness up front last season, just like about 15 other teams. It's not much fun being bullied and they plan to change.

There's no need to adjust the number one line, however. Pierre Turgeon, Derek King and Steve Thomas form one of the more effective units in the league. Even with Turgeon missing 15 games after being struck in the cheek by a puck in a pre-game warmup, they all had at least 30 goals. Thomas set a career high with 42.

The only downside was that their power play production fell off. The three had a cumulative total of 57 man-advantage goals two years ago, but fell to 37 last season.

Elsewhere, Benoit Hogue improved his goal total for the fourth year in a row, and Marty McInnis came into his own, scoring 25 goals and using his excellent speed for five short-handed markers.

Other positives include Travis Green improving from seven to 18 goals, and

Brad Dalgarno playing well as a checker.

The negatives include two-time 40 goal scorer, Ray Ferraro, who could manage only 21 goals and 53 points. At the halfway point he had just eight goals, at which time said he would eat his hat if he didn't score more than that in the second half. He had 13. How about a bite or two?

The nice thing about an off year by Ferraro is that it's often followed by a good one. In the full seasons he's played in the NHL, the point totals go like this — 77, 59, 50, 76, 54, 42, 80, 53. That means we can look for him the high seventies this year.

Turgeon, Green, Ferraro, and Ron Sutter, obtained from Quebec for Uwe Krupp, should take care of things in the middle.

Another possible is Todd Bertuzzi, who at 6-3, 240, is big, nasty, and can score. Everything they're looking for.

Besides Thomas and Dalgarno on the right side, there is tough guy Mick Vukota and Pat Flatley, a valuable player when he's not injured, which isn't very often. Yan Kaminsky, Dan Plante and Dave Chyzowski will also get a look. Plante tied for the lead in Islanders playoff scoring despite only playing one game. He had, uh... one point.

The left side is where they'll get the muscle. Besides King, Hogue and McInnis, they have David Maley and added Troy Loney in the summer. Brian Mullen, who had a stroke and sat out the season, is cleared to make a comeback as well.

They also drafted 6-4, 215 pound Brett Lindros, who doesn't have the skill of his brother, but is supposed to be meaner. He may be a year away, but it's clear the Islanders are in love with him and want him in the lineup as soon as possible. If he starts man-handling other clubs during training camp, you never know.

Bigger, tougher, stronger. That's the new motto of the Islanders.

COACHING: Al Arbour retires as one of the most respected and winningest coaches of all time. Only Scotty Bowman has more victories to his credit and no one has coached more than Arbour's 1,606 games.

His replacement is Lorne Henning, a former Islander player, who served as Arbour's assistant for nine seasons. Henning had a short stint as a head coach in Minnesota, but for just one full season, in 1985-86.

MANAGEMENT: Don Maloney hasn't made an impact deal that's paid off well yet, but he showed some nifty moves at this year's draft, trading up to get Brett Lindros, one pick before the Maple Leafs who were almost sure to grab him.

Maloney has also made a concerted effort to address a weakness, mainly size and power from the forward position.

He has taken some criticism by allowing the likes of Jeff Norton, Bill Berg and Glenn Healy to get away, but so far he hasn't traded a Brett Hull or a Doug Gilmour, like Cliff Fletcher and Doug Risebrough.

He's bound to make some mistakes but seems the type to learn from them.

He's still new on the job but he's already showing signs of becoming a good general manager. He isn't interested in quick fixes, preferring instead to bring the prospects along slowly. That's how you build a winner.

NEEDS: Size up front and a power play point man.

POTENTIAL NEW FACES: LW Troy Loney, Anaheim; C Todd Bertuzzi, 28-54-82, Guelph (OHL); C Ron Sutter, Quebec; LW Brett Lindros, 4- 6-10 with 94 PIM in just 15 games for Kingston (OHL).

McKENZIE'S BOTTOM LINE: The bottom line on the Islander season of a year ago is this: GM Don Maloney badly miscalculated in the area of goaltending and chemistry.

Maloney opted not to sign free agent goalie Glenn Healy after the Isles' stunning upset of the defending Cup champion Penguins two years ago, choosing instead to trade for Ron Hextall from Quebec.

It was a mistake.

Hextall simply didn't do the job for the Islanders last year. In hindsight, Healy would have been a much better choice. Only when Hextall finally put together a few weeks of solid play did the Islanders put themselves into the playoff picture.

As for chemistry, Maloney didn't move some of his excess offence up front — Benoit Hogue and/or Derek King — to get some much needed toughness and muscle up front. As a result, the Isles were poorly equipped to even supply a bit of a fight against the Rangers in the first round of the playoffs.

Are the Isles any better off heading into this season?

Not really.

Head coach Al Arbour has retired, replaced by capable assistant Lorne Henning. But if the man many concede to be the best coach in the business couldn't make this unit gel, what chance does Henning have?

The goaltending issue hasn't been addressed and if it isn't, the Islanders will be so far out of the playoff picture by Christmas it won't matter.

Maybe big Brett Lindros, the Isles' first-rounder, is ready to step in and offer some physical presence to a team that has virtually none. Then again, maybe not. Now, Hogue or King or both have to be moved to get some more grit, but their market value isn't as high as it was a year ago.

Islander fortunes also rest with a pair of defencemen — big Russian Vladimir Malakhov and Latvian wild card Darius Kasparaitis. On any given night, Malakhov can be the NHL's best blueliner but he's infuriatingly inconsistent. Kasparaitis can be a world-class pest and aggravating agitator, but he copped an attitude last season that didn't serve his development or his team's either.

If those two get their act together, the Islanders have a fighting chance of getting back into the playoffs. But they're still going to need a goaltender and some size and strength up front to make it all happen.

DRAFT PICKS

Just call Isles' GM Don Maloney's draft Brett and the Blazers.

The Islanders went out of their way — shipping veteran defenceman Uwe Krupp to the Quebec Nordiques — to get big power forward prospect Brett Lindros with the ninth choice overall. The Islanders were sitting with the 12th pick overall, but realized the Toronto Maple Leafs, at No. 10 thanks to a deal with the Nords, were prepared to take Lindros if he were still available. So they moved Krupp to Quebec, flip-flopped picks with Quebec and snagged some much needed physical presence.

Lindros' overall game is rough around the edges, but he'll give the Islanders exactly what they need. The Isles were manhandled by the Rangers in the playoffs. If 1993 first rounder Todd Bertuzzi, another not so gentle giant, and Lindros can step in this season, the Isles will have gone a long way toward getting Pierre Turgeon the kind of protection he needs to play his game.

After taking Lindros, though, the Islanders showed a strong affection for the Memorial Cup champion Kamloops Blazers. They got offensive defenceman Jason Holland inthe second round, big defenceman Jason Strudwick in the third round and mobile blueliner Brad Lukowich (nephew of former WHA-NHL player Morris Lukowich) in the fourth round. And well after the top goaltending prospects were chosen, the Isles picked up Guelph's Mark McArthur, a solid prospect who turn a few heads in time.

1993-94 KEYS
KEY DEALS:
After season:

* Obtained Troy Loney from Anaheim for Tom Kurvers

* Obtained Ron Sutter and Quebec's 9th pick overall at the draft for Uwe Krupp and their 12th pick.

KEY INJURIES: Pierre Turgeon (15), Uwe Krupp (39), Richard Pilon (56).

KEY STAT: If NHL games only lasted one period, the Islanders would have been battling for top spot overall in the league last season.

They showed an ability to jump out to an early lead, which they did 36 times by the first intermission. They also scored the second most goals in the first period.

It was their play afterwards which got them in trouble. Could that be something to do with their smaller stature, or perhaps their conditioning?

MOST TIMES LEADING AFTER THE FIRST PERIOD

1. NY Rangers	37
2. Chicago	37
3. NY Islanders	36
4. Florida	34
5. Buffalo	34
6. Dallas	33
7. Washington	33
8. Boston	32

New York Rangers

How big a factor was Mike Keenan in the Rangers Stanley Cup victory?

Put it this way. If not for him, "1940" would still be a fun thing to chant around Madison Square Gardens.

The year before he came aboard, the Rangers finished five games under .500 and out of the playoffs. That's all the physical proof you need.

We'll probably never know all the circumstances behind the bizarre summertime fiasco where Keenan claimed breach of contract and left the Rangers, signing two days later with St. Louis.

Subsequently, a trade was worked out to smooth things over between the two teams — Petr Nedved for Keenan, Esa Tikkanen and Doug Lidster — but Gary Bettman wasn't amused in the least and dished out all kinds of fines for conduct detrimental to the league.

It doesn't tarnish the Stanley Cup victory. The Rangers and their fans waited too long for it. It's all theirs.

But, they can forget about a repeat performance. It just isn't going to happen and probably wouldn't have even with Keenan still aboard.

It was a one shot deal anyway that came about partly through the use of older, experienced, character players who knew what it took to win.

1993-94 REGULAR SEASON AT A GLANCE

RECORD: 52-24-8

FINISH: 1st in Atlantic Division, 1st in Eastern Conference, 1st overall

HOME: 28-8-6 (1st)

AWAY: 24-16-2 (1st)

OVERTIME: 3-1-8 (4th)

VS OWN DIVISION: 21-8-3

VS OTHER DIVISIONS: 31-16-5

VS OWN CONFERENCE: 39-16-5

VS OTHER CONFERENCE: 13-8-3

FIRST HALF RECORD: 27-12-3

SECOND HALF RECORD: 25-12-5

GOALS FOR: 299 (4th-t)

GOALS AGAINST: 231 (3rd)

TEAM PLUS/MINUS: +39 (4th)

POWER PLAY: 23.0% (1st)

PENALTY KILLING: 84.6% (3rd)

PENALTY MINUTES: 20.1/game (10th)

1993-94 REGULAR SEASON LEADERS

GOALS: 52, Adam Graves

ASSISTS: 77, Sergei Zubov

POINTS: 89, Zubov

POWER PLAY GOALS: 20, Graves

SHORTHANDED GOALS: 4, Graves and Steve Larmer

GAME WINNING GOALS: 7, Larmer

PLUS-MINUS: +28, Brian Leetch

SHOTS: 328, Leetch

PENALTY MINUTES: 170, Jeff Beukeboom

1993-94 PLAYOFFS AT A GLANCE

RESULTS: Conference Quarterfinals - defeated NY Islanders 4-0 **Conference Semi-finals** - defeated Washington 4-1 **Conference Finals** - defeated New Jersey 4-3 **Stanley Cup Finals** - defeated Vancouver 4-3

RECORD: 16-7

HOME: 9-4

AWAY: 7-3

GOALS FOR: 3.5/game

GOALS AGAINST: 2.2/game

OVERTIME: 2-2

POWER PLAY: 21.2% (3rd)

PENALTY KILLING: 91.3% (1st)

PENALTY MINUTES: 16.5/game (5th)

1993-94 PLAYOFF LEADERS

GOALS: 12, Mark Messier

ASSISTS: 23, Leetch

POINTS: 34, Leetch

POWER PLAY GOALS: 5, Alexei Kovalev

SHORTHANDED GOALS: 1, Glenn Anderson, Messier

OVERTIME GOALS: 2, Stephane Matteau

GAME-WINNING GOALS: 4, Leetch, Messier

PENALTY MINUTES: 50, Beukeboom

PLUS-MINUS: +19, Leetch

SHOTS: 93, Graves

A LOOK AHEAD TO 1994-95

GOAL: Mike Richter had a 42-12-6 record in net, easily the best winning percentage in the league, and one of the best in NHL history.

The Rangers had to choose between Richter and Vanbiesbrouck last year. The decision to let the latter go would have been easily criticized had Richter not responded so well.

Backup Glenn Healy didn't perform up to expectations, earning only a 10-12-2 mark with a 3.07 GAA. Part of that can be blamed on inactivity. He played in the fewest games of his career.

With Canada's outstanding Olympic goalie Corey Hirsch also in the picture, that frees up Healy for trade bait.

Hey, maybe they can package him in a deal to St. Louis for Mike Keenan.

DEFENCE: This could be a trouble position for the Rangers. Without the discipline instilled by Mike Keenan, along with his persistent reminders, the whole thing could fall apart defensively.

In fact, it's very likely. And it might not be very pretty.

The best defense is a good offense. At least as far as Sergei Zubov and Brian Leetch are concerned. And they should know.

Never mind that Zubov also plays left wing, center and right wing, often all on the same shift. With point production like his, the defensive aspects can be overlooked. 89 points, 49 on the power play, almost unbelievable when you consider he spent time in the minors at the start of the season and was called by Keenan, "the least fit athlete on the team."

Leetch, with 79 points, tied for third in team scoring. He's no defensive dynamo either, but again it doesn't matter. He was a dominant force in the playoffs, leading the league in points, and earning the Conn Smythe Trophy.

Jeff Beukeboom, normally paired with Leetch, gives the Rangers a physical presence behind the blueline. Kevin Lowe, another ex-Oiler lends stability and leadership. So does Jay Wells, who is 35 years old, the same age as Lowe.

Alexander Karpovtsev is a young player who should improve with time. Just suiting up for 17 playoff games under Keenan means you've already passed some sort of test.

Rookies last season with short auditions included Joby Messier and Mattias Norstrom. Both are expected to have a future with the team.

FORWARD: Not as impressive as you might think, considering they're Stanley Cup champions. But, remember, defensemen Leetch and Zubov, were two of the top three scorers. After Adam Graves and his 52 goals, the next in line was Mark Messier, with only 26.

A couple years ago, nobody could have predicted that Adam Graves would ever be a 50 goal scorer. In the 1989-90 season, he had just nine goals for Detroit and Edmonton in 76 games. The following year he had just seven for Edmonton. Then in his first two seasons with the Rangers, after signing as a free agent, he had 26 and then 36.

The amazing thing about Graves is that he's not only a sniper, he's an outstanding defensive player. Fifty goal scorers who play well defensively are a rare commodity. Well, there is Fedorov and Shanahan, but still they're a rare breed.

Graves, along with Mark Messier, give the Rangers two of the better "character" players in the game. Leetch may have won the Conn Smythe Trophy, but Messier, through his inspired play and leadership, had as much to do with the Rangers winning as any player on the ice.

Steve Larmer can be included in that bunch as well. But, he and Messier aren't getting any younger. They're both 33 years old, well past the point where production is expected to wane.

The trade for Petr Nedved gives them a quality youngster, something they sorely needed. The 22 year old had 20 points in 19 games for St. Louis after signing with them as a free agent and creating a hulabaloo almost as great as the Keenan caper. In Nedved's last full season in the NHL, he had 38 goals and 71 points for Vancouver.

Alexei Kovalev is young too at just 21 years of age. He emerged towards the end of the season and in the playoffs. Although seemingly doomed early in the year because of his weak defensive play and selfish attitude a move from right wing to centre seemed to make all the difference. He became a useful commodity, one who could score enough to offset his defensive-j-shortcomings. He finished third on the team with 21 playoff points.

One incident earlier in the season gave a good indication of Keenan's regard for Kovalev at the time. Frustrated with the player's extended shifts, Keenan left him on for the last six minutes of a period and most of the first seven in the next. When he tried to come off, Keenan waved him away. At the end of the game, Keenan remarked sarcastically that Kovalev probably thought he was being rewarded. He was right. Kovalev said that's the way he likes to play all the time.

Nevertheless, considering his play in the playoffs, he isn't likely to be traded, but he drops some in value with the addition of Petr Nedved in the Keenan deal. That makes Messier and Nedved the men in the middle and Kovalev the odd man out, or at least likely to be moved back to wing.

Two ex-Oiler forwards won't be back. Craig MacTavish, an unrestricted free agent, signed with Philadelphia. Glenn Anderson will likely play in Europe.

That still leaves competent two-way players like Brian Noonan, Stephane Matteau, Mike Hudson and Greg Gilbert. They're Keenan type players, evidenced by the fact he coached them all before they came to New York.

Maybe they'll all be traded to St. Louis.

Other forwards include Sergei Nemchinov, Nick Kypreos, Mike Hartman, and Ed Olczyk.

How this group performs will have as much to do with the coach as anything. Without knowing who that man is at press time, it makes some analysis difficult.

Chances are, however, the forwards will join with the rest of the team in their fall from grace.

SPECIAL TEAMS: When you put out a power play and Brian Leetch and Sergei Zubov are manning the points, it doesn't get much better. Doesn't even matter that much who the forwards are, but a sniper like Graves (20 power play goals last year) helps considerably as do Messier and Nedved.

17 of Leetch's 23 goals and 9 of 12 by Zubov came with the man-advantage last season for the number one ranked power play in the league.

The penalty killing percentage was third best in the league. With all that defensive forward talent around they should remain up near the top.

COACHING: Colin Campbell has an incredibly tough act to follow, and it will be a thankless one at that.

MANAGEMENT: It's pretty hard to give much credit to Neil Smith for the

Stanley Cup win, unless you count hiring Keenan in the first place.

That'll do. He obviously knew there would be problems with Keenan, or at least suspected. But, his concern was making the Rangers winners.

That's not a bad guy to have running things.

NEEDS: An influx of youth on all fronts.

POTENTIAL NEW FACES: C Petr Nedved, St. Louis; D Joby Messier, Binghamton; D Mattias Norstram, Binghamton; G Corey Hirsch, Canadian Olympic Team.

McKENZIE'S BOTTOM LINE: With the departure of Mike Keenan, there is significant risk in forecasting another strong season for the defending Stanley Cup champions. Ask the Montreal Canadiens about the hangover they suffered last season after winning the 1993 Stanley Cup.

Factor in the upheaval of the whole Keenan fiasco and you have the ingredients for potential disaster.

But...

Because Rangers' GM Neil Smith did the expected and named Colin Campbell as the head coach, there'll be a good degree of continuity in terms of the team's style and on-ice approach.

Yes, the Rangers are an old team, but not as old as some would have you believe. With Mike Richter in net, Brian Leetch and Sergei Zubov on defence and Adam Graves and rising star Alex Kovalev up front, the Rangers have reasonably youthful talent and experience at all key positions. Plus, some of the oldsters (Mark Messier, Steve Larmer et al) aren't quite ready for the scrap heap just yet.

The key, in many respects, will be rebuilding the defence from the No. 4 through No. 6 spots. Leetch, Zubov and Jeff Beukeboom comprise the first three slots. The Cup win notwithstanding, the Rangers were vulnerable after that trio.

In some respects, the climate in New York might actually be better without Keenan. If he were still there, the rift between he and GM Smith would likely only widen. The only way it could all blow up in the Rangers' face would be if the team's veterans, especially Messier, aren't buying what the new man behind the bench is selling.

DRAFT PICKS

The Rangers didn't really need a top goaltending prospect. They have Mike Richter leading the way, soon to be backed up by Corey Hirsch, the former Kamloops Blazer stopper who looks as though he's going to be a good one.

But when you're picking No. 26 over-all, the last selection in the first round, you often do subscribe to the theory of taking the best player available. And in this case, that meant the Rangers taking Sault Ste. Marie Greyhound netminder Dan Cloutier.

It was surprising Cloutier fell that far. Pre-draft prognostications had him going to either Boston or Detroit in the first round, but Boston shocked everyone by taking Russian netminder Evgeny Ryabchikov and Detroit, knowing it was going to deal for a proven keeper in Mike Vernon, opted for a defenceman instead.

That left the Rangers looking at Cloutier.

Wise move, really. A team can never have too much goaltending. Cloutier's chances of one day playing in the NHL are better than most of the other prospects the Rangers were considering at No. 26, so even if New York finds it's stacked up at net when Cloutier is finally ready to play, another team will be more than willing to pay a premium for a goaltender.

Cloutier is a tough, competitive kid who is likely to finish out his junior career and require some minor pro seasoning before he's ready.

The rest of the way, the Rangers went with an intersting blend of skill and toughness. Much of that skill comes from the five Europeans they drafted and the toughness is centred on players such as Laval defenceman Sylvain Blouin (492 penalty minutes), Oshawa General scrapper Rick Boulton and Tacoma tough guy Jamie Butt.

1993-94 KEYS

KEY DEALS:

* Obtained Glenn Anderson, Scott Malone and a 4th round pick in 1994 for Mike Gartner.

* Obtained Brian Noonan and Stephane Matteau from Chicago for Tony Amonte and Matt Oates.

* Obtained Craig MacTavish from Edmonton for Todd Marchant

Post-Season:

* traded coach Mike Keenan to St. Louis along with Esa Tikkanen and Bruce Driver for Petr Nedved

KEY INJURIES: none

KEY STAT: It's been a long time since Stanley Cup victories for the New York Rangers. How Long?

Since 1954, all of the following took place before last season:

* They've played 3,882 regular season games.

* There have been 25,596 regular season goals scored in Ranger games — 12,612 for and 12,984 against.

* They've had 32 different coaches, 21 captains and nine general managers.

* Thirty-three Ranger players have been voted into the Hall of Fame.

* The Rangers have taken 31 regular season penalty shots, scoring on 16 of them. Opponents have had 31 penalty shots, scoring on 13.

* Almost 300 million fans have attended regular season games around the league, just since 1960.

* All six league presidents, and Commissioner Gary Bettman, held office.

Ottawa Senators

Let's try to look at the positives, shall we? Okay, here goes:

* the Senators had a 6-5-1 record against Pacific Division Teams.

* there was a team whose power play was worse (Anaheim).

* they won four big games more than their inaugural season.

* somebody on the team (Troy Murray +1 with Ottawa) actually finished with a plus.

* they beat Montreal twice, both times in Montreal.

* they won four overtime games.

* rookie Alexei Yashin had 30 goals and 79 points.

* if they hadn't had so many injuries they could have won at least three more games.

* they weren't mathematically elimated from the playoff race until February.

* they had a player on pace for 50 goals in Bob Kudelski, until they traded him.

* they got Radek Bonk in the draft.

* construction of the new Palladium should be under way by the time you read this.

See, it wasn't all bad. And keeping with the positive frame of mind, someday it will get even better.

1993-94 REGULAR SEASON AT A GLANCE

RECORD: 14-61-9

FINISH: 7th in Northeast Division, 14th in Eastern Conference, 26th overall

HOME: 8-30-4 (26th)

AWAY: 6-31-5 (26th)

OVERTIME: 4-4-9 (13th-t)

VS OWN DIVISION: 4-23-3

VS OTHER DIVISIONS: 10-38-6

VS OWN CONFERENCE: 5-46-7

VS OTHER CONFERENCE: 9-15-2

FIRST HALF RECORD: 8-31-3

SECOND HALF RECORD: 6-30-6

GOALS FOR: 201 (26th)

GOALS AGAINST: 397 (26th)

TEAM PLUS/MINUS: -149 (26th)

POWER PLAY: 14.5% (15th)

PENALTY KILLING: 73.3% (26th)

PENALTY MINUTES: 20.4/game (12th)

1993-94 REGULAR SEASON LEADERS

GOALS: 30, Alexei Yashin

ASSISTS: 49, Yashin

POINTS: 79, Yashin

POWER PLAY GOALS: 11, Yashin

SHORTHANDED GOALS: 2, Yashin, Phil Bourque

GAME WINNING GOALS: 3, Yashin, Dan Quinn

PLUS-MINUS: +2, Troy Murray Shots: 232, Yashin

PENALTY MINUTES: 214, Dennis Vial

A LOOK AHEAD TO 1994-95

GOAL: What the heck difference does it make? Patrick Roy couldn't have taken this team out of the basement. Goaltending should be their last priority. Once they have a team that can play in front of him, then it's time to worry about a goaltender who can make a contribution to the winning cause.

In the meantime, Craig Billington and Darrin Madelay can do as good a job as anyone else.

DEFENCE: There will be a number of new faces in the defense corps of the Senators this season. Three players — Sean Hill, Jim Paek, and Chris Dahlquist — were obtained in the off-season, and step right in as regulars.

Hill was obtained from Anaheim and can play on the power play; Paek, a stay-at-home defenseman, and former Penguin, was picked up for future considerations from Los Angeles; Dahlquist, 31 years old, was a regular on the Calgary defense last season.

Norm MacIver had an injury plagued year after leading Ottawa in scoring their first year in the NHL. MacIver suffered through a bruised heart and then a broken leg. If he's recovered he mans one of the points on the power play.

Brad Shaw provides more experienced and is no stranger to the power play either. Kerry Huffman, obtained on waivers from Quebec, during the season is also penciled in as a regular along with tough guy Dennis Vial.

That gives the Senators a much better defense than last year when 15 different players tried their hand at the position. Still not very good, but better.

In limbo are free agent Gord Dineen, and Steve Konroyd, as well as Canadian Olympian Derek Mayer and Darren Rumble, both of whom were offered termination contracts. They didn't sign with anybody else so they'll probably be battling for backup positions at training camp.

Others looking for full time employment are Dimitri Filimonov, Hank Lammens, big Francois Leroux, free agent signee Corey Foster and Kent Paynter.

At least there will be a battle for jobs this year. That's the first sign that they could be ready to move up from the ridiculous to the mediocre.

FORWARD: If the Senators are trying to build with strength up the middle, then they have three of the best building blocks in the game.

Alexei Yashin, Alexandre Daigle, and now Radek Bonk are all 20 or younger, and all have unlimited promise.

One of them on each of their top three lines will be entertaining to watch, despite the fact there's precious little to put out with them.

That means none of them will tear the league apart for awhile, and all will suffer their growing pains.

Daigle went through plenty last season. He got off to a great start with 12 points in his first six NHL games, laying early claim to the Calder Trophy and was even challenging for the scoring title. That was about all we heard from him. He almost completely disappeared by late season, finishing with 20 goals and 51 points. He didn't get a single vote in the Calder ballotting.

Instead, Alexei Yashin moved to the head of the class with a hot streak of scoring and some exciting play. He too, faltered, however, and ended up fourth in the Calder voting.

No big deal with either one of them. They showed they have talent. Consistency comes with experience, a competitive team, and somebody to pass to. Both have bright futures.

It probably didn't help either one when Bob Kudelski was traded. The only legitimate sniper, besides Sylvain Turgeon who was hurt for much of the year, was traded to Florida for spare parts despite the fact he was on pace for 50 goals.

Nobody's saying Kudelski was Mario Lemieux, but he took some pressure off the youngsters by popping in the goals. They had nobody else to do that unless

you count Dave McLlwain, who played above and beyond expectations. An underated fourth liner for much of his career, he put on a nice offensive show for a time when he played on the top line.

Of course, that's not where he belongs, and wouldn't be playing if there was anybody else.

Dan Quinn was brought in late season, a player no one else was willing to take a chance on with his checkered past. He responded well, with seven goals in just 13 games, but contract negotiations stalled and it appears he'll return to Europe.

Free agent signee Pat Elynuik, who played last season with Tampa Bay should be a regular somewhere on the right side and along with Turgeon could score more goals than normal considering the talent at centre.

After that, we have a group of terminal non-scorers who are there to make sure the other guys don't get pushed around. Troy Mallette, Claude Boivin and Scott (Sandman) Levins, will fill that role. That's if Levins can wake up in time to get to the games. Twice in one week last year he overslept, missing practise, and another time, he had to run after the bus to catch it.

Fill in the blanks with Evgeny Davydov, Andrew McBain (free agent), Phil Bourque and Michel Picard (free agent signee).

SPECIAL TEAMS: There's nothing special about these special teams. They were terrible last season.

Things will get better, because they can't get any worse. The power play especially, has to improve and it will with more people around who can handle that type of responsibility.

Penalty killing will improve too, with proven defensive quality having been added on forward and defense.

COACHING: He will be fired. He won't be fired. He will be fired. That's mostly what you hear about Rick Bowness, and will continue to hear until he's let go.

He could probably escape criticsm for last season's mess if Florida and Anaheim hadn't done so well. If they can do it with lousy players, why not Ottawa?

He will have to show some improvement with this year's edition of the Senators or he'll be shown the door.

MANAGEMENT: Randy Sexton didn't exactly distinguish himself in his first year as Ottawa general manager, but he didn't do irreparable harm either.

He made one lousy trade, giving away Bob Kudelski, on pace for 50 goals, to Florida for Evgeny Davydov and Scott Levins. Nobody would dispute that Kudelski had suddenly acquired some surprising trade value, and that it wouldn't be too bad an idea to trade him before he lost it, but to give him up for nothing wasn't too smart. Evgeny Davydov, a seven goal man, and dime-a-dozen tough guy Scott Levins, both spare parts at best, sure weren't it.

The young guys need experienced veterans around. To Sexton's credit, he saw there was a problem and went about fixing it, acquiring a whole bunch of players in that vein after the end of the season.

A test of Sexton's resolve will be the Yashin contract dispute. Yashin was apparently happy when he signed the five year deal but now wants it re-negotiated because he had a good season, and because he claims Sexton said they would. Yashin is threatening to sit out.

It will be interesting to see how it's handled.

POTENTIAL NEW FACES: C Radek Bonk, Las Vegas (IHL); RW Pat Elynuik, Tampa Bay; LW Randy Cunneyworth, Chicago: D Jim Paek, Los Angeles; D Corey Foster, Hershey (AHL); RW Michel Picard, Hartford; D Sean Hill, Anaheim; D Chris Dahlquist, Calgary.

NEEDS: Scoring from the wings, power play quarterback, and time. Lots of time.

McKENZIE'S BOTTOM LINE: If the Lightning find their situation troublesome, think how the poor Senators must feel.

The worst team in the NHL for the past two years running has had difficulty coming up with the formula for (relative) success that teams such as Florida, Anaheim, Tampa and San Jose have found.

The Senators' biggest problems have been behind their blueline. And what major steps have been taken to address them? None really.

Ottawa's team defence is still shoddier than it should be. Goaltending has also faltered.

The most significant off-season addition, assuming he could be signed, was Czech centre Radek Bonk, whose 42 goals for Las Vegas in the International League last season would suggest he's a ready-for-prime-time player.

Unquestionably, he'll be a help, especially if Alexei Yashin's contract hassles blow up into a full-fledged divorce. Alexandre Daigle, with a year's experience, is only going to get better, too.

But the other expansion teams proved that initial success if founded more on defence than offence. That seems to have been lost on the Senators, who look as though they're odds-on favorite to have the No. 1 pick in the NHL entry draft next year.

When the Senators finally arrive as a contending team, they'll arrive with a bang provided by some of the game's brightest young offensive stars. Until then, though, it's bound to be a sorry state of affairs.

DRAFT PICKS

If there were any NHL team that left itself open to second guessing at the '94 draft, it was the Ottawa Senators.

The Senators' most dire need is for help behind their own blueline, which made defenceman Oleg Tverdosky and Ed Jovanovski and goaltender Jamie Storr most attractive prospects indeed.

There were just two problems. Jovanovski went No. 1 to Florida and Tverdosky No. 2 to Anaheim. That left the Senators with a choice between the highly-touted netminder (Storr) or the player many consider to be the No. 1 talent in the class of '94 — Las Vegas Thunder centre Radek Bonk.

They went with Bonk, even though they already have two blue-chip talents at centre — Alexei Yashin from the '92 draft (No. 2 overall) and Alexandre Daigle (No. 1 from the '93) draft.

Is there going to be enough puck to go around for three young centres and their egos? Is there going to be enough bucks to go around?

It's quite possible only two of the three will be in Ottawa long term, since Yashin is unhappy with his financial lot in life and is looking for a new renegotiated contract that could lead to either a walkout or a trade or both.

In any event, as long the Senators can sign Bonk, they have the '94 draftee most ready to step in and contribute. His 42 goals in Las Vegas last season were no fluke, but it will also be interesting to see how Bonk's temperament melds on a third-year team that is struggling badly and showing no signs of getting much better because the issues of defence and goaltending haven't been addressed satisfactorily.

There will be some who suggest the Senators would have been better off taking their chances on Storr, but that was a risk they weren't prepared to take, especially when they had the top talent of the draft dropped into their lap.

1993-94 KEYS

KEY DEALS:

* signed free agent Dan Quinn

* obtained Steve Konroyd from Detroit for Daniel Berthiaume

* obtained Claude Boivin and Kirk Daubenspeck from Philadelphia for Mark Lamb.

* obtained Scott Levins, Evgeny Davydov and two draft picks for Bob Kudelski.

Post-Season:

* obtained Jim Paek from Los Angeles for future considerations

* obtained Sean Hill from Anaheim with 1994 ninth-round pick for 1994 third-round pick

* signed free agent Pat Elynuik and Randy Cunneyworth

KEY INJURIES: Dave McLlwain (18 games), Sylvain Turgeon (37), Brad Shaw (18), Norm MacIver (31).

KEY STAT: Bad enough that the Senators were the worst team in the NHL on special teams, but at even-strength nobody was even close to being as weak.

WORST TEAM PLUS/MINUS RECORDS

Ottawa	-149	Winnipeg	- 90
Edmonton	- 40	Hartford	- 34
Los Angeles	- 30	Tampa Bay	- 26
St. Louis	- 26	Philadelphia	- 20

Philadelphia Flyers

After four straight seasons of missing the playoffs it looked like the Flyers would end the dubious streak when they started off last year with an 11-3-0 record.

When all was said and done they had missed the playoffs for the fifth straight time.

After that initial blast, they went 24-36-10. What went wrong? Lindros was injured and missed 19 games, which didn't help, but it didn't hurt that much either. They still played .500 hockey without him.

Scoring wasn't a problem at all. They had plenty of firepower.

The difficulties were more in the defensive zone. Their defense was too young and inexperienced. So was their goaltending.

Not to worry. A new era starts (again) with Bobby Clarke (again) back in the picture. His first kick at the can in Philadelphia, between 1984-85 to 1989-90 produced three first place finishes, and two Stanley Cup final appearances. Mind you, Mike Keenan was the coach both times they reached the finals.

Last year in Florida, Clarke did an outstanding job at building a contender from nothing. He left his heart in Philadelphia, however, so he's back as both GM and president. A little older, a little wiser, he should help guide the Flyers back to respectability.

1993-94 REGULAR SEASON AT A GLANCE

RECORD: 35-39-10

FINISH: 6th in Atlantic Division, 10th in Conference, 18th overall

HOME: 19-20-3 (18th)

AWAY: 16-19-7 (16th)

OVERTIME: 3-5-10 (20th)

VS OWN DIVISION: 11-16-4

VS OTHER DIVISIONS: 24-23-6

VS OWN CONFERENCE: 28-24-8

VS OTHER CONFERENCE: 7-15-2

FIRST HALF RECORD: 20-19-3

SECOND HALF RECORD: 15-20-7

GOALS FOR: 294 (6th-t)

GOALS AGAINST: 314 (23rd)

TEAM PLUS/MINUS: -20 (19th)

POWER PLAY: 20.8 (5th)

PENALTY KILLING: 80.7 (18th)

PENALTY MINUTES: 20.2/game (11th)

1993-94 REGULAR SEASON LEADERS

GOALS: 44, Eric Lindros

ASSISTS: 67, Mark Recchi

POINTS: 107, Recchi 77

POWER PLAY GOALS: 14, Rob Brind'Amour

SHORTHANDED GOALS: 2, Lindros, Dave Tippett

GAME WINNING GOALS: 9, Lindros

PLUS-MINUS: +16, Lindros, Jeff Finley

SHOTS: 230, Brind'Amour

PENALTY MINUTES: 137, Dave Brown

A LOOK AHEAD TO 1994-95

GOAL: Dominic Roussel and Tommy Soderstrom are both young, inexperienced and after last year's performance, leave some question as to their ability to be number one goalies in the NHL.

Maybe they both had the sophemore jinx. Roussel, who started the season by winning eight games in a row, was at least decent with a 29-20-4 mark and a 3.34 GAA.

Soderstrom wasn't. He did have some medical problems generated from an irregular heart beat, however. His record was 6-18-4, with a 4.01 GAA. The goals against average was the worst in the league for netminders on teams other than Ottawa.

Not that the two were completely to blame. They didn't get much protection from the young defense in front of them.

These things are funny, though. One of the two could be playing in the all-star game this year. Nobody knows when a goaltender is going to move to the head of the class. Case in point: Dominik Hasek last season.

The Flyers can't wait much longer, however, for their young netminders to become Dominik Hasek. They need a legitimate number one goaltender, and they need it now.

Roussel and Soderstrom can fight it out for the backup and go through the learning process like everyone else.

Clarke, who had the pleasure of watching John Vanbiesbrouck in Florida last season, won't put up with incompetence in the nets for long. It wouldn't be a surprise if he makes a deal before the season starts.

DEFENCE: They are young, inexperienced, (sound familiar? — see goaltending) not defensive-minded enough, and don't use their size to full advantage.

In other words, they ain't so hot. But, the situation won't be difficult to fix. The Flyers don't need much offense from the blueline, they've got enough up front. They just need guys to stop the other team from scoring, keep the front of the net clear, and to make opposing forwards pay the price for venturing into their territory.

Those types are easier to find than scoring defensemen. Sometimes, the scoring ones you just luck into. Like Garry Galley. Not too many players wait until 30 before coming into their own as a scorer. And not too many have their two best seasons after that age.

Even more amazing, Galley managed all this after being diagnosed with Chronic Fatigue Syndrome. He had 70 points from the blueline last season, 35 on the power play.

He was also openly critical of since fired coach Terry Simpson, but man enough to admit it when the remarks in the press were attributed to an anonymous source.

Galley has no obvious help on the power play point. Yves Racine, who had 52 points last season, was dumped off to Montreal for underachiever Kevin Haller. Tough move to figure, especially with nobody to take his place.

Dimitri Yushkevich was penciled in as a power play pointman before the season started, but proved woefully inadequate. He could get another chance, and could still produce. Same with Haller who's only 23 years old.

The rest of the defenders who get the bulk of the playing time are stay-at-home types, which makes it difficult to understand why they played so poorly as a group.

Among them are: Jeff Finley, a tall player but not a physical one with only 24 PIM in 55 games; Rob Zettler, a more aggressive type who came over from San Jose; Ryan McGill, who dropped 126 penalty minutes from the season before; rookie Jason Bowen, who

wasn't quite as aggressive as advertised; and a surprise starter who came out of nowhere, Stewart Malgunas.

They're within grasp of becoming a force that could make life miserable for opposing forwards. But they need a veteran or two, a defensive type guy who can give them some stability and help out the younger players.

FORWARD: The Flyers were pretty close to having three 100 point players in their lineup last season. Recchi earned 107, Brind'Amour 97, and Lindros, who missed 19 games, also had 97.

Can't do much better than that unless you throw in Mikael Renberg, who had 38 goals and set a record for Swedish rookies with 82 points.

If Lindros is healty (and Lemieux is not), he will be the leading scorer and most valuable player in the NHL this season. Remember where you heard it.

Recchi is an underated player who has been overshadowed by big stars in his career, first Lemieux in Pittsburgh and now Lindros. But he doesn't feed off the big guys. He's self-sustaining and gets his points regardless. In the 19 games Lindros missed last season, Recchi had 32 points.

Brind'Amour just keeps getting better. After St. Louis gave up on him in the 1990-91 season when the left wing/center had just 49 points, he's had years of 77, 86, and now 97 points.

He played some left wing with Lindros and Recchi on the top line, but may be better suited as the second line center.

After the top four, there's not a lot in the way of scoring. Josef Beranek had 28, but was leading the league after goals in each of his first eight games. That tied him with Pavel Bure for the longest streak of the year. Beranek only had 16 points in the second half of the season so more consistency will be needed.

Brent Fedyk can do some scoring, especially when he's playing on the Crazy Eights line with Lindros and Recchi. Then again, who couldn't score with those guys. They make a nice fit when they're together.

That's it for proven scoring, besides Kevin Dineen, who has been slowed with ailments. Andre Faust is expected to contribute more there as well.

They don't need any more scoring anyway. What they need is some size and intimidation, something currently in short supply.

They did sign Craig MacTavish to help with the checking responsibilities. Mark Lamb, a free agent with compensation, is a good guy to have around as is Rob DiMaio, obtained from Tampa Bay.

Otherwise, they have to fill the slots with character players, preferably big ones, who will spend the majority of their time worrying about the other team's goal scorers and will make life difficult for them.

SPECIAL TEAMS: No surprise that the power play was so effective with the kind of forwards they have. They were fifth in the league. Surprisingly though, they traded away a valuable point man in Yves Racine, whom they obtained from Detroit during the season.

Penalty killing wasn't very good, ranking just 18th in the league. Part of the reason for that was a group of inexperienced defensemen. MacTavish will help out there from the forward position.

COACHING: The new coach is Terry Murray, which makes him the fourth on the Flyers in four years. Murray had some good success with Washington before being dumped last season when things didn't go quite so well.

The players won't miss Terry Simpson much. A lot didn't like him and some said so. Clarke says he likes Murray's communication skills much better than Simpson's, a factor gaining importance in this day and age.

Only one thing matters right now, and that's getting into the playoffs. If they don't make it, the Flyers will be looking for their fifth coach in five years.

MANAGEMENT: Clarke did a good job in his year in Florida. He made all kinds of deals to get the right players to make that team competitive. Roger Neilson did the rest.

Clarke has had success when he's had good coaches. While his drafting record has been weak, his trading record has been much better.

He has his supporters and others who think he's not a very good GM. One thing in his favor is the ability to recognize character players. And why not? He was one of the great character players of all time.

NEEDS: A veteran goalie, more experience on defense, somebody to help out on the power play point.

POTENTIAL NEW FACES: Craig MacTavish, NY Rangers; Kevin Haller, Montreal.

McKENZIE'S BOTTOM LINE: It seems incongruous that a team with a star the stature of Eric Lindros could miss the playoffs in consecutive years, but here's a news flash for you — it could happen again.

As dominant as Lindros can be — and good health willing, this is the year he really takes off for a 50-goal, 100-plus point season — the Flyers aren't going anywhere until they get NHL calibre netminding.

The only reason the Flyers missed the playoffs last season was because Tommy Soderstrom and Dominic Roussel couldn't get the job done between the pipes. It's that simple.

One of two things has to happen this year. Either Soderstrom or Roussel, or both, have to re-discover their fine form of two years ago. Or new Flyer GM Bob Clarke has to go out and find himself a reliable No. 1 goalkeeper who can put the Flyers over the top.

The Flyer defence could also use a boost, especially if Garry Galley is traded because of his dissatisfaction with his contract and the way he was treated last season. But the priority has to be goaltending.

New coach Terry Simpson takes over a solid, sometimes spectacular, lineup, led by Lindros, Calder Trophy finalist Mikael Renberg, Mark Recchi, Rod Brind'Amour and Kevin Dineen. Most non-playoff teams should be so lucky to have that kind of firepower up front.

Some believe Clarke may make some dramatic changes to the composition of the club, which would mean trading Recchi (if there's a taker on his multi-million dollar salary). But it seems the only thing the Flyers really need is a lot of help in net and a little on defence and they'll be poised to make the playoffs — finally.

DRAFT PICKS

What is there to say about a team that didn't make its first pick until No. 62 overall in the third round?

Not much.

The Flyers' top pick was Russian defender Artem Anisimov and they followed that with fourth-rounder Adam Magarrell, another blueliner but this time from Brandon of the Western League.

No question the Flyers need help on defence, but this wasn't the draft to supply it for the coming season.

The Flyers took a Swedish goaltender, Johan Hedberg, in the ninth round, which is all well and good for the long term. But the immediate challenge is to get their current Swedish netminder Tommy Soderstrom playing like he did two years ago.

1993-94 KEYS

KEY DEALS:

* obtained Yves Racine from Detroit for Terry Carkner

* obtained Rob Zettler from San Jose for Viacheslav Butsayev.

* obtained Mark Lamb from Ottawa for Claude Boivin and Kirk Daubenspeck

Post-Season

* obtained Kevin Haller from Montreal for Yves Racine

KEY INJURIES: Eric Lindros (19 games), Jason Bowen (22), Yves Racine (15).

KEY STAT: No team had more offense than the big four of Philadelphia last season - Mark Recchi, Eric Lindros, Rob Brind'Amour and Mikael Renberg.

With that kind of nucleus, the rest of the pieces can't be far behind.

MOST TOTAL POINTS FROM EACH TEAM'S TOP FOUR SCORERS

Philadelphia	383
Detroit	372
Los Angeles	361
Pittsburgh	353
Toronto	350
Calgary	344
Boston	335
NY Rangers	331
St. Louis	331

Pittsburgh Penguins

At the end of last year's regular season there were plenty of reasons to make Pittsburgh the favorites to win the Stanley Cup:

* They finished third overall in the league, and that was with Lemieux in the lineup for only 22 games.

* Lemieux was healthy again, or as healthy as he'd been all year.

* After getting Sandstrom and McEachern from Los Angeles, they were set up with three good scoring lines.

* They had already won two Stanley Cups with most of the same people.

* With many of the nucleus players getting on in years, it was good inspiration to go for it all.

* On paper, they were strong at forward, defense and in net.

One other measurement, however, couldn't be made until they went out on the ice, and that one fell far too short. They were a minus in heart and desire.

They were bounced by Washington in the first round, four games to two. They scored 12 goals in the six games, and in game number two, which they won 2-1, they were outshot 35-17. In the final game, they were zonked 6-3.

Not exactly the Penguin way, now is it. End of the line? Pretty close. They're older now, most of them a year or two past their prime. They won a couple Stanley Cups, and apparently aren't hungry for any more.

1993-94 REGULAR SEASON AT A GLANCE

RECORD: 44-27-13

FINISH: 1st in Northeast Division, 3rd in Eastern Conference, 3rd overall

HOME: 29-11-2 (2nd)

AWAY: 19-18-5 (10th)

OVERTIME: 4-2-13 (8th)

VS OWN DIVISION: 21-9-2

VS OTHER DIVISIONS: 23-18-11

VS OWN CONFERENCE: 35-19-6

VS OTHER CONFERENCE: 9-8-7

FIRST HALF RECORD: 21-12-9

SECOND HALF RECORD: 23-15-4

GOALS FOR: 306 (2nd)

GOALS AGAINST: 285 (19th)

TEAM PLUS/MINUS: +10 (12th)

POWER PLAY: 18.8% (13th)

PENALTY KILLING: 82.0% (10th)

PENALTY MINUTES: 19.3/game (7th)

1993-94 REGULAR SEASON LEADERS

GOALS: 41, Kevin Stevens

ASSISTS: 67, Jaromir Jagr

POINTS: 99, Jagr

POWER PLAY GOALS: 21, Stevens

SHORTHANDED GOALS: 2, Shawn McEachern (5 overall), Mullen

GAME WINNING GOALS: 9, Joe Mullen

PLUS-MINUS: +24, Martin Straka

SHOTS: 298, Jagr

PENALTY MINUTES: 199, Ulf Samuelsson

1993-94 PLAYOFFS AT A GLANCE

RESULTS: Conference Quarterfinals - lost to Washington 4-2.

RECORD: 2-4

HOME: 2-1

AWAY: 0-3

GOALS FOR: 12, 2.0/game

GOALS AGAINST: 20, 3.3/game

OVERTIME: None

POWER PLAY: 7.4% (15th)

PENALTY KILLING: 90.0% (2nd)

PENALTY MINUTES: 23.2% (14th)

1993-94 PLAYOFF LEADERS

GOALS: 4, Mario Lemieux

ASSISTS: 5, Larry Murphy

POINTS: 7, Lemieux

POWER PLAY GOALS: 1, Lemieux, Rick Tocchet

SHORTHANDED GOALS: none

OVERTIME GOALS: none

GAME-WINNING GOALS: 1, Jagr, Tocchet

PENALTY MINUTES: 26, Kjell Samuelsson

PLUS-MINUS: +2, Peter Taglianetti

SHOTS: 23, Lemieux

A LOOK AHEAD TO 1994-95

GOAL: Ken Wregget and Tom Barrasso had remarkably similar stats last year. Check out these numbers. Goals against average: Barrasso 3.36, Wregget 3.37; save percentage: Barrasso .893, Wregget .893; Wins: Barrasso 22, Wregget 21; Minutes played: Barrasso 2,482, Wregget 2,456; Goals against: Barrasso 139, Wregget 138; Shots against: Barrasso 1,304, Wregget 1,291.

The point of the above exercise? Just to show that the Penguins are fortunate to have two number one goaltenders, a rare commodity in the league today.

Sure, Barrasso is considered top dog, but he's injury prone, and streaky. When your number one goaltender is not available, it's good to be able to stick your other number one guy in net.

The numbers also show how

goaltending can be as much a team stat as an individual one.

The Penguins finished 19th overall in goals against average, despite the fact they let in the second fewest goals in their history. If they want to improve they should look at the team in front of the netminders. The last line of defense is just fine.

DEFENCE: Just about all the regular defensemen the Penguins employed last season are over 30 years old: Larry Murphy (33), Kjell Samuelsson (35), Ulf Samuelsson (30), Peter Taglianetti (31), and Mike Ramsay (33).

There isn't much to replace them with yet, however, so most will be on tap for another season. But, they're not getting any younger or any better.

Grant Jennings, Greg Hawgood and Greg Brown also played on the blueline, but none of them are likely to be regulars. Brown and Ramsay were both offered termination contracts.

There are a couple players who will be challenging for jobs from the farm club. One is Patrick Neaton, the heir apparent to one of the Penguin power play point spots. He had only 32 points in 71 games at Cleveland, so it's hardly a given.

Another youngster with a chance to make the grade is Chris Tamer. A physical defensive type, he played in five of Pittsburgh's six playoff games.

Murphy hasn't shown any indication yet that he's through, despite his age, moving up to lofty heights for defensemen. He surpassed the 900 point mark last season and is only eight behind Bobby Orr on the all-time

defenseman scoring list. The only others ahead of him are Paul Coffey, Ray Bourque, and Larry Robinson.

The Pittsburgh defense is big and strong, but they're not very offensive-minded, which is okay when you've got the kind of forwards the Penguins have. But, if last year is any indication, they're not all that great defensively anymore either.

Wholesale changes are in order in the near future.

FORWARD: Not many teams in the NHL can match the sheer scoring power of the Pittsburgh forwards. But, if they don't play any defense what good does it do?

Last season, they scored 299 goals, but gave up 285. 101 points and the third best record in the league, somehow.

The key, of course, is Lemieux. How much he can play. If he can play. If he wants to play anymore.

No question marks about Jaromir Jagr though. He's firmly established himself as a star. Still only 22 years old, he now has two 90 plus point seasons to his credit, finishing just one shy of the magic 100 mark last year.

Martin Straka is also only 22 as well, and also came though for them, scoring 30 goals in his second NHL season, after just three his first year.

That could be an indication of what could happen to Markus Naslund, the highly heralded Swedish right winger who was possibly the biggest disappointment in the league last season. In 71 games he could scored just four goals and seven assists. That's a difficult feat in itself, but it won't happen again.

Shawn McEachern is back in Pittsburgh for the second time, after being traded back and forth from Los Angeles. He likes Pittsburgh better apparently. He had eight goals in 49 games for Los Angeles and 12 in 27 for Pittsburgh.

Kevin Stevens isn't yet 30, and did well last season with 41 goals and 88 points coming back from a serious injury. He also had 21 power play goals. No one else made it to double figures.

Rick Tocchet is 30, but an old 30, with back problems that kept him out of 33 games last year and made his goal production drop from 48 to 13 and his point totals to drop from 109 to 40. Picking up proven goal-scorer Luc Robitaille for him seems like a steal for the Penguins.

Thirty-one year old Ron Francis seems to be getting better with age. He had 93 points last season, and 100 the year before. He's now past the 1,000 point career mark and moving into elite territory.

Joe Mullen is 36 years old, but he too doesn't play like it. He had 38 goals last season and 70 points. He's just 11 points shy of becoming the first American born player to reach the 1,000 point plateau.

Jim McKenzie, who was traded three times last year, gives them a tough guy for the fourth line, at least until they trade him. The status of Tomas Sandstrom is unknown, but it is expected he will play in Europe this season. Ed Patterson, a rookie last season, gives them some size on right wing. Also

patrolling the right side is Doug Brown, a journeyman type who showed some surprising scoring ability with 55 points, topping his previous season high by 21.

Can the veterans still perform? Can Mario Lemieux play more often? Can the youngster (as in Naslund) come through? Can they play better when the other team has the puck? Can they play well enough offensively so the other team doesn't get the puck?

Seems like a lot of questions. Doesn't it?

SPECIAL TEAMS: For a team with their firepower, finishing in the middle of the pack on the power play (13th) is inexcusable. They suffered the ultimate embarassment in the playoffs when they had as many goals scored against them as they scored with the man advantage. Mario Lemieux, on a more frequent basis, is bound to help any power play.

The penalty killing is mediocre (10th last season), sort of a team tradition. They finished in fourth place two years ago, but in the 17 years prior to that, they finished no higher than 11th, and in 12 of the 17 years, were 15th or worse.

COACHING: Some people like to judge coaches by their special teams' performance, where it's suggested he can make a big difference; and in the playoffs where strategy comes into play.

Eddie Johnston hasn't had much success at either. In five years of coaching, going back to 1979-89, he's made it to five playoff series and has one win to show for it, a best-of-five affair back in 79-80.

After stern taskmasker, Scotty Bowman, it was a sigh of relief for the Penguin players to get somebody more laid back like Johnson. They may have been grateful, but in the playoffs, at least, they looked more like the grateful dead.

MANAGEMENT: Ironically, the best deal Craig Patrick ever made to help this club was with coach Eddie Johnston, who was the Hartford GM at the time. That's when he got Ron Francis, Ulf Samuelsson and Grant Jennings for John Cullen, Zarley Zalapski and Jeff Parker.

He made another big deal this year, getting Sandstrom and McEachern, which at the time looked like all they needed to make a serious run for the Stanley Cup.

It didn't work out, but these things happen. Patrick has shown an ability to recognize talent and an even better ability to get those players on his team. He's not afraid to make big deals and he may need a couple this year.

Over the summer, Patrick picked up one of the better goal¬scorers in the game for somebody, Rick Tocchet, who didn't help them much last season anyway because of a bad back.

NEEDS: After Larry Murphy, the Penguins don't have a legitimate point man for the power play. And Murphy isn't getting any younger. If Markus Naslund comes through this year, they have a good young nucleus at the forward position along with Jagr and Straka. But some of the stars there now, like Francis, Tocchet and Mullen will need their skates filled by others soon. The Penguins hope it isn't all at once.

POTENTIAL NEW FACES: D Patrick Neaton, Cleveland; D Chris Tamer, Cleveland.

McKENZIE'S BOTTOM LINE: Tough to figure these Penguins.

If Mario Lemieux is back in the lineup and healthy — mentally and physically — then there is no choice but to consider them a force to be reckoned with.

But that's a big if. Lemieux showed in last spring's playoffs that he didn't have the physical stamina to fight through the extra attention a player of his stature gets. Worse yet is that he seemed to be mentally tired, falling well short of what it takes to be the NHL's brightest light.

Those who talked to Lemieux in the off-season sensed a lot of bitterness and hostility towards a game that he believes doesn't do nearly enough to let the good players play. He's always beefed there's been too much in the way of restraining fouls and the league has been negligent in policing them.

Whatever. The fact remains that the game isn't going to undergo any radical changes in this area. Lemieux is either going to have to put up with it — and overcome it — or call it quits.

And Lemieux isn't the Penguins' only concern.

Kevin Stevens showed last season that his horrific face plant of two springs ago, and the subsequent facial reconstruction surgery, had a dramatic impact on his game.

Can those two rediscover their form? The Penguins' hopes depend upon it.

Jaromir Jagr should take the next step up the ladder of superstardom, but the Pens are getting perilously old in a number of other key positions. Ronnie Francis will turn 32 this season. Larry Murphy, Ulf Samuelsson and Kjell Samuelsson are being asked to shoulder too large a load for their age and there's no bright light on the blueline coming to assume their mantle.

Netminder Tom Barrasso could well be key. If he's on his game, he's one of the league's best. But his attention span seems to have shortened some in the last year or two.

Coach Eddie Johnson faces a mammoth task — pulling together a collection of individuals who seem to still think of themselves as Stanley Cup champions. This is not an easy group to coach and at the first sign of trouble, the players will shift the blame to the coaching staff.

All in all, it's not a real pretty picture. But don't forget, we're dealing with a lot of talent, too. The pieces are all there to make something good happen, although the sense that it's beginning to slip away for good is most certainly there.

The Penguins could go either way this season, and much of it depends on big Mario's health and attitude, and how newcomer Luc Robitaille fits in.

DRAFT PICKS

The Penguins faced something of a conundrum at the '94 draft. Simply, what's their most pressing need?

A bright young defenceman to inherit the mantle from aging veterans Larry Murphy and Ulf Samuelsson? Or a centre, given that Mario Lemieux's future is in doubt and Ronnie Francis will be turning 32 this season?

According to their draft selections, give centre a slight edge over defence. The Penguins drafted five centres and five defencemen with their 14 picks, although the first two were pivots.

Seattle's Chris Wells will never be confused as Mario's replacement, but the 6-foot-6, 215-pound centre should help to eventually fill the void in the post-Lemieux era, however soon that arrives. The big power forward, who has played already played three years of major junior, is one of the hardest-working players in the WHL and has some offensive skill to go with the strong work ethic.

Just to make sure, though, the Penguins took another centre, a highly-skilled one, in Belleville's Richard Park, who was initially tabbed as a first rounder only to fall to No. 50 overall in the second round.

The Korean-born, California-raised and Toronto trained prospect is a good offensive player who has to learn to deal with pro-style traffic.

The Penguins finally did something for their defensive future when they took towering Brandon Wheat King defenceman Sven Butenschon with the first of three picks in the in the third round.

Buteschon, a late bloomer who is showing rapid improvement, is still a long-term project, but at 6-foot-5 and 201 pounds, he most certainly has Kjell Samuelsson-like dimensions.

The Pens' next pick was notable for the bloodlines. Their second third-rounder was Greg Crozier, the towering left winger from Lawrency Academy who is the son of former NHL coach Joe Crozier. He, too, is a project, one who was rated to go higher than he did.

1993-94 KEYS

KEY DEALS:

* acquired Shawn McEachern and Tomas Sandstrom from Los Angeles for Marty McSorley and Jim Paek.

Post-Season:

* obtained Luc Robitaille from Los Angeles for Rick Tocchet

KEY INJURIES: Mario Lemieux (62 games), Tom Barrasso (30), Rick Tocchet (33).

KEY STAT: The Penguins led the league in wins by one goal, and winning percentage by one goal. Pretty impressive, huh? Not really, because it means they weren't nearly as dominant as they were previously.

They were still winning, yes, but not by as much. In games decided by three or more goals last season, the Pens only had a record of 14-15.

Compare that to the previous year when their record for the same category was 30-7.

BEST ONE GOAL WINNING PERCENTAGES		
Pittsburgh	20-7	.741
Dallas	17-8	.680
NY Rangers	16-9	.640
San Jose	19-11	.633
St. Louis	19-12	.613
Calgary	14-10	.583
Montreal	11-10	.550
Boston	13-11	.542

Quebec Nordiques

Talk about your disasters. One season, 104 points and a promising future. The next, just 76 points and out of the playoffs.

What went wrong? An easier question to answer would be what went right?

Nothing.

It didn't help that Steve Duchesne was a holdout and that Owen Nolan was injured for most of the season.

It didn't help that Mats Sundin took a dive, along with Mike Ricci and Andrei Kovalenko, or that the promise wasn't fulfilled by the likes of Valeri Kamensky, Martin Rucinsky and others.

It didn't help that Pierre Page seemed to be having a running battle over something or other with half the team.

It didn't help that the players didn't respond to Page's attempts to put the word "defense" into their vocabulary.

So, who's to blame? The players certainly, for one. But, they blamed Page. Page blamed himself, the players, and even the media for creating dissention. Guy Lafleur blamed Marcel Aubut. Aubut ultimately blamed Page because he fired him.

The Nords lacked character. That was the bottom line. They made some attempts to get it from St. Louis in Ron Sutter, Garth Butcher and Bob Bassen. The first two didn't want to go to Quebec in the first place and hated it when they got there. Among other things, they complained about the weather, if you can believe it. One's from Alberta, the other's from Saskatchewan.

Doesn't matter now anyway. Butcher is off to tropical Toronto and Sutter is in balmy Philadelphia.

When the season was over, the Nords traded Mats Sundin, along with Butcher to Toronto for Wendel Clark and Sylvain Lefebvre. Two players with character who won't complain about the weather.

Quebec has a new coach, a new general manager and a new lease on life.

1993-94 REGULAR SEASON AT A GLANCE

RECORD: 34-42-8

FINISH: 5th in Northeast Division, 12th in Eastern Conference, 19th overall

HOME: 19-17-6 (15th)

AWAY: 15-25-2 (21st)

OVERTIME: 0-0-8 (tied for 13th)

VS OWN DIVISION: 13-15-3

VS OTHER DIVISIONS: 21-27-5

VS OWN CONFERENCE: 22-32-6

VS OTHER CONFERENCE: 12-10-2

FIRST HALF RECORD: 17-20-5

SECOND HALF RECORD: 17-22-3

GOALS FOR: 277 (15th-t)

GOALS AGAINST: (21st)

TEAM PLUS/MINUS: +5

POWER PLAY: 15/6 (23rd)

PENALTY KILLING: 79.6 (22nd)

PENALTY MINUTES: 19.3/game (8th)

1993-94 REGULAR SEASON LEADERS

GOALS: 32, Mats Sundin

ASSISTS: 64, Joe Sakic

POINTS: 92, Sakic

POWER PLAY GOALS: 13, Mike Ricci

SHORTHANDED GOALS: 3, Ricci

GAME WINNING GOALS: 9, Sakic

PLUS-MINUS: +16, Craig Wolanin

SHOTS: 279, Sakic Penalty Minutes: 159, Steven Finn

A LOOK AHEAD TO 1994-95

GOAL: The Nords are set in net until at least the 21st century. Stephane Fiset is only 24, Jocelyn Thibault is 19, and Garth Snow is just 25.

Fiset got the bulk of the action last season, but Thibault was impressive making the jump directly from junior, and Garth Snow is another highly regarded prospect who comes to them from the U.S. Olympic team.

At one point last season, Quebec had four goaltenders on their NHL roster. That won't happen this year. All three of the above-mentioned need playing time. That means one will go to the minors or perhaps more likely, one will be used in a trade where they should command some good value.

DEFENCE: A definite weakness last season, both offensively and defensively.

The acquisition of Sylvain Lefebvre will help. He won't be a factor offensively, but he doesn't make many mistakes when the opposition has the puck. He'll be their steadiest defenseman.

What they need is offense. Somebody to replace Duchesne. They didn't find that person last season, eventually reaching the desperation stage when they obtained Tommy Sjodin from Dallas, a player who only got on the ice for the power play, and didn't even do that well. He'll be back in Europe this season.

The Nords also acquired Uwe Krupp from the Islanders at the draft. He can play on the power play, but he's no Duchesne.

There's also not much toughness behind the blueline. Steven Finn provides some, but registered his lowest penalty minute total last season in seven NHL seasons.

He's been around that long? Craig Wolanin took some heat last year because Page wasn't convinced of the seriousness of a nagging groin injury. The 27 year-old is heading into his ninth NHL season and will snag another regular spot on the blueline. He led the team with a +16 last season.

Curtis Leschyshyn, the third pick in the 1988 draft grabs another spot on the Quebec blueline.

That leaves Alexei Gusarov, Mike McKee, Brad Werenka, Dave Karpa (also a forward) and Adam Foote to battle it out for the remaining ice time.

The problem here is that the Nordique have a good supporting cast without the headliners.

It's doubtful it will stay that way, however. Pierre Lacroix has already shown he will address weaknesses. He'll get aroun d to this one as well sooner or later.

FORWARD: The core group of forwards have the potential to be among the best in the league.

Peter Forsberg should prove to be one of the more exciting players in the game and may very well be the rookie of the year.

Most of the rest, like Joe Sakic, Mike Ricci, Andrei Kovalenko, and Martin Rucinsky are coming off disappointing seasons. Rucinsky is a free agent and could sign with a European team.

Iain Fraser had an impressive rookie campaign, and Scott Young squeezed himself back into the picture when the other highly touted forwards couldn't do the job.

Owen Nolan, back from injury, and Wendel Clark give the team two quality snipers. Clark, however, is among the most frequently injured players in the game.

Others in line for jobs include Rene Corbet, a right winger who led his AHL team in scoring with 37 goals and 77 points, and was named rookie of the year. He was up and down a couple times with Quebec last season, but could stick this time.

Claude Lapointe, Bob Bassen and Chris Lindberg give the team some quality third and fourth liners.

You could project a first line of Joe Sakic between Wendel Clark and Owen Nolan. A good second line would probably see Forsberg between Kamensky and Kovalenko or Young.

That leaves Ricci as a third line center if Forsberg lives up to his press clippings. That could change though. Ricci was the most traded player in the league last season, in the press anyway.

This is a pretty good offensive mix. There are snipers, playmakers and toughness. They should definitely score more goals this season.

The only negative point is that they're still not strong defensively. That makes it a tough call for the coaching staff. Do you let them do what they do best, which is score goals? Or do you try to mold them into a better defensive unit, which in the current NHL, means a better chance of winning?

SPECIAL TEAMS: Both were dismal last season. The power play went from one of the best two years ago to one of the worst. They dropped from 101 man-advantage goals to just 67. The difference was Steve Duchesne and his 82 points.

He still hasn't been replaced. They need somebody in his mold badly. If they get him, Clark and Nolan will be popping in the power play markers on a regular basis.

COACHING: It was clearly time that Page stepped down as coach. He was given the option of retaining the GM position but chose not to.

His fault or not, he had lost the respect of the players. They weren't happy with Page, and Page wasn't happy with them.

The new man in town, Marc Crawford, has guided the Toronto farm team in St. John's to some good success the past three years. He was considered one of the prime coaching candidates not yet in the NHL.

Crawford will have his work cut out for him on and off the ice where the Quebec press is one of the toughest in the business.

The real question is, will Crawford be smart enough to allow the offensive players to be offensive, or will he be smart enough to make them play defense as well.

MANAGEMENT: Pierre Lacroix has no GM experience, but he's been a player agent for 20 years. He knows the game, the players, the other GMS, and obviously the contractual side of the business.

His experience might even be considered better than that of a normal general manager.

He said right out of the box that his initial goal was to improve team chemistry. He's already done that. It looks like he's going to get rid of the whiners as fast as he can. Good move, who wants 'em anyway.

At the draft, Lacroix did a good job of manipulating and trading his first round picks.

Already he looks like a winner.

POTENTIAL NEW FACES: Peter Forsberg, Sweden; Wendel Clark, Toronto; Sylvain Lefebvre, Toronto; Rene Corbet, Halifax;

NEEDS: Offensive defenseman.

McKENZIE'S BOTTOM LINE: The Nordiques will be this season's New York Rangers, which is not to say they're going to win the Stanley Cup.

It is, however, to say they've got a good shot at being the top team in the Northeast Division after missing the playoffs last spring.

The Rangers went from first to worst to first in their division over a three-year span. Watch for the Nords to more closely resemble the 104-point team of two years ago than the playoff pretender of a year ago.

Start with a new fresh face behind the bench in Marc Crawford. He's young and relatively inexeperienced but he has a nice touch and a talented team to work with. New GM Pierre Lacroix went out and did what predecessor Pierre

Page only dreamed about, infusing some grit, character and defensive help to a team badly in need of attitude adjustment.

The addition of Wendel Clark up front — so long as he stays healthy — will vastly improve the Nords' mindset, as will the insertion of rock-solid Sylvain Lefebvre and reliable veteran Uwe Krupp on the blueline.

Players such as Joe Sakic, Mike Ricci and highly-touted newcomer Peter Forsberg will benefit from the departure of Mats Sundin to Toronto. Now, there'll be enough puck to go around. Forsberg, incidentally, is the leading contender for rookie of the year honors. If Paul Kariya signed with Anaheim, it should be a two-man race.

The only major area of concern is in net. Stephane Fiset has to step to the fore to show he can be a No. 1 goalie in the NHL. Failing that, the Nords will still look to youngster Jocelyn Thibault, who despite his immense talent had no business being in the NHL last season. A general tightening of the defence will help the goaltenders, but they have to take it upon themselves to get to the next level.

Then there is coaching. As a bench boss, Page sometimes seemed to be an impediment. Crawford is by no means soft, but he'll be more of a players' coach and should benefit from the surge often accorded to first-year coaches.

All signs point to the Nords as being back on the rise again and there aren't many teams in the Northeast Division that can say that this fall.

DRAFT PICKS

The Nordiques were a lot less concerned about the 1994 draft itself than what the '94 draft could do for them in terms of immediate help.

New GM Pierre Lacroix didn't waste any time revamping the talent-laden Nords, completing the blockbuster trade with Toronto (bringing in Wendel Clark and Sylvain Lefebvre, among others) and flip-flopping draft picks with the Islanders to secure more defensive help, in the form of veteran Uwe Krupp.

The net result, as far the draft was concerned, was that the Nordiques went from having the ninth and 10th picks overall to the 12th and 22nd picks. They did with those two selections what they planned to do if they'd been picking back to back at nine and 10. That is, acquire some long-range help on the blueline.

More importantly, the D-Day wheeling and dealing helped to bolster the Nords' defensive unit for this season and inject some much needed character, too.

The Nords' top pick (12th overall) was Saskatoon defenceman Wade Belak, a 6-foot-4, 213-pound behemoth, followed (22nd overall) by Boston area high schooler Jeff Kealty, a rangy 6-foot-4 and 175 pounds. Belak is more of a classic banger while Kealty shows signs of being able to do more with the puck. In both cases, though, the ETA is a few years down the road.

The Nords' second-round pick, Czech centre Josef Marha, was one of the more highly-skilled prospects available. If he'd been chosen in the first round, it wouldn't have come as a large surprise to anyone.

1993-94 KEYS

KEY DEALS:

* obtained Bob Bassen, Ron Sutter and Garth Butcher for Steve Duchesne and Denis Chasse

Post Season:

* Obtained Wendel Clark, Sylvain Lefebvre, Landon Wilson and the 22nd pick in 1994 draft from Toronto for Mats Sundin, Garth Butcher, Todd Warriner and the 10th pick in the 1994 draft.

* Obtained Uwe Krupp and 12th overall pick in 1994 draft from the New York Islanders for Ron Sutter and 9th pick in 1994 draft.

KEY INJURIES: Owen Nolan (78 games)

KEY STAT: This is a short list. A very short one. It's shows the only teams in NHL history that have had 100 points in one season and missed the playoffs the next.

Oddly enough, all three times it has happened have been once in each of the past three years.

	Year	Points	Next
QUEBEC	92-93	104	Out of playoffs
NY Rangers	91-92	105	Out of playoffs
Calgary	90-91	100	Out of playoffs

Tampa Bay Lightning

It was a good news, bad news type of season for the Tampa Bay Lightning, just as you would expect for a second year team.

Good News: The Lightning improved by 18 points. Bad News: They still finished last in their division and third last in the conference.

Good News: They allowed only 251 goals, eight best in the league. Bad News: They could only score 224, second fewest behind Ottawa.

Good News: The penalty killing ranked sixth in the league. Bad News: The power play was 24th.

Good News: The Lightning could have made the playoffs with a good late season run. Bad News: They didn't, finishing 13 points behind the last spot.

Good News: Brian Bradley led the team in scoring once again. Bad News: He scored 22 fewer points and 18 less goals than the season before.

Good News: Tampa Bay outshot their opponents in 51 games. Bad News: They only won 20 of those games.

Good News: They were 15-10-4 against the Northeast Division. Bad News: They were 5-19-5 versus the Atlantic Division.

Good News: 31 of their games were decided by one goal. Bad News: They lost 18 of them.

Good News: They were 4-0-0 versus Ottawa. Bad News: They were 0-3-2 versus rival Florida.

Good News: The Lightning went through one stretch where they recorded a 9-3-2 mark. Bad News: They went through another where they were 0-8-1.

1993-94 REGULAR SEASON AT A GLANCE

RECORD: 30-43-11

FINISH: 7th in Atlantic Division, 12th in Eastern Conference, 21st overall

HOME: 14-22-6 (24th)

AWAY: 16-21-5 (18th)

OVERTIME: 3-4-11 (20th)

VS OWN DIVISION: 5-20-5

VS OTHER DIVISIONS: 25-23-6

VS OWN CONFERENCE: 20-29-9

VS OTHER CONFERENCE: 10-14-2

FIRST HALF RECORD: 14-23-5

SECOND HALF RECORD: 16-20-6

GOALS FOR: 224 (25th)

GOALS AGAINST: 251 (8th-t)

TEAM PLUS/MINUS: -26 (20th-t)

POWER PLAY: 14.7 (24th)

PENALTY KILLING: 82.7 (6th)

PENALTY MINUTES: 18.8/game (5th)

1993-94 REGULAR SEASON LEADERS

GOALS: 28, Petr Klima

ASSISTS: 40, Brian Bradley

POINTS: 64, Bradley

POWER PLAY GOALS: 10, Klima

SHORTHANDED GOALS: Three players tied with one.

GAME WINNING GOALS: 6, John Tucker

PLUS-MINUS: +9, Tucker

SHOTS: 181, Denis Savard

PENALTY MINUTES: 135, Roman Hamrlik (Enrico Ciccone overall with 226)

A LOOK AHEAD TO 1994-95

GOAL: Daren Puppa did everything asked of him and more. He finished ninth among goaltenders with his 2.71 goals against average and earned four shutouts.

He'll be backed up this year probably by J.C. Bergeron, who has served his apprenticeship in the minors and is ready for prime time.

Last year's backup, Wendel Young, was offered a termination contract, but nobody signed him, so he could return as well.

DEFENCE: They dearly need a quarterback for the power play, but otherwise there is some good young talent, some steady NHL defensemen, and more help on the way.

Roman Hamrlik started showing some of the promise the Lightning had for him when they made him the first overall choice at the 1992 draft. Unfortunately, he hurt his knee while playing for the Czech team at the world championships and will have a long summer of rehabilitation and rest. He's only 20 years old, however, so his future is bright.

Chris Joseph made an impression after coming over from Edmonton for Bob Beers. The Oilers gave up on the fifth overall pick from the 1987 draft, but he finally started coming into his own with Tampa Bay, spending time on the power play.

Shawn Chambers is another big guy at 6-2, like Hamrlik and Joseph, although he doesn't play like it. He led all defensemen in scoring on the team with 34 points.

Marc Bergevin, at 29, is the steadying influence, while Enrico Ciccone is the muscle. He accumulated 226 penalty minutes with Washington and Tampa Bay. Rudy Poeschek, who also plays forward, handles that stuff as well.

A number of young players received auditions during the season and might earn their way into a spot on the team.

They include Eric Charron, Chris LiPuma and Cory Cross.

The best defensive product in the organization is Drew Bannister, who played with Sault Ste. Marie last season. He was a member of Canada's national gold medal winning junior team, and was named the team's MVP.

There's no superstar on the defensive unit, but that's not necessarily the bad news. As a group, they're young, big, tough, and any team that plays against them will know they've been in a game.

FORWARD: While the Lightning defense is rough and rugged, the forward unit isn't. Worse, they don't score very often.

Many of them are journeymen filling up space until somebody emerges as a star to carry the team.

Petr Klima was once considered that type of player. Actually, lots of times he was considered that type of player. He scored 28 goals to lead Tampa last season. You never know if he's had a good season or not because whatever he does everybody expects more.

The flaky Czech turns 30 this year so it's clear he's never going to accomplish what was predicted of him at one time. He does, however, give the Lightning some good trade bait. If they don't deal him, the threat is at least good enough to provide motivation. He's admitted as much himself, suggesting he plays harder when he hears the rumours. Klima likes the weather in Tampa Bay.

Brian Bradley is still the team's top center, leading them in points for the second year in a row. His goal production, however, dropped from 42 to 24.

Chris Gratton, the third pick overall in 1993 had an okay rookie season. He didn't burn up the league with just 13 goals, but he showed flashes of things to come, with 10 multi-point games. During a 17 game stretch in the second half, he had 17 points. He will improve this year and it will only be a matter of time before he's a big scorer, as well as a physical presence on the ice.

Denis Savard is still around to play center along with steady defensive player Marc Bureau. Adam Creighton was offered a termination contract last season, but he signed it and will be back for another go at it.

The new kid on the block may be Aaron Gavey, a third round selection in 1992 who has come on strong since then. He had 102 points for Sault Ste. Marie in the OHL in 60 games last season.

On the left side, stop-gap players like Mikael Andersson Gerard Galant, and perhaps Rob Zamuner or Jason Ruff, will earn playing time.

Klima plays left or right wing, spending much of last year on a line with Gratton and Danton Cole.

First round draft pick Jason Wiemer has a spot on the left wing when he's ready. Phil Esposito says he doesn't like to rush prospects, but each of his first rounders so far have been in the lineup, so it could just be that Wiemer is ready. He has drawn comparisons to Cam Neely.

Danton Cole was a pleasant surprise for the Lightning last season. His 20 goals were third on the team, and he even got a third place vote in Selke Trophy balloting for the best defensive forward.

John Tucker, who scored six of his 17 goals in the last five games of the season, also patrols right wing along with tough guy Jim Cummins. Pat Elynuik was lost to free agency and signed with Ottawa.

SPECIAL TEAMS: The power play was horrendous with the third worst percentage in the league. Adding insult to injury, they also allowed 20 shorthanded goals. There's not a lot of hope for improvement until they get a quarterback for the point.

Penalty killing was good, ranking an impressive sixth. Actually, that's quite remarkable when you consider that the year before they were dead last. Danton Cole had a lot to do with that.

COACHING: If you can't score goals, the next best thing is to make sure the other team doesn't score any either. Terry Crisp made sure they were good at that part of the game.

A coach can only do the best with what he has to work with. He's already proven he can win with a good team (Calgary) and now he's proving he can at least be competitive with a weak one.

MANAGEMENT: It appeared Phil Esposito would step down as GM after the season to take a job with ESPN. He decided against it when the money wasn't right. For this year, anyway.

That could mean his heart isn't in the job anymore as Tampa GM and he's looking for new challenges. Reports of friction between him and upstairs were denied, but who knows.

His reputation as Trader Phil took another beating this year. He didn't make many moves, utilizing much needed patience with a new team. He knows there's no point rushing things because they're not going to win the Stanley Cup for a while.

He has already built a decent defense, and there's some good talent coming from the forwards.

This is their third season now. Decent trade bait is available, so maybe this is the year Esposito starts living back up to his reputation.

NEEDS: Power play quarterback. Goals. Toughness and size on the wings.

POTENTIAL NEW FACES: D Drew Bannister, 7-43-50, Sault Ste. Marie (OHL); C Aaron Gavey, 42-60-102, Sault Ste. Marie (OHL); LW Jason Ruff, Atlanta (IHL); LW Jason Wiemer, 45-51-96 with 236 PIM for Portland (WHL); G J.C. Bergeron, Atlanta; C Brent Gretzky, Atlanta.

McKENZIE'S BOTTOM LINE: This is where the grim reality of life in the NHL should set in for a team like the Lightning.

Under GM Phil Esposito and head coach Terry Crisp, the Lightning have seldom been outworked in their first two seasons in the NHL. It is for that reason, they are a moderately competitive team that can never be taken lightly.

But it's one thing to go from an

expansion team to a respectable, hard-working non-playoff team. It is, however, yet another to take that next step to true playoff contender.

It's simply difficult to infuse enough new talent into the lineup to make a considerable difference from one year to the next. And while top prospects such as Roman Hamrlik, the defenceman taken No. 1 overall in the 1992 entry draft, and power centre Chris Gratton, the No. 3 pick in the 1993 draft, will only get better with experience, it's asking too much for them to advance entire levels in only a one- or two-year span.

It really boils down to this: How much better will the Lightning be this year than they were a year ago? Perhaps only marginally. The immediate thrill of that first expansion season is long gone. Now, the Lightning have to face the facts and come to terms with being in a dogfight with teams (Washington, Philadelphia, the Islanders, Hartford etc.) who have better talent and are further along the path to becoming a playoff team.

Maybe Tampa will surprise, but if they're to come close to a playoff spot, they're going to need some of the more talented playoff-seekers to falter.

DRAFT PICKS

Two years ago, the Lightning nabbed a top defensive prospect (Roman Hamrlik) with its first-round pick. Last year, it was a power centre (Chris Gratton).

This year? A power winger in the Cam Neely mold, in Portland Winterhawk Jason Wiemer.

Wiemer's mobility is the one area of his game that requires work but he does so many other things — score, hit, fight and lead — that he's tabbed by most as a can't miss player.

In keeping with the emphasis on size and strength, the Lightning picked up massive 6-foot-3, 224-pound centre Colin Cloutier from the Brandon Wheat Kings in the second round. He was hindered by a variety of injuries last season but has the potential to develop into a fearsome power forward.

Tampa Bay went to the other end of the spectrum for its third-rounder, 5-foot-9, 169-pound Vadim Epanchintsev from Moscow Spartak. In fact, the Lightning drafted Epanchintsev's whole line from Spartak, including his wingers Dmitri Klevakin and Yuri Smirnov. All three are diminutive by NHL standards but possess excellent speed and skill.

Another name worth noting on the Lightning list is sixth-rounder Daniel Juden, a U.S. high school centre who is the cousin of Philadelphia Phillies' pitcher Jeff Juden.

1993-94 KEYS
KEY DEALS:
* obtained Jim Cummins from Philadelphia for Rob DiMaio
* obtained Enrico Ciccone from Washington for Joe Reekie
* obtained Chris Joseph from Edmonton for Bob Beers

KEY INJURIES: Wendell Young (53 games), Adam Creighton (25), John Tucker (18), Shawn Chambers (18), Roman Hamrlik (20).

KEY STAT: It was bad enough that the Lightning only scored 57 power play goals, just three away from the fewest in the league. But adding insult to injury, they also gave up 20 short-handed markers for a net power play production of only 37 goals.

MOST SHORT-HANDED GOALS AGAINST

Tampa Bay	20
Quebec	18
Winnipeg	17
Dallas	16
Florida	15
St.Louis	14
Ottawa	14
Detroit	14
Philadelphia	14

Washington Capitals

The Capitals had been disappointing their fans the same way for so long it was time they did it differently.

So instead of a great regular season followed by a lousy playoffs, they had a lousy regular season and then did okay in the playoffs.

For 11 straight years prior to last season they had made post-season play. Three times they had at least 100 points and on four other occasions they broke 90. A record over .500 every season but one.

Six times over that span they were knocked out in the first round. Four times they made it as far as the second. The only time they went further, to the Conference finals, was the one season in 11 that they didn't have a .500 record.

Yup, that's the Caps. Last year, they were in danger of not even making the playoffs. If they had lost their last three games instead of winning them, they would have finished behind expansion Florida.

Then they go out and knock off Pittsburgh, one of the Stanley Cup favorites. And it wasn't even all that hard.

In the next round, however, they had their hands full with the Rangers. But who didn't?

During the season, coach Terry Murray was fired for the team's inconsistent effort and Jim Schoenfeld resurrected. The team responded to Schoenfeld's brand of coaching almost immediately, and sported a 19-12-6 mark the rest of the way.

It's not unusual for players to come up with an inspired effort when a new coach comes on board; they've all got something to prove. Continued success is another story.

One of these days the Capitals are going to do everything right. But, their fans won't be holding their breath waiting for it.

1993-94 REGULAR SEASON AT A GLANCE

RECORD: 39-35-10

FINISH: 3rd in Atlantic Division, 7th in Eastern Conference, 12th overall

HOME: 17-16-9 (17th)

AWAY: 22-19-1 (7th)

OVERTIME: 2-2-10 (13th-t)

VS OWN DIVISION: 13-15-4

VS OTHER DIVISIONS: 26-20-6

VS OWN CONFERENCE: 25-28-7

VS OTHER CONFERENCE: 14-7-3

FIRST HALF RECORD: 19-19-4

SECOND HALF RECORD: 20-16-6

GOALS FOR: 277 (15th-t)

GOALS AGAINST: 263 (12th)

TEAM PLUS/MINUS: +18 (9th)

POWER PLAY: 18.1% (18th)

PENALTY KILLING: 81.6% (13th)

PENALTY MINUTES: 23.9/game (23rd)

1993-94 REGULAR SEASON LEADERS (WITH WASHINGTON)

GOALS: 29, Dimitri Khristich

ASSISTS: 44, Mike Ridley (Joe Juneau overall with 66)

POINTS: 70, Ridley (Juneau 85 overall)

POWER PLAY GOALS: 10, Khristich, Ridley

SHORTHANDED GOALS: 2, Ridley, Sylvain Cote

GAME WINNING GOALS: 5, Randy Burridge

PLUS-MINUS: +30, Cote

SHOTS: 217, Kevin Hatcher

PENALTY MINUTES: 305, Craig Berube

1993-94 PLAYOFFS AT A GLANCE

RESULTS: Conference Quarterfinals - defeated Pittsburgh 4-2 **Conference Semi-finals** - lost to NY Rangers 4-1

RECORD: 5-6

HOME: 4-1

AWAY: 1-5

GOALS FOR: 2.9/game

GOALS AGAINST: 2.9/game

OVERTIME: None

POWER PLAY: 9.1% (14th)

PENALTY KILLING: 88.5% (3rd)

PENALTY MINUTES: 23.3/game (15th)

1993-94 PLAYOFF LEADERS

GOALS: 4, Juneau, Ridley, Michal Pivonka

ASSISTS: 8, Cote

POINTS: 10, Ridley

POWER PLAY GOALS: 2 Juneau

SHORTHANDED GOALS: 1, three tied

OVERTIME GOALS: none

GAME-WINNING GOALS: 1, three tied

PENALTY MINUTES: 37, Hatcher

PLUS-MINUS: +7, Ridley

SHOTS: 40, Hatcher

A LOOK AHEAD TO 1994-95

GOAL: It may or may not be a good thing that the Caps go into the season with four different goaltenders vying for the number one job. They are, in no particular order: Don Beaupre, Rick Tabaracci, Byron Dafoe and Olaf Kolzig.

Beaupre was offered a termination contract with the Caps but didn't sign with another team during the allotted time, so he'll be back. But, he doesn't seem an integral part of the big picture anymore. He's 33 and while he had lots of ups last season, there were also lots of downs. Inconsistency, a plague troubling the whole team, was his problem.

Tabaracci got into 32 games and he too had consistency problems. He was either giving up a lot of goals, or none, or very few. For example, during one stretch, he gave up five goals against Hartford and Quebec, lasting only about half the game in each effort. His next three outings featured two one goal efforts versus Philadelphia and the Rangers and a shutout against Anaheim. Then he gave up five again in consecutive games to Tampa Bay and Boston. Then, he shut out New Jersey.

What's up with that? In Portland (AHL), Dafoe got most of the work, but Kolzig had a slightly better goals against average and a better winning percentage.

One of the above, besides Beaupre, will have to emerge as the number one man. Beaupre has experience and can jump into the fray when somebody falters or needs a break.

DEFENCE: Two seasons ago, the Caps put on a collective offensive display from their defensemen never before been seen in the NHL. Last year it was somewhat more modest.

Kevin Hatcher took the biggest dive,

going from 34 goals to 16 and 79 points to just 40. That's not so odd for him, his career has always been a roller-coaster ride. The 28 year old's last five seasons and their points: 54-74-54-79-40. According to the pattern, this ought to be a big season for him.

Sylvain Cote, surprisingly, led all defensemen with 51 points and led the team with a plus 30.

Calle Johansson is another who contributes offensively, but like Cote, isn't going to strike fear into opposing forwards, physically at least.

Joe Reekie might, though. He was an excellent pickup from Tampa Bay for Enrico Ciccone. The trade wasn't popular among Tampa players who understood the value of having Reekie in the lineup.

Jim Johnson also gives them another strong stay-at-home type.

John Slaney hasn't overwhelmed since being drafted ninth overall in the 1990 draft, but maybe his time has come. When Jim Schoenfeld took over the team, he seemed to like Slaney and gave him more playing team, including every game in the playoffs. The Newfoundland born player can be a big force offensively.

Others who could see time on the blueline include Jason Wooley, Todd Nelson and Russian Sergei Gonchar.

Brendan Witt, who played this season back in junior for Seattle, had the team made last season, but couldn't agree on a contract with the Caps. There is some question whether he ever will.

Overall, not a bad defensive unit - mobility, scoring power, some toughness, and some good defensive types.

FORWARD: Petr Bondra was supposed to score 50 goals; he got 24. Michal Pivonka was supposed to get 100 points; he got 50. And so on and so on.

A disappointing year from the scorers, finally getting some welcome help when they obtained Joe Juneau from Washington for Al Iafrate. He finished tops on the team, not a particularly difficult feat.

Their second leading scorer, Mike Ridley, was dispatched to Toronto in a draft day deal that brought the Caps right winger Rob Pearson. Ridley has been one of the more dependable Caps for many years, but he is 31 years old and there's lots of centers ready to move up the depth chart.

Washington has a lot of forwards who can play different positions, but on paper behind Juneau at center will be Pivonka and Dale Hunter, both hoping to rebound from bad seasons, Hunter's due mostly to injury and suspension.

Steve Konowalchuk could be ready to break out. The 21 year old had 11 of his 12 goals and 22 of his 26 points in the second half of the season.

Dave Poulin is still around for his checking ability and up and coming Jason Allison was scoring champ, MVP and most gentlemanly player in the Ontario Hockey League last season. He was also named the CHL player of the year.

On the left side is Dimitri Khristich who led the team with a paltry 29 goals; excellent two-way player Kelly Miller; Randy Burridge, who made a good comeback last season after injuries; Todd Krygier, always good for 30 points (usually exactly 30); and Craig Berube, one of the tougher guys in the league,

who can contribute offensively.

Right wing has Bondra, who forgot to show up last year; Pat Peake, who could be ready to move up and start piling up the points, Keith Jones, who made a nice contribution, and Rob Pearson, who is a restricted free agent.

A change of scenery might be a big help to Pearson. He's not a gifted skater, and he does dumb things on the ice, but he's right there to protect his teammates when the going gets rough. If you give the 23 year old the right linemates (like Juneau for starters) he could turn into a sniper.

If all or some of the Cap forwards regain their scoring touch of two years ago — and at least some should — then they will be a decent offensive unit.

Nothing special though in any event.

SPECIAL TEAMS: No problem finding point men for the power play, even with Al Iafrate gone, but some, like Kevin Hatcher are going to need comeback seasons. Cote, Johansson, and John Slaney can contribute back there as well. Up front, Juneau will combine with whomever shows up to play this year. A return to form by Dale Hunter would help. He only scored one power play marker last season after being a major contributor the year before.

There's some good defensive forwards to do the penalty¬killing, most notably, Kelly Miller. They could miss Mike Ridley in that role, but if Dave Poulin is healthy again, it will make up for it.

COACHING: Jim Schoenfeld is a motivator type and got them fired up for awhile when he replaced Murray. The Caps only lost once in his first 11 games on the job.

He has his work cut out for him motivating this bunch again. The up and down careers of many of them show the talent is there if somebody can bring it out.

MANAGEMENT: What more can David Poile do? Year after year he puts a good product out on the ice and year after year they falter in the playoffs. In 12 years on the job, he's had a winning season every year but one and made the playoffs every time. Only once did they get past the second round of the playoffs.

That's not his fault. Is it? He is one of the better traders in the league, locating and filling needs. Joe Juneau is a good example. Poile traded from strength - offensive defensemen - and shipped Iafrate to Boston for a big time scoring threat in Juneau.

He does everything that appears necessary to make the team a winner.

As long as the regular season lasts, anyway.

NEEDS: A number one goaltender, or somebody to establish themselves as such. Scorers who are consistent.

POTENTIAL NEW FACES: C Jason Allison, 55-87-142, London (OHL); D Todd Nelson, Portland (AHL); RW Rob Pearson, Toronto; C Jeff Nelson, Portland (AHL); D Sergei Gonchar, Russia; G Byron Dafoe, Portland (AHL); D Olaf Kolzig, Portland (AHL).

McKENZIE'S BOTTOM LINE: Coach Jim Schoenfeld's task with the Caps is to avoid the pitfalls he faced in a similar situation with the New Jersey Devils a few years back.

If you recall, Schoenfeld came to the Devils in mid-season and led them to the conference final against the Boston Bruins. It was supposed to be a portent of things to come. But the Devils stumbled after that and Schoenfeld was ultimately dismissed.

Rightly or wrongly, he picked up the reputation as a great reliever, the kind of guy you want to come into a tough situation, as it was in Washington when Terry Murray was fired last season, and turn around the year. Schoenfeld only added to the image when he led the Caps to a first-round win over the Pittsburgh Penguins last spring.

Now, the fiery redhead must show that his inspirational, rah-rah ways will play over the course of an 84-game season.

The trading of Al Iafrate to Boston for Joey Juneau gives Schoenfeld a gun in his arsenal that previous Cap coaches simply haven't had. For the Caps to make the playoffs, Juneau has to step his play up to the superstar level.

And the Caps' Euro-connection — Dmitri Khristich, Peter Bondra and Michal Pivonka — have to step to the fore with some goals. Dale Hunter will have to continue to shoulder a larger load than he should, especially with utility man Mike Ridley now in Toronto.

Team defence has never been a problem for Washington teams and that isn't likely to change this year so long as

Kevin Hatcher and Sylvain Cote remain healthy and happy.

The crucial issue for the Caps is goaltending. Whether it's Rick Tabaracci or Byron Dafoe or Don Beaupre (if he's still on the scene), someone has to step forward and prove he's a No. 1 goaltender in the NHL. That may be a reach and where the Capitals are likely to be at season's end — in another battle for the last playoff spot — goaltending could well decide the issue.

The good news for the Caps, for now anyway, is that their chief rivals for the final playoff spot — Philadelphia and the Islanders — have the same or worse goaltending problems. Besides, one of the kids (Tabaracci or Dafoe) could turn out to be the genuine article.

What's in Washington's favor is that the Caps usually find a way to get the job done, as opposed to the Flyers of recent years, who seem to find a way to let the playoffs slip away.

DRAFT PICKS

What the Caps really need is a blue-chip scoring star, but what was available was something else. Something pretty good, too.

That's why the Caps flip-flopped draft picks (Nos. 16 and 10) with the Toronto Maple Leafs, paying the price of veteran centre Mike Ridley to move up to get Kamloops Blazer defenceman Nolan Baumgartner.

Baumgartner looks as though he's going to be a good one. The Caps

believe you can never have too many good defenceman.

Bob Brown, GM of the Blazers, said Baumgartner can be favorably compared to former Blazer and now King Darryl Sydor. Brown said Baumgartner is perhaps even mentally tougher than Sydor was at the same age and that Sydor learned the mental toughness of aspect of the game while it comes naturally to Baumgartner.

Baumgartner is a rangy defenceman with good puck skills and decent offensive instincts. But he's also capable defensively and doesn't mind throwing his weight around. He has the potential to be a leader, although he still will require some seasoning.

The Caps also had another first-rounder, 15th overall, which was used to take Russian winger Alexander Kharlamov, the son of the late, great Valeri Kharlamov.

Valeri is not nearly as flashy offensively as his father was, but he is a strong two-way talent who is looking to carve his own niche away from the shadow of the Russian hockey legend.

1993-94 KEYS

KEY DEALS:

* obtained Joe Juneau from Boston for Al Iafrate

* obtained Jim Johnson from Dallas for Alan May and 1995 7th round pick.

* obtained Joe Reekie from Tampa Bay for Enrico Ciccone

Post-Season

* obtained Rob Pearson and 10th pick in 1994 draft from Toronto for Mike Ridley and 16th pick.

KEY INJURIES: Dale Hunter missed 32 games with injuries and suspension.

KEY STAT: What goes up, must come down. At least that's the way it looked in Washington last year. Listed are the top six scorers from 1992-93 and how they fared last season, including the point difference. Some players were affected by injuries and suspensions, but even projected totals over the same number of games would leave large variances.

1992/93 — 1993/94

	GP	G	A	Pts	GP	G	A	Pts	Diff
Peter Bondra	83	37	48	85	69	24	19	43	-42
Mike Ridley	84	26	56	82	81	26	54	70	-12
Kevin Hatcher	83	34	45	79	72	16	24	40	-39
Dale Hunter	84	20	59	79	52	9	29	38	-41
Michal Pivonka	69	21	53	74	82	14	36	50	-24
Dimitri Khristich	64	31	35	66	83	29	29	58	-8

WESTERN CONFERENCE

WESTERN CONFERENCE
PREDICTED ORDER OF FINISH

1. DETROIT
2. ST. LOUIS
3. VANCOUVER
4. TORONTO
5. DALLAS
6. CALGARY
7. CHICAGO
8. WINNIPEG
9. SAN JOSE
10. LOS ANGELES
11. EDMONTON
12. ANAHEIM

Anaheim Mighty Ducks

Before the season started, the only thing funny about The Mighty Ducks of Anaheim was their name. By season end, the only thing funny about The Mighty Ducks of Anaheim was still their name.

So what happened to all the yuks, the goofy antics we've come to expect from expansion teams?

Fortunately, the Ottawa Senators are still around to take care of that sort of thing because there was none of that in Anaheim. They had one of the best seasons in expansion history. Coach Ron Wilson molded a group of castoffs, rejects, misfits and spare parts into a force nobody could afford to take lightly.

Open season on Ducks? Never happened. Just ask the Stanley Cup winning Rangers. The Ducks swept their two game season series, making them one of only two teams to accomplish that (Detroit was the other). Just ask the Jets who lost all four games against them, or the Oilers who lost five of six, or the Flyers or Islanders who have yet to beat the Ducks, or the Maple Leafs who were shut out by them at home.

That's just for starters. Some more highlights from the Ducks first NHL season:

* They won six more games than the Stanley Cup finalist Los Angeles Kings and out-pointed Edmonton, Hartford, Winnipeg and Ottawa.

* Their 33 wins tied them with Florida for the most ever by an expansion team.

* Nineteen road wins were the most ever by a first year team, and 11 more than Ottawa has in two seasons combined. Amazingly, the Ducks were just one game under .500 away from home.

* The 122 goals Anaheim allowed in 42 road games were the second fewest in the Western Conference, behind only Chicago.

* They were in the playoff race until the last week of the season.

* Their team goals against average was 2.97, tenth best in the league.

* Outside of California, they had a record of 19-15-3; against the 21 "established" teams they had a record of 31-36-5.

* They averaged 16,989 fans per game (98.9% of capacity) and sold out their last 25 home games.

Not bad for starters. Not bad at all.

1993-94 REGULAR SEASON AT A GLANCE

RECORD: 33-46-5, 71 points

FINISH: 4th in Pacific, 9th in Western Conference, 20th overall

HOME: 14-26-2 (25th)-

AWAY: 19-20-3 (13th)

OVERTIME: 2-5-5 (24th)

VS OWN DIVISION: 11-18-1

VS OTHER DIVISIONS: 22-28-4

VS OWN CONFERENCE: 23-30-3

VS OTHER CONFERENCE: 10-16-2

FIRST HALF RECORD: 16-24-2

SECOND HALF RECORD: 17-22-3

GOALS FOR: 229 (23rd)

GOALS AGAINST: 251 (8th-t)

TEAM PLUS/MINUS: -9 (18th)

POWER PLAY: 14.4% (26th)

PENALTY KILLING: 82.7% (7th)

PENALTY MINUTES: 17.9/game (3rd)

1993-94 REGULAR SEASON LEADERS (WITH ANAHEIM ONLY):

GOALS: 23, Bob Corkum

ASSISTS: 31, Terry Yake

POINTS: 52, Yake

POWER PLAY GOALS: 3, Stephan Lebeau and Troy Loney

SHORTHANDED GOALS: 3, Corkum

PLUS-MINUS: + 20, Bobby Dollas

SHOTS: 206, Joe Sacco

PENALTY MINUTES: 272, Todd Ewen

A LOOK AHEAD TO 1994-95

GOAL: Guy (not as in Lafleur) Hebert (not as in Lambert) was born in Troy, New York, so resist the urge to use the French pronunciation, no matter how tempting. You may, however, mention him in the same breath as some of the great French-Canadian goalies currently playing in the NHL.

Hebert was outstanding for the Ducks with a 2.83 GAA, a .907 save percentage and two shutouts in 52 games. The first Anaheim pick in the expansion draft (second overall) is still only 27 years old so he should be a mainstay in their nets for some time to come.

Ron Tugnutt was just as steady before being traded to Montreal for Stephan Lebeau. But, the team needed some kind of offense, so he was expendable.

In stepped Mikhail Shtalenkov, former Moscow Dynamo goalie, whom the Ducks felt had served his apprenticeship in the minors. The 28-year old proved a capable backup in 10 games with a 2.65 GAA.

If anything goes wrong, the farm team in San Diego boasts John Tanner and Allan Bester, former Toronto Maple Leaf netminder who started in the IHL all-star game.

Definitely not a worry position for the Ducks.

DEFENCE: They were the great unwanted; the unwashed; the unloved. And on opening night against Detroit, they did nothing to improve their reputations in a 7-2 losing effort. In the first period alone, the Red Wings pumped 20 shots against Hebert and held a 3-0 lead. Mark Ferner and David Williams each finished the game a minus 4. Williams didn't play again for another month.

That's the bad news. The good news is that it never again got quite as bad. They didn't allow as many as seven goals in a game for the rest of the season. Williams ended up at plus 8, and Bobby Dollas, injured for that opening game, finished at a plus 20, incredible for an expansion team.

For Dollas it was a long time coming. A first round draft pick (14th overall) for the Winnipeg Jets in 1983, he never came close to the potential expected of him. He didn't score his first goal until the 1990-91 season after being bounced around in the minors and from organization to organization. In 1987, he was traded to Quebec for Stu Kulak.

Who? Exactly. While Dollas was their best defenceman, Alexei Kasatonov was their all-star representative. At 36, however, he was deemed expendable for youth and was shipped to St. Louis for Maxim Bets.

Bill Houlder held down one of the power play points, and David Williams spent some time there as well. Another journeyman, Randy Ladouceur proved dependable on defence.

Nikolai Tsulygin, a 1993 second round draft pick, at 6-3, 200 pounds, is expected to make the team this year as a defensive defenseman.

The Ducks needed an offensive defenseman and a power play point man and they got it with their second overall draft pick. Oleg Tverdovsky has been compared to Bobby Orr in some quarters (probably not Don Cherry's though). He is touted as an outstanding skater, passer and shooter. A perfect fit for the Ducks.

They also obtained Tom Kurvers at the draft from the Islanders for Troy Loney. Kurvers is an experienced power play specialist.

FORWARD: The Ducks weren't expected to be a high scoring team and so it was no surprise when they weren't.

There were some individual flashes of scoring ability but nothing much on a consistent basis: Anatoli Semenov when he wasn't injured; Terry Yake, who had 15 goals in the first half and only six in the second; Joe Sacco, who had three goals in the first half and 16 in the second; and Bob Corkum, the big surprise, with 51 points after earning just 10 the previous season.

In all, there were 15 Ducks who set career highs in points, which wasn't particularly difficult to do for most of them because 20 players also set career highs in games played. Even the Grim Reaper, Stu Grimson, set a career mark in points with six.

The problem is, few of them are likely to improve on those totals in the coming year. Almost all are role players who played their part to the hilt and understudied others.

There are some scorers on the horizon: Paul Kariya, if he ever signs; Valeri Karpov, if he ever signs; and Maxim Bets, who needs more experience.

The biggest disappointment for the Ducks was probably Steven King, the first forward they selected in the expansion draft. It was a nightmare season for him. He didn't score, then didn't play, and then finally ended his season on February 8th when he had reconstructive surgery on his shoulder.

A pleasant late season surprise was free agent acquisition John Lilley, who came on board after playing for the U.S. Olympic team, and had seven points in the Ducks last 13 games.

SPECIAL TEAMS: Dead last on the power play. And that's where it will stay until they get some legitimate scorers. Defenceman Bill Houlder, a power play specialist, led the team with 17 power play points. By comparison, Brian Leetch on the Rangers had 53. Tim Sweeney had six power play markers to lead the team. Pavel Bure and Brett Hull tied for the league lead with 25.

It should be somewhat better if they sign Tverdosky. He and Tom Kurvers would handle the power play points, making everyone in front of them a little more effective.

Now, the penalty killing unit — that's a different story. Seventh in the league, outstanding. Mostly, they just had to play the way they did at even strength, which was defense all the way. The forwards used speed to their advantage. Players such as Corkum, Sacco and Valk handled things up front, while Dollas and Ladouceur were prominent on the blueline.

COACHING: This was Ron Wilson's first test as a head coach anywhere, and he passed with flying colors. An assistant under Pat Quinn in Vancouver for three seasons, he took one look at the roster handed him and knew they weren't going to win any shootouts.

So, he became a salesman. He sold them on the idea of playing defence first and foremost, and he sold them on the team concept. The players bought it all, assembled the package, and it worked.

There were no superstars around like they had been accustomed to on other teams, Wilson told them, so they had to do it themselves. They did.

A good measure of a team's discipline is how well they play on the road. That's where they can concentrate on the style of play they've been taught, and not have to worry about entertaining the fans at home. The Ducks travelled well, setting an expansion road record with 19 wins.

At the same time, Wilson didn't endear himself to his coaching brethren or other management around the league. When Wilson accused Vanbiesbrouck and others of using illegal goalie pads, Clarke thought perhaps he should just worry about his own team and wait until he's been around a little longer before he started running his mouth off. "He's not exactly Al Arbour," said Clarke.

No, Wilson isn't Al Arbour, but he had just three fewer wins then him last year.

MANAGEMENT: Michael Eisner, the Chairman and CEO of The Walt Disney Company, knows entertainment, so maybe the rest of the NHL should just defer to his judgement and institute shootouts for tie games. Okay, maybe not, but it's nice to have some fresh thinking around the NHL.

As for the management closer to ice level, no problems there. Ferreira knows what he's doing, has an excellent management staff with good backgrounds in scouting and is patient enough to put together a team the right way.

TEAM NEEDS: Goals. Signing the players they already own would be a good start. Depth everywhere else.

POTENTIAL NEW FACES: C Paul Kariya, Canadian Olympic Team; RW Valeri Karpov, Russia; Nikolai Tsulgin, Russia, and Oleg Tverdovsky, Russia are all expected to sign and play. Also Tom Kurvers, NY Islanders.

Jarrod Skalde has proven he can score in the minors, (63 points in 57 games with San Diego of the IHL and a team leading 15 points in 9 playoff games) but he's going to have to show some consistency. He had nine points in his first nine games with the Ducks after being called up but then went into a tailspin with no points in his next 10 games. Back he went to the minors.

Maxim Bets was acquired from St. Louis for 36 year old defenseman Alexei Kasatonov and a sixth round pick. That's not a heck of a lot to give up for someone with the press clippings of Bets. He had 116 points for Spokane of the WHL before joining the Ducks for three games (no points) and then going to San Diego for the playoffs (two assists in nine playoff games). It looks like he will be a project.

McKENZIE'S BOTTOM LINE: How the Mighty have fallen. Just kidding.

In their initial NHL season, the Ducks finished ahead of established teams in Los Angeles, Edmonton and Winnipeg. While there is a chance the same could happen this year, don't necessarily count on it.

Winnipeg and Los Angeles should be improved. Maybe Edmonton, too.

Which is not to say the Ducks won't be better either, although that depends almost entirely on whether they can sign 1993 first-rounder Paul Kariya.

Kariya is an exceptional talent with Gretzky-like qualities. He's already had an impact in two world junior championships, one world championship and the 1994 Olympics. The Ducks could desperately use his offensive wizardry and the lustre he would bring to any NHL organization.

As the 1994-95 season approached, though, the Ducks still hadn't signed Kariya and there were indications that maybe, just maybe, they wouldn't be able to accomplish it. That would be devastating to an organization in its infancy and send all the wrong messages to the Ducks' fan.

Disney, which owns the Ducks, have a reputation in the entertainment industry as being notoriously frugal. The Ducks' management team would prefer to term it as fiscally responsible.

Whatever you call it, if it results in not being able to sign Kariya, the organization will have taken a huge step backwards. Last season's strong showing will be quickly forgotten.

If the Ducks realize they can't sign Kariya, the logical step is to trade him before the season to someone who can — and will. Because if Kariya sat out this one season — his only option in that case would be to play next spring briefly for Canada's entry at the 1995 world championships — he could become an unrestricted free agent at season's end.

Having said all that, if the Ducks can get Kariya and 1994 first-rounder Oleg Tverdosky, the Ukrainian-born, Russian-trained defenceman, in the lineup this season, they'll be more exciting to watch. That won't necessarily translate into the relative success they had a year ago, when they received the traditional first-year expansion boost that will be missing this year.

DRAFT ANALYSIS

Some were surprised when the Mighty Ducks chose Ukrainian-born, Russian-trained defenceman Oleg Tverdosky with the No. 2 pick overall. They shouldn't have been.

In a short draft history — all of one year — the Ducks have shown an attraction for things Russian, witness last year's selection of five Russians among their 11 draftees, including second pick Nikolai Tsulygin and third pick Valeri Karpov (both of whom are expected in the lineup this season).

Besides, Tverdosky, who has drawn comparisons to Bobby Orr but is probably much closer in potential stature to countryman Sergei Zubov or perhaps Brian Leetch, is a blue-chip

offensive talent. The Ducks hope to do with Tverdosky what they couldn't do with No. 1 pick Paul Kariya a year ago — that is, sign him.

After taking Tverdosky, the Ducks looked for offensive help up front, choosing Swedish centre Johan Davidsson and Red Deer right winger Craig Reichert. Davidsson is an immensely-gifted talent, but physically immature (5-foot-10, 170 pounds) and something of a long-term project. Reichert is a 20-year-old, passed over in last year's draft, who scored 52 goals and 119 points in the WHL last season.

The Ducks' final two picks were intriguing. They got Finnish centre Tommi Miettinen 236th overall, even though he was rated by NHL Central Scouting as the 17th best European available, and Sault Ste. Marie Greyhound tough guy Jeremy Stevenson, a 20-year-old who re-entered the draft after not being signed by the Winnipeg Jets, the team that chose him in the third round of the 1992 entry draft.

1993-94 KEYS

KEY DEALS:

In-Season

* obtained Stephan Lebeau from Montreal for Ron Tugnutt

* obtained Maxim Bets and 1995 6th round pick for Alexei Kasatonov.

Post-Season

* Obtained Tom Kurvers from the NY Islanders for Troy Loney.

KEY INJURIES: Anatoli Semenov (35 games), Troy Loney (21).

KEY STAT:

MIGHTY DUCK FIRSTS

GAME: 7-2 loss to Detroit at home

GOAL: Sean Hill

ASSISTS: Bill Houlder and Terry Yake

PENALTY: Sean Hill Shot: Sean Hill

WIN: 4-3 over Edmonton, October 13 (third game).

SHUTOUT: Guy Hebert - Dec. 13 at Toronto, 1-0.

HAT TRICK: Terry Yake - Oct. 19 at New York Rangers.

GOAL AGAINST: Aaron Ward, Detroit

STARTING LINEUP: Goal - Guy Hebert Defence: Alexei Kasatonov Defence: Randy Ladouceur Center: Anatoli Semenov Left Wing: Troy Loney Right Wing: Terry Yake

Calgary Flames

Since the Flames last won the Stanley Cup in 1989, they've been eliminated in the first round of the playoffs each time they've made it to the post-season. That means four of the last five years.

Time to sound the fire alarm? Nah. There's nothing wrong with this team that a couple breaks couldn't cure.

Even though they were plagued by injuries all season long, the Flames still earned 97 points, good enough for first in the weak Pacific division and sixth overall.

The playoff collapse wasn't pretty. Up 3-1 on Vancouver, they lost the last three games of the series in overtime. An inch here or there, however, and it could have been Calgary in the finals instead of the Canucks.

In game seven overtime, Robert Reichel took a pass from Theoren Fleury and lit up the red light behind Kirk McLean. Instant replay clearly showed the bad news, however. It hadn't crossed the goal line.

It will be a different team this year without Al MacInnis, and he will be missed. Phil Housley is about as good a replacement as there is, but at press time he was making noise that he didn't want to report.

Mike Vernon will also be missed. He was one of the most dependable goaltenders around the league for many years, despite the abuse he took at times during his Calgary tenure.

The Flames have so much depth, however, at every position, that it's unlikely the loss of the two will have a major effect on the success of the team. And it certainly won't stop them from getting past the first round of the playoffs.

1993-94 REGULAR SEASON AT A GLANCE

RECORD: 42-29-13

FINISH: 1st in Pacific Division, tied for 3rd in Western Conference, tied for 7th overall

HOME: 25-12-5 (5th)

AWAY: 17-17-8 (12th)

OVERTIME: 3-2-13 (10th)

VS OWN DIVISION: 20-8-4

VS OTHER DIVISIONS: 22-21-9

VS OWN CONFERENCE: 28-21-7

VS OTHER CONFERENCE: 14-8-6

FIRST HALF RECORD: 21-15-6

SECOND HALF RECORD: 21-14-7

GOALS FOR: 302 (3rd)

GOALS AGAINST: 256 (11th)

TEAM PLUS/MINUS: +49 (3rd)

POWER PLAY: 21.2% (4th)

PENALTY KILLING: 80.6% (19th)

PENALTY MINUTES: 22.0/game (18th)

1993-94 REGULAR SEASON LEADERS

GOALS: 41, Gary Roberts

ASSISTS: 54, Al MacInnis

POINTS: 93, Robert Reichel

POWER PLAY GOALS: 16, Theoren Fleury

SHORTHANDED GOALS: 3, German Titov, Roberts

GAME WINNING GOALS: 7, Joe Nieuwendyk

PLUS-MINUS: +38, Frank Musil

SHOTS: 324, MacInnis

PENALTY MINUTES: 243, Ronnie Stern

1993-94 PLAYOFFS AT A GLANCE

RESULTS: Conference Quarterfinals: lost to Vancouver 4-3

RECORD: 3-4

HOME: 1-3

AWAY: 2-1

GOALS FOR: 20

GOALS AGAINST: 23

OVERTIME: 0-3

POWER PLAY: 11.4% (12th)

PENALTY KILLING: 85.4% (5th)

PENALTY MINUTES: 24.7/game (16th)

1993-94 PLAYOFF LEADERS

GOALS: 6, Fleury

ASSISTS: 6, MacInnis, Roberts

POINTS: 10, Fleury

POWER PLAY GOALS: Five players tied with one

SHORTHANDED GOALS: 1, Mike Sullivan

OVERTIME GOALS: None

GAME-WINNING GOALS: 2, Fleury

PENALTY MINUTES: 34, Sandy McCarthy

PLUS-MINUS: +5, MacInnis

SHOTS: 32, MacInnis

A LOOK AHEAD TO 1994-95

GOAL: The Flames had more depth at this position than any other team in the league, so they were able to trade Mike Vernon.

At the start of last season, they kept four goalies on the roster in an attempt to audition backups for Vernon who was number one in Calgary for eight years. In six of those seasons, he was selected to play in the all-star game.

1990 first round draft pick Trevor Kidd won the competition over Andrei

Trefilov and Jeff Reese, and handled it nicely.

Trefilov created somewhat of a sensation when he recorded a shutout in just his fourth NHL start, and then did it again in his fifth. The former Moscow Dynamo netminder had a 2.50 GAA in 11 games, tops on the team. In Saint John he was 3.42 in 28 games with an .894 save percentage.

Jeff Reese, the fourth goaltender who started the season with the Flames, was deemed expendable and traded to Hartford.

Yet another goalie with a future is yet another first-rounder in Jason Muzzatti, who handled the bulk of the workload in Saint John, recording a 26-21-3 mark and a GAA of 3.74.

Look for Kidd and Trefilov to split the chores for a while until somebody emerges as number one. No bets on who it'll be.

DEFENCE: The Calgary defense has been revamped, not rebuilt. Lots of new faces. But, good quality faces.

Housley replaces MacInnis as the quarterback on the power play. He doesn't have his shot, but who does. He gets in the same range of points, however. He was felled by injuries for much of last season, but the year before earned a career high 97 with Winnipeg.

Gary Suter was traded to Hartford last season. He had many good years as the power play point partner of MacInnis, but he had outlived his usefulness in Calgary. Zarley Zalapski and James Patrick, both of whom can play the point with the man advantage, came over in the deal.

Dan Keczmer also showed the ability to help out on the power play with 14 extra-man points. Even Trent Yawney can stand back there when needed.

Frank Musil won't put the puck in the net, but he'll work hard at keeping it out. He finished with a plus 38 last season. His combined total for the last two years is an impressive plus 66.

Steve Chiasson, obtained in the Vernon deal, will prove to be a valuable member of the Flame defense. He's as dependable as they come defensively and also has some offensive capabilities in his repertoire.

A mobile nineties style defense with some good defensive types give the Flames one of the best units in the league.

FORWARD: The Flames had three 40 goal scorers, the most of any team. Gary Roberts (41), Robert Reichel (40), and Theoren Fleury (40), could have easily been joined by Joe Nieuwendyk (36) had he not missed 20 games with injuries.

The Flames have everything. Good goal scoring ability, good defensive forwards such as Joel Otto, Mike Sullivan and Kelly Kisio, and more than enough toughness with Ronnie Stern (243 PIM), Sandy McCarthy (173 PIM), and Paul Kruse (185 PIM), not to mention Gary Roberts (145 PIM) and Theoren Fleury (186) who do both.

First year Flame, German Titov, had an excellent start with 17 goals and 29 points in the first half before tailing off with 10 goals and 16 points in the last half.

Wes Walz, a free agent signee, who bounced around the minors after getting chances with Boston and Philadelphia, was a pleasant surprise, earning 38 points in just 53 games.

Michael Nylander proved to be a good playmaker, but because of defensive deficiencies, sat out most of the playoffs.

The Flames were a plus 49 at even strength last season, behind only Detroit and New Jersey. The ability to play well at even manpower shows a strength that's more important than scoring on the powerplay.

SPECIAL TEAMS: The downside of having such a rough and ready team is that they spend a lot of time in the penalty box. The Flames had 465 shorthanded situations, the most in the league. By comparison, Tampa Bay allowed 130 fewer power plays.

Even though their power play was one of the best, it wasn't much value because the Flames allowed more goals shorthanded t han they earned with a man advantage.

In the past, their strategy with the man advantage was simple: work the puck around and somehow get it back to MacInnis who would let the booming shot go. That will be changed some this year, but there's no shortage of snipers up front who can drive it home.

COACHING: Dave King said something interesting after the Flames lost in the first round of the playoffs. He suggested that perhaps they put too much energy into playing hard every night during the regular season and didn't have anything extra to give for the playoffs.

Does that mean he might take it easier on the troops next year? Not likely.

He demands a full effort from all his players all the time. If not, you're in the doghouse and in the press box. Paul Ranheim was one player who learned. Later in the season he was punished even further when he was traded to Hartford. Even fiery Theoren Fleury invoked the wrath of King who suggested Fleury come to play every night or he wouldn't be playing at all.

King might be among the top five coaches in the league, but he'll have to do something in the playoffs before he gets that kind of recognition.

MANAGEMENT: No matter what Doug Risebrough does over the rest of his management career he will always be remembered for THE trade. Then again, the man he made the deal with, his predecessor Cliff Fletcher, once traded away Brett Hull.

Risebrough is making strides towards making people forget his lowest GM moment (not quite yet, however - see Key Stat).

Risebrough tested the waters again last year in a big deal with Hartford, obtaining Michael Nylander, James Patrick and Zarley Zalapski from Hartford for Ted Drury, Paul Ranheim and Gary Suter.

After the season, he was busy again, shaking up the team with some big deals.

POTENTIAL NEW FACES: Not a lot of room for newcomers, but the Flames like to bring up a player or two every year. C Cory Stillman (35-48-83 at Saint John), LW Vesa Viitakoski (28-39-67 at Saint John), D Kevin Wortman (17-32-49 at Saint John), C David Struch (18-25-43 in 58 games for Saint John).

McKENZIE'S BOTTOM LINE: This is one of those predictions that is tailor-made to come back and haunt you.

The Flames shouldn't be nearly as good as they were a year ago, when they finished first in the Pacific Division.

Mike Vernon is gone, replaced by one of Trevor Kidd, Andrei Trefilov and Jason Muzzatti (bet on the latter being one of the two Flames' starters).

Al MacInnis and Gary Suter, the twin cannons on the Flames' blueline, have been replaced by Phil Housley, Zarley Zalapski and James Patrick.

Joel Otto is another year older. Joe Nieuwendyk seems another day closer to being traded to another team.

If you were plotting the Flames' fortunes on a graph, logic dictates a downward trend for this season.

But there's something about head coach Dave King that should make any forecaster wary. One gets the feeling that King is liable to do more with less than he has in the past two seasons, when it could be argued he did less with a lot more.

King has never really liked the chemistry on his hockey team since he arrived two years ago. Now, it's drastically altered and, for better or worse, the Flames are much closer to becoming Dave King's team. He made a little go a long way with Canadian Olympic teams.

Remember, though, that the Flames are hardly devoid of talent. Gary Roberts is one of the preeminent left wingers in the game and Robert Reichel is an emerging star at centre.

Having said all that, the indicators point down for Calgary this season. Just put an asterisk beside the prediction to allow for King to work some magic with this group.

DRAFT PICKS

Flames' GM Doug Risebrough went into the draft wanting to add size and strength. He accomplished that with the first-round selection of Chris Dingman, a 6-foot-3, 231-pound left winger from the Brandon Wheat Kings. The knock on Dingman is that he's injury prone — he played only 45 games last season because of knee and shoulder injuries — and that he lacks quickness. The skating issue is to be expected, given Dingman's enormous physical presence at such a young age. Besides, he showed marked improvement in that area, so the best is obviously yet to come. Some scouts believe Dingman could easily shed a few pounds to give himself an extra gear. He didn't do bad offensively last season, though, scoring 21 goals and 41 points in only 45 games, but his true value will be as a banging winger.

The Flames made an interesting D-day trade with the New Jersey Devils. Calgary sent its third-round pick (71st overall) to New Jersey for the Devils' third-rounder (77th overall) plus the Devils' fourth-and fifth-rounders, too.

In order to move up six places in the third round, so they could take big Tri-City American defenceman Sheldon Souray, the Devils gave up an additonal two draft picks.

Just for the heck of it, keep an eye on Souray's development as compared to the progress of the three players the Flames took with those Devil draft picks — scoring winger Chris Clark from the Springfield Olympics, high-scoring but diminutive Spokane Chiefs' centre Ryan Duthie and talented but physically immature Swede Nisse Ekman.

1993-94 KEYS

KEY DEALS:

* obtained James Patrick, Zarley Zalapski, and Michael Nylander from Hartford for Gary Suter, Paul Ranheim and Ted Drury.

* obtained Dan Keczmer from Hartford for Jeff Reese.

Post-Season:

* obtained Steve Chiasson from Detroit for Mike Vernon

* obtained Phil Housley and 1996 and 1997 second round picks for Al MacInnis and a 1997 fourth round pick

KEY INJURIES: Joe Nieuwendyk (20 games), Kelly Kisio (33), Gary Suter (44 games before trade), Mike Vernon (16), Trent Yawney (25).

KEY STAT: Lest we forget. There were only a few reporters in the Toronto Maple Leaf dressing room (including this one) when the biggest (in numbers) trade in NHL history was announced. Russian Alexander Godynyuk was the most confused of the bunch. His command of the English language wasn't very good and he didn't understand what was going on. He wasn't the only one.

Calgary got: Gary Leeman — 23 points in 59 games for Calgary. Traded to Montreal for Brian Skrudland who was lost in the expansion draft to Florida. Alexander Godynyk — 7 points in 27 games. Lost to Florida in expansion draft. Craig Berube — 17 points in 113 games. Traded to Washington for a fifth round draft pick. Michel Petit — 48 points in 134 games. Offered termination contract this year. Jeff Reese — 17-6-3 record in 39 games. Traded to Hartford for Dan Keczmer.

Toronto got: Doug Gilmour — 287 points in 206 games. Still with Toronto. Jamie Macoun — 65 points in 198 games. Still with Toronto. Kent Manderville — 24 points in 100 games. Still with Toronto. Rick Wamsley — Toronto goaltending coach Rick Nattress — 16 points in 34 games with Toronto. Now retired.

TALLY TO DATE: Calgary — 95 total scoring points Toronto — 392 scoring points and counting

Chicago Blackhawks

The number one star of the 1993-94 Chicago Blackhawk hockey season is...(drum roll, please) Chicago Stadium. And, of course, the fans who made it so special.

We will all "remember the roar" but for a while at least Chicago fans will also remember the bore of last season and remember the snore of the playoffs.

The Hawks ended up only three games over .500 and scored the fewest goals number of goals in 16 years. In the playoffs, they were shut out in three of six games in going down to defeat to the Maple Leafs.

Much of the action last season was off the ice where happy campers were difficult to find.

Larmer was unhappy with his contract and was eventually traded after refusing to play; other players were unhappy with their contracts and the coaching style of Darryl Sutter; Sutter was unhappy with the playing style of some of the players, Sutter and Roenick carried a running feud through the press all season long.

Sutter's tried to indoctrinate a defense first style of play. It made sense. After Roenick, and perhaps Joe Murphy, the Blackhawks had the firepower of a peashooter.

If they could concentrate on play in the neutral and defensive zones and work together as a team, just maybe they could be successful.

That's what Buffalo did. The difference is that the Sabres bought into the approach and the Blackhawk players didn't. When Roenick, the number one player on the team, isn't committed to it and is openly critical, it won't work.

1993-94 REGULAR SEASON AT A GLANCE

RECORD: 39-36-9

FINISH: 5th in Central Division, 6th in Western Conference, 13th Overall

HOME: 21-16-5 (14th)

AWAY: 18-20-4 (14th)

OVERTIME: 2-5-9 (22nd)

VS OWN DIVISION: 14-15-1

VS OTHER DIVISIONS: 25-21-8

VS OWN CONFERENCE: 30-24-2

VS OTHER CONFERENCE: 9-12-7

FIRST HALF RECORD: 20-18-4

SECOND HALF RECORD: 19-18-5

GOALS FOR: 254 (19th)

GOALS AGAINST: 240 (5th)

TEAM PLUS/MINUS: +18 (9th-t)

POWER PLAY: 17.5% (19th)

PENALTY KILLING: 83.4% (5th)

PENALTY MINUTES: 25.3 (25th)

1993-94 REGULAR SEASON LEADERS

GOALS: 46, Jeremy Roenick

ASSISTS: 61, Roenick

POINTS: 107, Roenick

POWER PLAY GOALS: 24, Roenick

SHORTHANDED GOALS: 5, Roenick

GAME WINNING GOALS: 6, Michel Goulet

PLUS-MINUS: +21, Roenick

SHOTS: 281, Roenick

PENALTY MINUTES: 212, Chris Chelios

1993-94 PLAYOFFS AT A GLANCE

RESULTS: Conference Quarterfinals - lost 4-2 to Toronto

RECORD: 2-4

HOME: 2-1

AWAY: 0-3

GOALS FOR: 1.7/game

GOALS AGAINST: 2.5/game

OVERTIME: 1-1

POWER PLAY: 13.8% (10th)

PENALTY KILLING: 71.9% (15th)

PENALTY MINUTES: 20.2/game (8th)

1993-94 PLAYOFF LEADERS

GOALS: 4, Tony Amonte

ASSISTS: 6, Roenick

POINTS: 7, Roenick

POWER PLAY GOALS: 2, Gary Suter

SHORTHANDED GOALS: None

OVERTIME GOALS: 1, Roenick

GAME-WINNING GOALS: 1, Roenick and Amonte

PENALTY MINUTES: 25, Joe Murphy

PLUS-MINUS: 4, Roenick, Amonte

SHOTS: 29, Chelios

A LOOK AHEAD TO 1994-95

GOAL: Ed Belfour played 70 games last season, the third time he's reached that plateau, the most of any goaltender in NHL history. The Western Conference starter in the all-star game tied for the league lead with seven shutouts and was second with 37 wins.

He'll be a busy man again this year. Backup Jeff Hackett is an NHL goalie, he just hasn't had much success. He was 2-12-3 for the Blackhawks last season, and has a career record of 24-94-6. His winning percentage is the lowest of any goalie in NHL history with at least 100 games between the pipes. Not all his fault, of course, but still....

The Blackhawks, no doubt, wished they still had Dominik Hasek, whom they traded for Stephane Beauregard, whom they traded for Christian Ruuttu. It's a moot point anyway, because with Belfour in the nets, Hasek would never have gotten the break he needed to prove himself.

DEFENCE: The defense rests. Or at least they did for much of last year. Injuries and suspensions meant there were few times when their top six defenseman could all suit up in the same game.

Not that they were the same top six that often anyway. Pulford suggested the team wanted to get younger on defense, and they were earlier in the year. That was scrapped with little fanfare and in true Blackhawk fashion, much of the youth was traded away.

After obtaining Keith Carney from Buffalo early on last season, the ages of their top seven defensemen were: Chelios - 31, Steve Smith - 30, Bryan Marchment - 24, Cam Russell - 24, Frank Kucera - 25, Neil Wilkinson - 26 and Carney - 23. A good mix of experience and toughness but not many good puckhandlers in the bunch.

The way they line up for this season: Chelios - 32, Smith - 31, Gary Suter - 30, Eric Weinrich - 27, Robert Dirk - 28, Russell - 25, Greg Smyth - 28, and Carney - 24.

They traded away the youth for experience and in the process became more mobile, perhaps in preparation for the move to the new arena and the bigger ice surface.

That mobility will help them move the puck better, but some of those players aren't known for their defensive abilities. On a team without much scoring power up front, it could be the wrong mix.

FORWARD: There isn't a team in the league that relies on one forward to do as much as Roenick. He can do lots, but he can't do everything.

The man needs a left winger. A no-lose assignment, you'd think. A ticket to pile up lots of assists and goals. But everybody keeps falling short. Michel Goulet would have been ideal earlier in his career, Stephane Matteau couldn't do it after about seven strikes, and nobody else has been able to step in.

Things could be different this year. Joe Murphy, a left-handed shot will probably play on the left side while Amonte patrols right wing.

If Amonte can return to form it could be one of the more potent lines is the league.

Now, if they could only also play Roenick on the second line. They did sign free agent Bernie Nicholls, who was shuffled aside in New Jersey last year, and at 33 can't be expected to be an offensive force anymore.

They need scoring there and they don't have it. Patrick Poulin was being touted as one of the best left wingers in the game two years ago, but flopped badly. He's still young, however, and could come around. Paul Ysebeart used to be a scorer, but he couldn't find the net last year either. Nobody at center behind Roenick has shown an ability to score much.

Lots of competent checkers on the Blackhawks, among the best groups in the league. They're led by Dirk Graham and Brent Sutter, both of whom excel in the role, but both of whom aren't getting any younger.

Among the youth, center Jeff Shantz showed something last year as a two way player, as did winger Steve Dubinsky. Right winger Sergei Krivoksarov is another good possibility to crack the lineup, although he didn't exactly shoot the lights out in Indianapolis with 19 goals and 26 assists in 53 games.

Eric Lecompte is a big left wing/center who scored 39 goals and 88 points with Hull in the Quebec League last season. He was their first round pick in 1993. Another prospect is Andy MacIntyre, a fourth rounder from 1992 who scored 54 goals for Saskatoon in the WHL.

SPECIAL TEAMS: Jeremy Roenick scored 24 goals with the man advantage, just one away from leading the league, and the most in Blackhawk history. So, how does a one man power play rank overall in the NHL? Nineteenth last season.

It could improve this year with specialist Gary Suter manning one of the points on a full time bases. Chelios, Weinrich and Smith are others who are no strangers to the power play point.

Again, however, not much help for Roenick up front. Here's a thought. How about a power play unit with Roenick and four defensemen.

The penalty killing percentage was fifth overall. There's plenty of good checking forwards to handle those duties. And Roenick spends plenty of time there as well, earning five shorthanded goals, second only to Brendan Shanahan in the league.

COACHING: Darryl Sutter has earned a reputation for telling it like it is. And then spends a lot of time telling the press that what it is, isn't. Or something like that.

No problem, he said, about his feud with Roenick, over and over again. No problem, he said, about Ed Belfour, who threw his stick in Sutter's direction after being pulled from a game. No problem, no problem, no problem.

That's a lot of problems for someone without any problems. The next time he doesn't have a problem, he could be looking for a job.

MANAGEMENT: Bob Pulford says he doesn't plan to remain as general manager for much longer. Hmm...now let's see. Who might be a good candidate to take over. Hey, how about rehiring Mike Keenan? Yeah, that's the ticket.

NEEDS: Goals, goals, and more goals. Left wingers who can score, centers who can score, right wingers who can score and prospects who can score.

POTENTIAL NEW FACES: Lots of big scorers in junior, especially on left wing where it's needed most. Could be time for one or two, or more, to make the jump. LW Eric Lecompte, 39-44-88, Hull (QMJHL); LW Andy McIntyre 54-35-85, Saskatoon (WHL); LW Ethan Moreau 44-56-98, Niagara Falls (OHL), RW Mike Prokopec, 52-58-110, Guelph

(OHL), LW Eric Daze, 59-48-107, Beauport (QMJHL), Bodan Savenko, 42-49-91, Niagara Falls (OHL); C Eric Manlow, Kitchener (OHL) 28-32-60 in 49 games.

McKENZIE'S BOTTOM LINE: Any team with Ed Belfour in net, Chris Chelios and Gary Suter on the blueline and Jeremey Roenick, Joe Murphy and Tony Amonte up front should not be discounted from making some noise this season.

Especially when it's the hard-working Chicago Blackhawks, playing out of the new United Centre across the road from the old Stadium.

But don't count on it.

The problem with the Blackhawks is that they rely too heavily on Belfour, Chelios and Roenick. This Hawk team didn't look awe-inspiring in last spring's playoff loss to Toronto and there is every reason to believe Chicago is now about to head to the downside of the mountain.

Adding free-agent centre Bernie Nicholls should help what has been a woefully weak position behind Roenick. And so long as Amonte and Murphy put the puck in the net, the Hawks' offence won't be as one-dimensional as it used to be. But the patented Hawk toughness is no more. The loss of players such as Bryan Marchment, Jocelyn Lemieux, Stephane Matteau, Stu Grimson and Mike Peluso have helped to emasculate one of the NHL's nastiest teams. Sure, they can score more goals than they used to, but do they compete as hard as they did?

Based on what we saw in the playoffs — beyond Chelios, Suter and Roenick — the answer is a definite no.

The Hawks have precious little young talent on the way up. That could change in a year or two, when Ethan Moreau and Eric Lecompte, two first-round left wingers, burst onto the scene. It's imperative, then, the Hawks start getting some mileage from underachieving Patrick Poulin, a potential star who has something the Hawks desperately require — size, strength and scoring from the left wing.

Chicago will go as far as Belfour, Chelios, Suter and Roenick take them, which without the proper support, won't be far enough.

DRAFT PICKS

No question what the Blackhawks saw as their most pressing need at the draft — help on the left side.

The Hawks have virtually no scoring on the left wing. All their offence is at centre (Jeremy Roenick) and on the right side (with Joe Murphy, Tony Amonte etc.) So it was no surprise when they took Niagara Falls Thunder left winger Eathan Moreau in the first-round. The three-year OHL veteran scored 44 goals and 98 points in 59 games, playing (in the second half of the season anyway) alongside centre Jason Bonsignore. Moreau moves well for a big man and has a good shot, which was hindered somewhat last season by a broken bone in his hand that required some post-season surgery. While no one is predicting immediate impact for Moreau, the vision of him skating alongside Roenick isn't out of the question.

With their second-round pick, the Hawks went back to the left side and took Jean-Yves Leroux from Beauport of the Quebec League. Leroux doesn't have the same offensive touch as Moreau, but he's a big, strong kid who plays an up-and-down pro-style banging game.

Another notable pick for Chicago was fourth-rounder Steve McLaren, a defenceman from the North Bay Centennials. He's probably a longshot to crack the Hawk lineup, but it won't be from lack of effort. McLaren was involved in what had to be the most spectacular fight of the 1993-94 season. He went toe-to-toe with Kamloops Blazer tough guy Chris Murray (drafted by Montreal) at the 1994 Memorial Cup in a scrap the scouts are still talking about.

1993-94 KEYS

KEY DEALS:
* obtained Patrick Poulin and Eric Weinrich from Hartford for Steve Larmer and Bryan Marchment
* obtained Gary Suter and Randy Cunneyworth from Hartford for Frank Kucera and Jocelyn Lemieux
* obtained Tony Amonte and Matt Oates from NY Rangers for Stephane Matteau and Brian Noonan
* obtained Paul Ysebeart from Winnipeg for a 1995 3rd round draft pick.
* obtained Robert Dirk from Vancouver for a 1994 4th round pick
* obtained a 1994 4th round pick from Los Angeles for Kevin Todd.

KEY INJURIES: Steve Smith (27 games), Christian Ruuttu (20), Dirk Graham (17).

KEY STAT: Over the last two seasons, the Chicago Blackhawks have exactly six goals courtesy of rookies. No other team can claim such poor production.

It's by design, however. Pulford likes his veterans. Chicago hasn't missed the playoffs since 1969 and he's been in the organization since 1977, so obviously that philosophy hasn't hurt them that much.

The Blackhawks need scoring, however, and they have lots in the junior leagues. It could be time to reverse the trend.

FEWEST GOALS BY ROOKIES

1992/93

CHICAGO	0
Minnesota	6
Toronto	6
Ottawa	10
Buffalo	12
Montreal	13

1993/94

Dallas	2
NYI Islanders	2
NY Rangers	3
Toronto	5
San Jose	5
CHICAGO	6

FEWEST TOTAL LAST TWO YEARS

CHICAGO	6
Dallas	8
Toronto	11

Dallas Stars

The Stars were a huge hit in their first season in Dallas. The Texan fans took to the team like...oh, Minnesotans to a college hockey game.

Average attendance was 16,119. There were 21 sellouts, including the last 13 in a row.

Mind you, after January, the winter alternative was the Dallas Mavericks, who couldn't win at home, or anywhere else.

There's no point trying to compete with the Cowboys in a popularity contest. It's a football town, first and foremost, and always will be. But, in their first season at least, the Stars had their share of attention.

Whether that continues is probably a matter of how well the team performs on the ice.

After a season in which they missed the playoffs, the Stars established a franchise record with 42 wins, surpassing the old mark of 40 set in 1982-83. The 97 points were also a franchise high, just the third time they've reached the nineties.

The club didn't make money for owner Norm Green, but it didn't lose near as much as in Minnesota.

Green, meanwhile, was embroiled in controversy. One press report said that he was already threatening to move the team if the city didn't do something about the lack of luxury boxes at Reunion Arena. Green denied it emphatically.

Elsewhere, he had to deal with sexual harassment charges stemming from his Minnesota days. He denied those too, eventually settling out of court.

In the playoffs, the Stars looked like they would make a serious run. They disposed of St. Louis in four straight in the first round. But, they ran into a brick wall, a.k.a. the Vancouver Canucks, and went down to defeat in five games. As it turned out, there wasn't much shame in that.

1993-94 REGULAR SEASON AT A GLANCE

RECORD: 42-29-13

FINISH: 3rd in Central Division, 3rd in Western Conference, 7th overall

HOME: 23-12-7 (7th) Away: 19-17-6

(8th) Overtime: 6-3-13 (6th)

VS OWN DIVISION: 12-13-5

VS OTHER DIVISIONS: 30-16-8

VS OWN CONFERENCE: 29-19-7

VS OTHER CONFERENCE: 13-10-6

FIRST HALF RECORD: 20-15-7

SECOND HALF RECORD: 22-14-6

GOALS FOR: 286 (9th)

GOALS AGAINST: 265 (14th)

TEAM PLUS/MINUS: +8

POWER PLAY: 18.4% (15th)

PENALTY KILLING: 84.1% (4th)

PENALTY MINUTES: 22.8 (21st)

RECORD: 5-4

HOME: 2-2

AWAY: 3-2

GOALS FOR: 3.0/game

GOALS AGAINST: 3.1/game

OVERTIME: 1-1

POWER PLAY: 20.4% (4th)

PENALTY KILLING: 82.9% (8th)

PENALTY MINUTES: 16.6/game (6th)

1993-94 REGULAR SEASON LEADERS

GOALS: 50, Mike Modano

ASSISTS: 57, Russ Courtnall

POINTS: 93, Modano

POWER PLAY GOALS: 18, Modano

SHORTHANDED GOALS: 3, Mike McPhee

GAME WINNING GOALS: 6, Dave Gagner

PLUS-MINUS: +19 Derian Hatcher

SHOTS: 281, Modano

PENALTY MINUTES: 333, Shane Churla

1993-94 PLAYOFF LEADERS

GOALS: 7, Modano

ASSISTS: 8, Paul Cavallini, Courtnall

POINTS: 10, Modano

POWER PLAY GOALS: 3, Gagner

SHORTHANDED GOALS: none

OVERTIME GOALS: 1, Cavallini

GAME-WINNING GOALS: 2, Modano

PENALTY MINUTES: 35, Churla

PLUS-MINUS: Four tied at +1

SHOTS: 48, Modano

A LOOK AHEAD TO 1994-95

GOAL: It's funny how some things work out. Boston and Dallas switched goalies before the start of last season, with Andy Moog going to the Stars, and Jon Casey moving to the Bruins.

At the end of the year, Casey's stats (30-15-9, 2.88) were better than Moog's (24-20-7, 3.27), but it was the Bruins who wished they hadn't made the deal. Casey was offered a termination contract at the end of the

1993-94 PLAYOFFS AT A GLANCE

RESULTS: Conference Quarterfinals: Defeated St. Louis 4-0;Conference Semi-Finals: Lost to Vancouver 4-1 season and eventually signed with St. Louis.

Moog became only the 10th goaltender in NHL history to win 300 games. He had some rough outings during the year, but most of the time gave them a good game.

The big surprise was Darcy Wakaluk. Instead of sitting quietly back in his accustomed role as second banana, he stepped up and did an outstanding job. His 2.64 goals against average was seventh best in the league (Moog was 28th) and he recorded an 18-9-6 record.

He was chosen over Moog to start in the playoffs and was a huge factor in their sweep of St. Louis in the first round. Moog was in 55 games last season compared to 36 for Wakaluk. Look for a more even split this year.

DEFENCE: A good quality, solid defense corps with depth. There are eight NHL caliber rearguards here with a good mix of experience, dependability, size and youth.

No Ray Bourque, mind you, but they can get the job done defensively and make a contribution in the other end of the rink.

Team captain, Mark Tinordi, at 6-4, 205 is the leader but is also one of the most injury prone players in the league. In seven NHL seasons, he's yet to play as many as 70 games in one year. He's coming off a broken femur suffered in late February that put him out of action for the season.

Craig Ludvig, at 6-3, 215 and Mike Lalor, 6-0, 200, obtained from San Jose at the trading deadline, are two defensive defensemen both over 30 years old who provide stability and experience.

Grant Ledyard, a free agent signee, had his best NHL season at the age of 32. He took up residence at one of the power play points and was their second leading power play point producer with 26, behind only Modano. His 46 points overall represented his best production in 10 NHL seasons. And as a bonus, he played all 84 games, the first time he's come even close.

Paul Cavallini played the point on the power play and also did a decent job. In the playoffs, his nine points in nine games were second on the team in scoring.

Tommy Sjodin was expected to be back there with the man advantage, but since that was the only time he was invited to go on the ice, he was a luxury the team couldn't afford. He was dispatched to the minors and eventually Quebec.

On the side of youth there's Doug Zmolek (23), obtained from San Jose with Lalor; Richard Matvichuk (21), a first rounder in 1991 who looks to be ready to step into a full time job; and Derian Hatcher (22), who sometimes needs to be reminded he's 6-5, 205, but could very well be an NHL all-star some day.

They could still use a quarterback for the powerplay, but as they stand, opposing forwards are not going to have a lot of fun playing against the Stars.

FORWARD: Mike Modano finally stopped hanging around the perimeter and got into the thick of things. The result was his first 50 goal season.

Gainey convinced him to go to the net more often and use his height to more advantage. Even Modano was surprised by the results. The first overall draft pick in 1988 will be entering his fifth full NHL season, but he's just turned 24 years old. Next step? A 100 point season.

Russ Courtnall was always the type of player who skated too fast for what he was able to do with the puck. Maybe, at 28, he's slowed down some because he had no such problem last year. He had his best point season with 80, and set a team record for right wingers with 57 assists. As long as he keeps setting up Modano there's no reason to think he can't duplicate his output.-j-î Dave Gagner is a streaky player, although that's within the confines of the season, not from year to year. His 32 goals put him over the 30 goal mark for the sixth year in a row.

From there, the scoring power drops considerably. Mike Craig was supposed to step up but has been a disappointment, only scoring 13 goals last year after two seasons of 15. Trent Klatt was expected to do better as well, but both are still young and could still break out at some time.

The rest of the lineup features defensive forwards who scored more than they should be expected to. Neal Broten had an outstanding season. The 34 year old is never going to score 100 points again, but 52 points, fourth on the team, was an unexpected bonus.

Dean Evason, Mike McPhee, Brent Gilchrist, Paul Broten, Shane Churla and Alan May are all role players who fit well into the Bob Gainey system.

The good news is that there's lots of depth at centre and right wing. The bad news is that there's almost nothing on the left side.

The only natural left-wingers in the lineup are Mike McPhee and Alan May. Everybody else took turns moving to their off-wing and away from centre. That clearly is a concern for Gainey, and he will try to rectify that somehow before the start of the season.

Curiously, on a team that doesn't have much scoring, the Stars traded away Ulf Dahlen for defensive help. Dahlen suits the Sharks offense, but maybe he didn't suit Bob Gainey's defensive system.

The Stars can get by with Modano doing most of the scoring, and most of the rest playing defensively, but they're in serious trouble if he's hurt for any extended period.

Some more scoring power could be on the way in the package of center Todd Harvey who was finally signed. The prolific junior isn't big, but he's competitive and has been compared to Bobby Clarke.

SPECIAL TEAMS: As could be expected from two of the best defensive forwards to play the game, Bob Gainey and Doug Jarvis, they put together one of the best penalty killing units in the league, ranking fourth.

Broten, McPhee, Evason, and Gilchrist handled the forward spots most of the time, with Tinordi, Ledyard, Hatcher and Ludvig sharing the duties in the back.

The power play was adequate, which is all that can be expected. There's no quarterback on the point, just lots of guys who can do a capable job.

COACHING/MANAGEMENT: Bob Gainey must have the biggest doghouse in the league. Just about everybody spends some time in it.

Indifferent play won't be tolerated by Gainey, and once the player has the message he'll usually respond. If he doesn't, Gainey can't stand to have him around.

This is Gainey's fourth year as coach of the Stars and each season has seen an improvement in winning percentage. He gets the type of player he wants, those he know will fit the system and follow the "team first" party line.

So far, so good.

NEEDS: Left wingers and a few players who can score. Solid at defense, goal, and with defensive forwards.

POTENTIAL NEW FACES: Gainey isn't the type of coach who likes to use a lot of rookies. Those who do make it to the big team, however, should be ready when they get there, or they won't stay long. The only projected new face is Center Todd Harvey, 34-51-85 in 49 games for the Detroit Jr Red Wings.

McKENZIE'S BOTTOM LINE: This should be the year Mike Modano takes off into the strata of superstardom.

The slick centre finally hit the prestigious 50-goal mark last season (in only 76 games) but he's still looking for that big 100-point season. If GM-coach Bob Gainey cuts him just a little slack from the Stars' rigid defensive system and finds a little extra icetime for the flashy young American, Modano could become one of the league's most electrifying players.

Last season was a critical year for him. He proved to Gainey, and himself, that he could play the pro-style game in heavy traffic. He went from being a periphery player to a man in the middle. He was a force in the first round of the playoffs against St. Louis, something less than that in the Stars' disappointing second round loss to the Canucks.

As for the Stars overall outlook, there is no reason to predict a fall for Gainey's team. Nor is there any rationale to forecast a huge surge.

The Stars' basic premise is to employ big strong players, especially on defence, who like to use their size to advantage. A crucial factor this season will be the return to health of team captain and defensive anchor Mark Tinordi, who badly broke his leg last season while chasing down a puck for icing. If Tinordi comes back to 100 per cent — and that is the prognosis — then the Stars have a rallying point. Young D-men Derian Hatcher and Rich Matvichuk are only going to get (bigger and) better.

Up front, there's plenty of toughness (Shane Churla, Alan May etc.) and good skill, too (Modano, Dave Gagner, Russ Courtnall). But the Stars' goal-scoring from the left side is almost non-existent. In an ideal world, Gainey would like to have more offensive punch, but not at the expense of team defence, which was his trademark as a Hall of Fame player.

It will be interesting to see how the Stars' goaltending shakes down this season. Darcy Wakaluk seemed to emerge as the No. 1 goaltender in the playoffs last spring, with Andy Moog still very much part of the picture. Wakaluk and Moog give the Stars adequate netminding, but in the Central Division (home of Ed Belfour, Felix Potvin, Curtish Joseph and now Mike Vernon), it might need to be better than that.

DRAFT PICKS

Like division-rival Chicago, the Stars desperately require scoring from the left side. Their first-round pick this year, Jason Botterill of the University of Michigan, will supply it, but not for at least a couple of years.

The hulking winger with a decent offensive touch is a project who intends to spend at least one year, and possibly more, at Michigan, where he scored 20 goals and 39 points in 36 games. There's no question his skating needs some work, but he proved at the 1994 world junior championships that he doesn't look out of place when up against the fastest in the world. He went in as a longshot to earn a spot of the Canadian national junior team entry and although he was a utility man for Canada, he handled himself well.

His combination of size and strength, plus the scoring touch, will endear him to Stars' GM-coach Bob Gainey.

The Stars' second-round pick, centre Lee Jinman of the North Bay Centennials, could turn out to be one of the steals of the draft. Jinman isn't big by pro standards — 5-foot-10, 155 pounds — but then neither was Doug Gilmour. Jinman embraces many Gilmour-like qualities, especially in the areas of work ethic and offensive creativity. He'll have to prove that he can do his thing in much heavier pro traffic but, given time and careful nurturing, he could turn out to be a gem.

Surprisingly, of the eight players drafted by Dallas, only one (Botterill) was more than 6 feet or 200 pounds. Shocking, really, when you consider Gainey's appreciation of big, strong physical Stars.

1993-94 KEYS

KEY DEALS:
* obtained Mike Lalor and Doug Zmolek from San Jose for Ulf Dahlen.
* obtained Gord Donnelly from Buffalo for James Black and undisclosed draft pick
* obtained Alan May from Washington for Jim Johnson and future considerations

KEY INJURIES: Mark Tinordi (23 games).

KEY STAT: You can't ask more from a coach than improvement from the year before. At his current rate, Bob Gainey should break the 100 point barrier this season.

He's improved the team's record each of his four seasons as coach of the Stars.

BOB GAINEY COACHING RECORD

Year	Record	Points	Difference
90-91	27-39-14	68	
91-92	32-42-6	70	+2
92-93	36-38-10	82	+12
93-94	42-29-13	97	+15

Detroit Red Wings

For a team that had such a great season, the Detroit Red Wings sure had a crummy season.

Forget the fact that they had 100 points, good for first in the Western Conference. Forget the fact that they led the league in scoring by 50 goals, the highest margin since the Edmonton Oiler glory days.

It was a disappointing year because so much more was expected of them. They were humiliated in the playoffs by the longshot San Jose Sharks, bounced in the first round for the second consecutive season.

The perceived culprit? Goaltending. The perceived scrapegoat? GM Bryan Murray, who lost his job after the season.

No team had a more publicized need than the Wings did for a goaltender. Just about every decent netminder in the league was rumored to be heading for the Motor City at one time or another.

Finally, they got Bob Essensa from Winnipeg when they really wanted Bill Ranford or Grant Fuhr. Bowman lost confidence in Essensa by the time the playoffs rolled around and they were right back where they started.

Maybe the culprit wasn't so much the goaltending as the players in front of them. There's so much offensive firepower that it's tough not to get caught up in it, or up the ice.

Scotty Bowman is used to coaching talented teams, and he's used to getting the best out of them, especially at playoff time. He has six Stanley Cup rings to prove it.

Didn't work this time. He had difficulty with their attitudes and egos all season long. And the players had difficulty with him.

That may be the real problem with this team, if you can call two 100 point seasons in a row a problem.

There are no excuses anymore now that they've obtained Mike Vernon in the off-season for Steve Chiasson, who may have been their best two-way defenseman.

If Vernon isn't the answer, than the problems lie elsewhere and they'll have to come to grips with it.

1993-94 REGULAR SEASON AT A GLANCE

RECORD: 46-30-8

FINISH: 1st in Central Division, 1st in Western Conference, 4th overall

HOME: 23-13-6 (8th)

AWAY: 23-17-2 (3rd)

OVERTIME: 5-2-8 (2nd)

VS OWN DIVISION: 13-13-4

VS OTHER DIVISIONS: 33-17-4

VS OWN CONFERENCE: 27-20-7

VS OTHER CONFERENCE: 19-10-1

FIRST HALF RECORD: 24-14-4

SECOND HALF RECORD: 22-16-4

GOALS FOR: 356 (1st)

GOALS AGAINST: 275 (16th)

TEAM PLUS/MINUS: +69 (2nd)

POWER PLAY: 20.8% (5th-t)

PENALTY KILLING: 80.9% (17th)

PENALTY MINUTES: 21.1/game (15th)

1993-94 REGULAR SEASON LEADERS

GOALS: 56, Sergei Fedorov

ASSISTS: 64, Fedorov

POINTS: 120, Fedorov

POWER PLAY GOALS: 19, Ray Sheppard

SHORTHANDED GOALS: 4, Fedorov

GAME WINNING GOALS: 10, Fedorov

PLUS-MINUS: +48, Fedorov

SHOTS: 337, Fedorov

PENALTY MINUTES: 275, Bob Probert

1993-94 PLAYOFFS AT A GLANCE

RESULTS: Conference Quarterfinals - Lost to San Jose 4-3

RECORD: 3-4 Home: 2-2 Away: 1-2 Goals for: 3.9/game

GOALS AGAINST: 3.0/game

OVERTIME: None

POWER PLAY: 14.3% (9th)

PENALTY KILLING: 83.3% (7th)

PENALTY MINUTES: 14.0/game (2nd)

1993-94 PLAYOFF LEADERS

GOALS: 5, Dino Ciccarelli

ASSISTS: 7, Fedorov

POINTS: 8, Fedorov

POWER PLAY GOALS: 2, Steve Chiasson

SHORTHANDED GOALS: 1, Nicklas Lidstrom, Kris Draper

OVERTIME GOALS: None

GAME-WINNING GOALS: 2, Shawn Burr

PENALTY MINUTES: 14, Ciccarelli

PLUS-MINUS: +6, Paul Coffey

SHOTS: 23, Paul Coffey

A LOOK AHEAD TO 1994-95

GOAL: Are we all happy now?

Mike Vernon has played in the all-star game in six of the last eight years. If he isn't the answer, there isn't one.

Bob Essensa got a raw deal. Make no mistake about it, he's a quality goalie. He just went to the wrong place at the wrong time.

He wasn't the number one choice, or number two, or probably even number three. He heard the criticism and it couldn't have done much for his confidence.

He got off to a poor start and didn't play well in the playoffs. In between, he did a respectable job, earning a 2.62 goals against average.

Essensa is used to playing behind a team that worries more about the opposing end, so he can do as well as anybody in that situation. What the Red Wings really want is a miracle worker. There are precious few of those around and even fewer available for trade.

Chris Osgood was a pleasant surprise in the Red Wing nets. He had a 23-8-5 record with a 2.86 goals against average in 41 games. There was even some talk about him as a Calder Trophy candidate.

He's not considered a number one goaltender in the Detroit scheme of things because he's still too young. He did get the call for much of the playoffs, however, and responded well. His 2.35 GAA was fifth best among playoff goaltenders with at least 240 minutes played.

There's no room for all three, so expect Essensa to be dealt for a quality defenseman to replace Chiasson.

The Red Wings are so good offensively that it cuts down on opposing shots. The difference is that those shots are often from quality opportunites, when the forwards or defensemen get caught behind the play.

In the majority of cases, teams make goaltenders, not the other way around.

Detroit ought to make one for themselves.

DEFENCE: They're aging, they're offensive minded, and they don't have a huge physical presence.

The flip side of that is that they're experienced, contribute a lot offensively and are mobile.

Nevertheless, it appears that the glass is half empty. Mark Howe is 39 years old, and one of the most injury prone players of the last decade, and still he's counted on to provide a stabilizing influence to the defense.

That's not a particularly good sign. Paul Coffey played in his 13th straight all-star game, and passed the 1,000 mark in games played. He will be 33 years old this season. Another excellent year under his belt, but how many more?

Vladimir Konstantinov has been called the dirtiest player in the league, but at under six feet in height isn't much of a physical presence.

Nicklas Lidstrom handles things well in the opposing end of the rink and apparently his own as well, finishing with a very impressive +43. But, his lack of aggressiveness is illustrated by a ridiculously low 26 penalty minutes.

Steve Chiasson will be missed. He was dependable, one of the few that could be counted on to play solidly and consistently both ways.

The Wings attempted to add some size when they got Sergei Bautin from Winnipeg in the Essensa deal. The Soviet born first round draft pick is a product of Mike Smith's failed regime, and won't play unless the Wings are desperate.

There may be some help on the way. There are three decent prospects in Jason

York, Aaron Ward and Dimitri Motkov.

FORWARD: When the number one offensive team has room for four rookies on the forward lines you know the rest of the league is in trouble for a long time to come.

Sergei Fedorov, who was already heralded as one of the best two-way players in the game, blew the competition out of the water last season. He had 56 goals, 64 assists, was a +48 and took home the MVP and best defensive forward trophies.

His reputation would be even further enhanced if he could carry his team through a playoff round or two. He had just one goal in their opening round loss to San Jose.

Steve Yzerman lost 26 games due to injuries, forcing him to miss out on his seventh consecutive 100 point season. He still managed to score 82 points in just 58 games.

Yzerman is the subject of trade rumours and with the talent the Wings have up front, dealing the 29 year old isn't such a far-fetched idea. When he was injured, Detroit had a record of 16-8-2, as Fedorov picked up the slack and then some.

Three players busted out of the pack last season: Ray Sheppard, Vyacheslav Kozlov and Keith Primeau.

Sheppard, the One Dollar Man (he was once sold for that much) had 52 goals in his seventh NHL season, topping his rookie year high of 38.

Kozlov had 34 and will only get better. The same thing for the LW/C fiery Primeau, who jumped from 15 goals to 31.

Primeau has a curious habit of fighting with his teammates and doesn't take kindly to practical jokes. When he complained about not getting an assist during a game, his teammates had somebody announce a scoring change over the public address system during practise. Funny, to everyone but Primeau, who got into it with Steve Chiasson and then dropped the gloves with Bob Probert. Ironically, the league later changed the scoring on the goal and awarded him his assist.

With the emergence of the above three, Dino Ciccarelli took a drop in ice time and point production, going from 97 to 57, although he did miss 18 games. The right winger went over the 500 goal and 1,000 point marks last season and should reach the 1,000 game mark this season. He's still one of the best s - - - disturbers in front of the other team's goalie, but his days are numbered.

Left winger Shawn Burr asked to be traded early in the season when he sat out four of the first five games. In the sixth game he got into action and was awarded the third star of the game. In the next contest he got a hattrick. In his next 31 games he only managed three more goals. He could get his wish and be moved before the start of the season.

Left wing is one position, however, where they need a veteran like Burr. Along with Kozlov, there's second year defensive specialist Micah Aivazaoff and talented playmaker Greg Johnson. The latter is small at 5'10", 173, but he should get more ice time this year and make a contribution.

Left winger Bob Probert is history.

The Wings did everything possible for him, and then some, but Probert didn't respond, again and again. His off-ice problems continued in the summer and Detroit finally conceded they couldn't help someone who wouldn't help himself. There was demand for Probert's services after he was released by Detroit, and he ended up signing with Chicago, with permanent suspension looming.

A couple other youngsters showed promise last season. Darren McCarty established himself early as one of the league's toug h guys and can contribute with scoring as well. Right winger Martin Lapointe is highly regarded, and it's just a matter of time before Mike Sillinger comes into his own.

A lot of teams are drooling over the young talent the Red Wings have at forward. They can't all play regularly in Detroit, so somebody could be moved for defensive help.

SPECIAL TEAMS: The power play should be strong again (6th last season), with so many snipers up front, and Coffey and Lidstrom patrolling the points.

The penalty killing percentage was only 17th last year, but they make at least part of it up with an offensive style when down a man. They scored 22 short-handed goals to lead the league.

Fedorov had a league-high 11 short-handed points, while Yzerman and Primeau added six each.

COACHING/MANAGEMENT: Bowman has a record that stands on his own.

He drives players nuts and wears out his welcome eventually, but before that he'll take them to a Stanley Cup, or pretty close.

Communication isn't his big strength, but when you have six Stanley Cups to your credit, the players can adjust to your style, not the other way around.

Despite their offensive superiority, the team never seemed to play the way Bowman wanted. He criticized their defensive committment, and even had a tough time getting the players to take shifts for the proper amount of time.

They didn't get the message until he had each line skate at full speed during a practise for the average time of their shifts during the previous game.

Bowman will probably be happier with Murray gone because it will give him the opportunity to get the players he wants and get rid of the ones he doesn't. And that should be more than just one or two.

NEEDS: Big, strong, physical defensive defensemen and Ken Dryden in the nets.

POTENTIAL NEW FACES: There's not much room for new people up front where they're already stacked with youth. The defense is a different story. Jason York, Aaron Ward and Dimitri Motkov all served apprenticeships at Adirondack last year. One or two of them will be give the opportunity to make the jump.

McKENZIE'S BOTTOM LINE: There simply is no good reason to not pick the Red Wings to finish first in the Western Conference. They did it last season and all signs point to the Wings being a better team this year.

The much talked about Wings' goaltending woes have, it would seem, been silenced with the acquisition of veteran Mike Vernon from the Calgary Flames. That move is likely to have far greater ramifications in the playoffs — or so the Wings would like to think — than in the regular season.

In any case, the Wings have what it takes to be the best in the West over 84 games and their playoff hopes look to be stronger than they have for the past few springs anyway.

Now that Scott Bowman has, for all intents and purposes, taken over as GM from Bryan Murray, more changes are in store.

The acquisition of Vernon didn't come without a price — defenceman Steve Chiasson, the Wings' best two-way man on the blueline. He will be missed.

And as much as some might consider the Vernon move to have addressed the team's critical flaw, consider this notion: The real reason Detroit has failed in the post season has more to do with poor team defence than it does with goaltending.

The Wings' overall play in their own end needs work. This will necessitate some new personnel who think defence first and have the skill to execute it and renewed commitment from those already there.

Even though Steve Yzerman's return date from serious neck surgery is up in the air, the Wings still have plenty of offensive firepower, led by Hart Trophy winner Sergei Fedorov. This should be

the season Keith Primeau comes into his own both as physically dominant player and point producer, too.

The Wings are in the unenviable position of having to justify their existence with a strong playoff. Anything they do in the regular season isn't going to be good enough.

And while Vernon may be the post-season answer, this is a club that still needs considerable work on its defensive play before being declared a legitimate Cup contender.

DRAFT PICKS

The Red Wings could have drafted a goaltender in the first round — Dan Cloutier of the Sault Ste. Marie Greyhounds was still available — but Scott Bowman figured there's no point in getting a boy to do a man's job. Besides, in Chris Osgood (his giveaway in Game 7 against San Jose notwithstanding), the Wings have a fine young goaltender with potential. What they really needed was a proven stopper and on Day 2 of the draft, the Wings went out and got Mike Vernon.

That allowed Detroit to continue its focus on building the blueline for the future. When the Wings took Russian defender Yan Golubovsky, a rangy kid who has the potential to be a two-way man, it was the second consecutive year they opted for a European defenceman in the first round. Last year it was big Swede Anders Eriksson.

There's some question as to when players such as Eriksson and Golubovsky will arrive on the scene in

Detroit. Suffice to say, the Wings, as they did in the Vernon case, will have to look for some quicker fixes until the youngsters are ready to play — and contribute — a couple of years down the road.

Detroit did, however, use two of its 10 picks this year on goalies. The first was in the fifth round (Granby's Frederic Deschenes) and the second was in the eighth round (Jason Elliot of the Kimberly, B.C., junior team).

1993-94 KEYS

KEY DEALS

* obtained Bob Essensa and Sergei Bautin from Winnipeg for Tim Cheveldae and Dallas Drake Post Season:

* obtained Mike Vernon from Calgary for Steve Chiasson

* obtained a 1995 third round draft pick from Winnipeg for Sheldon Kennedy.

KEY INJURIES: Steve Yzerman (26 games), Shawn Burr (25), Dino Ciccarelli (17), Terry Carkner (11), Dallas Drake (18 games before trade to Winnipeg), Mark Howe (33).

KEY STAT: For the second straight season, Detroit led the league in goals scored. And for the second straight season, they were knocked out of the playoffs in the first round.

In fact, except for the Rangers winning the Stanley Cup this year, none of the top four scoring teams over the last two years have lasted very long in the playoffs.

MOST GOALS 1993-94

	Goals	Playoff exit
Detroit	356	1st round
New Jersey	306	2nd round
Calgary	302	1st round
Pittsburgh	299	1st round
NY Rangers	299	Won Stanley Cup

1992-93

Detroit	369	1st round
Pittsburgh	367	2nd round
Quebec	351	1st round
Vancouver	346	2nd round

Edmonton Oilers

Somebody forgot to tell the Oilers that training camp was over. So, they just kept right on going until April.

As training camps go, it was pretty successful. Just about everybody in their organization got playing time, few overextended themselves, and management got a good look at players who would soon be too good for the team so they could start working on deals to trade them.

The Oilers started off with a 3-18-3 mark. Winning just one game with this mishmash should have been cause for rejoice. Instead, coach Ted Green was fired. Like it was his fault.

Okay boys, I want you all to play like you're legitimate NHLers, say, twice as good as you are now, and maybe we can have a winning record.

It would be like a car manufacturer firing the salesman because the car didn't work properly.

Still, somehow, Glen Sather managed to spark the team when he took over behind the bench. Their record the rest of the way was a respectable 22-27-11. Maybe he threatened some of them with long term contracts.

The Oilers are a young team made up mostly of players other organizations no longer wanted. It's a nice way to manage your budget, but that's about it.

It's tough to figure out who to feel sorry for the most. Sather, because that's the way he had to operate with his financial contraints, or the fans, because they're the ones who have to watch the product on the ice.

1993-94 REGULAR SEASON AT A GLANCE

RECORD: 25-45-14

FINISH: 6th in Pacific Division, 12th in Western Conference, 23rd overall

HOME: 17-22-3 (21st)

AWAY: 8-23-11 (23rd)

OVERTIME: 1-6-14 (23rd)

VS OWN DIVISION: 9-18-5

VS OTHER DIVISIONS: 16-27-9

VS OWN CONFERENCE: 17-33-6

VS OTHER CONFERENCE: 8-12-8

FIRST HALF RECORD: 12-24-6

SECOND HALF RECORD: 13-21-8

GOALS FOR: 261 (18th)

GOALS AGAINST: 305 (22nd)

TEAM PLUS/MINUS: -40 (24th)

POWER PLAY: 18.4% (16th)

PENALTY KILLING: 80.5% (20th)

PENALTY MINUTES: 22.1/game (19th)

1993-94 REGULAR SEASON LEADERS

GOALS: 33, Jason Arnott

ASSISTS: 50, Doug Weight

POINTS: 74, Weight

POWER PLAY GOALS: 11, Shayne Corson

SHORTHANDED GOALS: 1, Weight, Kirk Maltby

GAME WINNING GOALS: 7, Scott Pearson

PLUS-MINUS: +12, Dean McAmmond

SHOTS: 197, Igor Kravchuk

PENALTY MINUTES: 199, Kelly Buchberger

A LOOK AHEAD TO 1994-95

GOAL: Bill Ranford is one of the best goaltenders in the world. Without him, the Oilers don't reach double figures in wins.

Last season, he averaged 34 shots per 60 minutes and played in 71 games, the most in his career.

The backup chores were handled capably by rookie Fred Braitwaite.

After that, the cupboard is bare. The Oilers even sent termination contracts to their number one and number two men in Cape Breton.

At the draft, they passed up the opportunity to select highly touted Jamie Storr, who was available for two of their selections, so they must feel comfortable at this position, and committed to signing Ranford.

DEFENCE: If Ranford has problems sleeping at night there's good reason. The defense on his team may be the worst in the league and the softest physically.

After Luke Richardson, one of the best open-ice bodycheckers in the league, there's very little separating opposing forwards from a clear path directly to Ranford.

Fredrik Olausson, Igor Kravchuk, Boris Mironov and Bob Beers all handle the puck well, but they're not physical players.

Kravchuk had only 16 penalty minutes, which could be some kind of record low for a defenseman. Olausson had 30, another ridiculously low total. Mironov had more, at 101, and is big at 6-2, 192, but opposing players go wide on him and wave on their way by.

Adam Bennett is another big defenseman who doesn't exactly make opposing forwards cringe in fear. He missed much of the season after undergoing knee surgery.

Dave Manson was a definite presence on defense, but he had a terrible year and was traded to Winnipeg in the Mironov deal.

With the exception of Richardson,

there is nobody on the blueline that played with the Oilers before the start of last season. By the end of this season, we could very well see another complete turnover.

One welcome addition would be Nick Stadjuhar, the 16th pick last season in the draft. He could be their quarterback on the power play. At the very least he'll be one of their best defensemen as soon as he laces on the skates for his first game.

FORWARD: In his very first NHL game, center Jason Arnott scored the winning goal. There's little doubt that last year's 7th pick overall in the draft is a winner himself. A close second in Calder Trophy balloting behind Martin Brodeur, Arnott scored 33 goals, which is like scoring 40 or more for another team.

That's because there's very little in the way of help. Only a handful of Edmonton forwards would be regulars with most decent NHL teams.

Put center Doug Weight and left winger Shayne Corson in that category. Weight was expected to carry the scoring load, and he did, with 74 points. He even scored on his first four shots of the season. If he had scored on his other 184 shots, the Oilers would have at least made the playoffs.

On the right side is Steven Rice, a bruiser type who likes to hit. He's not a great scorer, but if they can get 20 goals out of him it will be a bonus. Zdeno Ciger also started to come into his own, improving from 36 to 57 points.

Not much depth at that position, however. It got so bad for the Oilers last season that they had to move defenseman Ilya Byakin up to the right wing.

Kelly Buchberger is another regular there, and although his scoring has dropped considerably (from 20 goals two years ago, to 12, to just three last season), he's still a force, at least physically.

Others with an opportunity on the right side are Kirk Maltby who had 11 goals in 68 games in his rookie season, a rare homegrown draft pick in the lineup; David Oliver, the Hockey News U.S. College player of the year; and whomever else wanders onto the team bus.

Not bad at center with Arnott and Weight, but a bunch of question marks after them. Dean McAmmond will get a chance to show he can stick. U.S. Olympian Todd Marchant got in a few games after he was obtained from the Rangers for Craig McTavish. Peter White, the top scorer at Cape Breton, got the call for a while, and Tyler Wright, the 12th pick overall in the 1991 draft, who needs to add more offense to his game, could get a chance.

Big Jason Bonsignore is their man of the future, which in the Oiler scheme of things is the present. The sixth pick overall in this year's draft wasn't getting the same raves he was receiving a year earlier, but he still has a chance to be a blue chip player. He isn't supposed to show it this year, but the Oilers had good success with Arnott, who was selected seventh, so they may give him a try right away.

It's not as if bringing prospects along slowly has worked well for them in the past. The drafting record of the Oilers over the last 11 years is the worst in the league in the first round. Before Arnott, none of their previous nine first rounders has landed a regular job in the NHL. Mind you, a lot of them were late first-rounders because of past Oiler success.

Left wing is headed up by Corson. After that, two former high draft picks of the Toronto Maple Leafs — Scott Thornton and Scott Pearson — patrol that wing, both with limited scoring ability. Vladimir Vujtek didn't show much, but he's still only 22, so he will have more opportunity.

Louie DeBrusk has shown an ability to play it tough in the past, but he has had problems with alcohol and the law.

The forwards on this team are very young. Some will develop into consistent NHL performers, some will be traded, and some will disappear without a trace.

We'll learn much of that after training camp, which ends April 9 of next year.

SPECIAL TEAMS: Not much in the way of a legitimate sniper on the power play, although Arnott seems capable of handling that role as he matures. He had 10 extra-man markers in his rookie season.

There are, however, lots of defensemen who can handle the puck on the points with the man-advantage. Olausson, Mironov, Beers and Kravchuk actually give them considerably more strength than most. Also on the way is Nick Stadjuhar, who may eventually be the best of the bunch.

Compared to the other parts of their game, ranking 16th in the league in power play percentage isn't bad. They won't be among the best this season, but they could move up a notch or two.

One of the features of penalty-killing units in recent years is to take advantage of opportunities and try to score - maybe a quick break up the middle, catching the other team off guard.

None of that for the Oilers. They had just two short-handed markers, 20 fewer than league leading Detroit, and four less than San Jose and Pittsburgh, who had the next fewest at six.

COACHING: Glen Sather is looking for a coach. Two may be better than one. A co-coaching arrangement involving George Burnett, who led Cape Breton to the AHL championship two years ago, and Ron Low, who worked as an assistant last season, is a possibility. At press time, nothing had been announced. The odds are that Burnett for sure will be behind the bench in some capacity.

It's a no-win situation in any event. There's only so much a coach can do when a team is so outclassed. Ted Green found that out when he was dumped last season.

Glen Sather may end up behind the bench again later this year. That might not be so bad, though, because he's still a good coach who seems to get the most out of his players. (Burnett was hired as we went to press.)

MANAGEMENT: It appears the Oilers lease with the Northlands Coliseum has been fixed to Pocklington's satisfaction.

That may mean more money to spend on the on-ice product. Maybe.

You likely won't recognize this team by half way through the season.

Sather's not afraid to make trades. He gives the players a chance, but not a big one. He sours on them quickly and away they go to make their mark in the world with some other team.

He seems to be high on getting Europeans, but they're also dispatched quickly.

As for Peter Pocklington, maybe we won't be hearing as much from him this year. That will be a relief to many. About the only place he didn't threaten to move the team in recent years has been Mexico City, and that's only because they don't have a suitable NHL arena there.

NEEDS: Left wing, centre, right wing, and defense.

POTENTIAL NEW FACES: D Nick Stadjuhar, 34-52-86, London (OHL); C Tyler Wright, Cape Breton; C Jason Bonsignore, 22-64-86, Niagara Falls (OHL); RW David Oliver, 28-4-68, Michigan (CCHA).

Stadjuhar was a second team all-star in the OHL, while Oliver was the MVP in the CCHA and was named The Hockey News College Player of the Year.

McKENZIE'S BOTTOM LINE: There is good news and there is bad news for fans of the Oilers.

The good news is that all indicators point to netminder Bill Ranford being with the team over the long haul. It it were going to be otherwise, the Oilers would have either traded Ranford to the Red Wings and/or chosen up-and-coming goalie Jamie Storr in the '94 entry draft. And make no mistake, Ranford is a tremendous asset to have. It's forgotten that he's one of the league's very best stoppers because he plays on a non-contending team that has shown no semblance of defence for the past few years.

As for that bad news, it's that the Oilers' rebuilding phase which includes a plethora of talented youngsters is still in its most formative stages and won't result in a playoff spot. Not this year anyway.

The Oilers are starting to put together an impressive array of young talent, especially up front. But there's no guarantee — actually, it would be doubtful — that 1994 draftees Jason Bonsignore and Ryan Smyth will have the same sudden impact that 1993 first-rounder Jason Arnott had. Ditto for Sweden's Mats Lindgren, a fine two-way talent and 1993 first-rounder who came over from the Winnipeg Jets in the Dave Manson trade. Those four blue-chip talents should ensure a potent attack, but it's a good two or three years away from manifesting itself.

The Oilers' biggest problem, Ranford's excellent netminding notwithstanding, is preventing goals. The defence unit lacks a marquee talent, although Russian veteran Igor Kravchuk is a better player than he is given credit for. The trading of Manson — a good move for the Oilers, incidentally, given the future prospects they received — diminishes the unit's physical presence in the short term. Luke Richardson will be asked to be the heavy and Freddie Olausson the blaster from the point.

Assuming the Oilers handed the coaches' reins to George Burnett — the official announcement wasn't going to be made until mid-August — it's a commendable hiring. Burnett, as stoic as they come, is one of the bright young coaches in the game. He was a solid defensive forward when he played junior and understands the importance of playing without the puck. It's a lesson the Oilers need to learn because the offensive part of the game, especially as their draftees mature, is going to come naturally anyway.

For this year, though, the Oilers will not only struggle to make the playoffs, they'll have to look over their shoulder to make sure they aren't caught by the other non-playoff teams and finish last in the division — again.

DRAFT PICKS

It was a big draft for the Oilers. Big kids. Lots of them.

The Oilers drafted 16 players in all — more than any other NHL club — and not one of them was under 6 feet tall.

By virtue of the Dave Manson trade with the Winnipeg Jets, the Oilers had two picks in the top six and came away with Jason Bonsignore, the Niagara Falls Thunder centre who tries to pattern his game after Mario Lemieux's, and hard-driving left winger Ryan Smyth of the Moose Jaw Warriors, who Oiler chief scout Barry Fraser dared to compare to Glenn Anderson.

Bonsignore, Smyth, last year's exceptional first-rounder Jason Arnott and Swede Mats Lindgren (picked up in the Manson trade) give GM Glen Sather a talented but young nucleus up front with which to rebuild the once vaunted Oiler attack.

One subplot to keep in mind is that the majority of Oiler scouts wanted to use the No. 6 pick overall to take Bonsignore's winger Ethan Moreau from Niagara Falls, but Fraser apparently overruled them and went with Smyth. It will take a few years for the verdict to be returned, but that will be an interesting developmental matchup to keep an eye on.

After the first two rounds, not surprisingly, the Oilers put a premium on big, strong physical defencemen to begin filling a primary need on the rebuilding club. Notable amongst that group was North Bay's Corey Neilson and Portland's Brad Symes.

1993-94 KEYS

KEY DEALS:

* obtained Adam Bennett from Chicago for Kevin Todd

* obtained Fredrik Olausson and a 7th round pick in 1994 for a third round pick and futures (Craig Fisher).

* obtained Todd Marchant from the New York Rangers for Craig MacTavish

* obtained Boris Mironov, Mats Lindgren and a first and fourth round draft pick in 1994 from Winnipeg for Dave Manson

KEY INJURIES: Shane Corson (20 games).

KEY STAT: If you're a rookie, this must be Edmonton. No fewer than 15 rookies had playing time for the Oilers last season.

ROOKIES BY TEAM (at least one game)

Edmonton	15
Quebec	13
Ottawa	12
Buffalo	10
Montreal	11
Calgary	10
Philadelphia	10
Detroit	9
St. Louis	9
Toronto	9
NY Islanders	8
Boston	8
Florida	7
Hartford	7
Pittsburgh	7
Tampa Bay	7
Washington	7
Winnipeg	7
Los Angeles	6
Vancouver	6
New Jersey	6
Chicago	5
San Jose	5
Anaheim	5
NY Rangers	5
Dallas	1

Los Angeles Kings

One season, Stanley Cup finalists with a bright future; the next, a bigger joke than the expansion Ducks.

Bruce McNall, Chairman of the NHL Board of Governors one year; Bruce McNall, sitting in front of a grand jury explaining his finances the next.

Barry Melrose, NHL glamour boy one season; weirdo the next. Tony Granato, 37 goals and 82 points one year; stick¬swinging goon with seven goals and 21 points the next. Wayne Gretzky, great player one year; great player the next. There, you see, all that positive thinking wasn't completely lost. But, Anthony Robbins would still do well to disassociate himself from this bunch. Or is it the other way around?

To be fair, the Stanley Cup finalist edition of the Kings weren't that great a team. They had a nice playoff run but during the regular season they only finished four games over .500 and gave up more goals than they scored.

It could have been that last season they thought they were better than they really were. Hmm...more dangers of positive thinking.

The one truly bright moment of the season was Wayne Gretzky setting the all-time NHL mark in goals, surpassing Gordie Howe. The latter suggested his WHA goals should count in the overall scheme of things, but it's not even worth arguing the point.

And here's something really positive for King fans to think about. This season can't possibly be as bad as last year.

1993-94 SEASON AT A GLANCE

RECORD: 27-45-12

FINISH: 5th in Pacific Division, 10th in Western Conference, 22nd overall

HOME: 18-19-5 (19th)

AWAY: 9-26-7 (24th)

OVERTIME: 3-3-12 (13th-t)

VS OWN DIVISION: 12-14-6

VS OTHER DIVISIONS: 15-31-6

VS OWN CONFERENCE: 18-28-10

VS OTHER CONFERENCE: 9-17-2

FIRST HALF RECORD: 17-21-4

SECOND HALF RECORD: 10-24-8

GOALS FOR: 294 (6th-t)

GOALS AGAINST: 322 (24th)

TEAM PLUS/MINUS: -30 (22nd)

POWER PLAY: 20.7% (7th)

PENALTY KILLING: 80.5% (21st)

PENALTY MINUTES: 24.0/game (24th)

1993-94 REGULAR SEASON LEADERS

GOALS: 44, Luc Robitaille

ASSISTS: 92, Wayne Gretzky

POINTS: 130, Gretzky

POWER PLAY GOALS: 24, Robitaille

SHORTHANDED GOALS: 4, Gretzky, Jari Kurri

GAME WINNING GOALS: 6, Rob Blake

PLUS-MINUS: +16, John Druce

SHOTS: 304, Blake

PENALTY MINUTES: 322, Warren Rychel

A LOOK AHEAD TO 1994-95

GOAL: Nobody was faulting Kelly Hrudey for the team's performance last season even though they finished third from the bottom in goals against average. He faced an average of 36 shots per 60 minutes, and probably twice as many quality shots as goalies on better teams.

Robb Stauber, his backup, faced an average of 37. The Kings took Jamie Storr seventh overall at the draft.

He's considered a potential franchise player, but it's unlikely he will be subjected to the nightly shooting gallery right away.

DEFENCE: It would be interesting to watch an exhibition game between the King forwards and the King defensemen. The scoring power is about the same — four of the nine top scorers on the team were rearguards — and the defensive ability would be similar.

The score would probably by 18-17. McSorley would have to play half the game for both sides, because he played up and back last season; that means only one fight, between Warren Rychel and Doug Houda; no hitting; and two suspensions, one to Granato and another to McSorley. After the game, Melrose would say that none of his teams played like they were interested in winning and McNall would forget to include the game receipts as income.

Oops, cheap shot there. The McNall bit that is. Cheap shots aren't something you're likely to get very often from the King defense. Lots of shots on net, yes.

They're not intimidating in the least, defensively. Offensively, you'd be hard pressed to find three better young talents on the same team than Rob Blake, Alexei Zhitnik and Darryl Sydor.

All were inconsistent during the season. They're young, however, and consistency comes with experience.

McSorley gives them some much needed toughness. He wasn't the savior he was predicted to be, however. The Kings were only 6-16-6 with him in the lineup after they got him back from the Penguins. He had a groin problem, however, and couldn't play to his fullest capability. A new season should help.

After the nucleus, are a bunch of defensive-minded types that you think would fit in with the young offensive go-getters. People like Donald Dufresne, Tim Watters, Charlie Huddy and Michel Petit who was signed as a free agent from Calgary.

There's some hope at this position. Maybe all they need is some of the forwards coming back to help out once in a while. And some of the defensemen with them.

FORWARD: Coach Melrose is big on positive thinking, but last year's forwards were positively stinking. Similar to the wit of that last sentence.

Hard to imagine a team with Wayne Gretzky, Luc Robitaille, Jari Kurri, Tony Granato, Shawn McEachern and Tomas Sandstrom being such a flop.

But they were. As a group, defense was not in their vocabulary, and offensively, only Gretzky and Robitaille were putting the puck in the net on a regular basis.

McEachern and Sandstrom were traded, Granato sat out half the season with injuries and suspension, and the rest of the mishmash didn't come through.

Without Gretzky, the Kings might not have finished ahead of Ottawa. He earned 92 assists, broke the all-time goal scoring record, won another scoring title with 130 points, and took home the Lady Byng Trophy. The bad news was that he was -25, worst on the team.

Nobody's ever accused Gretzky of being a great defensive player, so he's excused.

Robitaille dropped to a career low 44 goals from a career high of 63 the previous season. He was shipped to Pittsburgh for Rick Tocchet, a curious move because he's still only 28 and one of the top-scoring left-wingers to ever play the game.

Tocchet, a right-winger, is one of the most valuable players around when he's healthy, but he missed 33 games last year, dropping from 48 goals to 14. He's also 30 years old.

Jari Kurri is still hanging in there, but at the age of 34, don't expect him to contribute for much longer.

Tony Granato had himself a bizarre season. The goal light was on, put the puck wasn't in the net. First, he jumped off the bench to tackle Ranger Tony Amonte, who happened to be on a breakaway. Then, he smashed Blackhawk Neil Wilkinson over the head with his stick, earning a 15 game suspension, the second highest in NHL history. In between wackiness, he scored just seven goals. For a player who has averaged 36 goals a season, that's just more insanity.

The rest of the forward unit is just spare parts. It wouldn't make a difference if they were there or not.

And it's likely most will be in the "not" category before long.

Melrose complained his forwards were too small. Which they were.

They were also too soft. And just plain lousy. When teams are weak at something, they tend to overcompensate. In a year or two the Kings may have the biggest, toughest forwards in the league.

Help may be on the way in wingers Kevin Brown, 6-1 213, big time scorer for Detroit in the Ontario League, and Keith Redmond, 6-3, 205, who was up and down from Phoenix.

Two key free agents were signed in the off-season. One is Rob Brown, strictly a scorer. He had 155 points and was named MVP in the IHL last season. He doesn't play defense so he should fit in well on the Kings.

Same thing for Yanic Perreault, a gifted minor league scorer. He had 105 points in 62 games for St. John's in the Toronto organization last season. The Maple Leafs were never going to give him much chance of making their team, partly because he doesn't play defense either. That shouldn't be a problem in Los Angeles.

COACHING: Barry Melrose has a reputation of being a good motivator. Not necessarily a master tactician, but somebody who can get his players to perform up to their potential.

He did it two years ago, but failed miserably last year. Can he do it again? Probably, if he lasts long enough.

Besides alienating management, he alienated a lot of players, benching almost everyone on the team at some time or another.

He called them a bunch of "Fat Cats." He said they didn't have any grit, guts, courage, ordiscipline. That just about covers it.

Maybe it's a new Anthony Robbins motivational technique, perhaps to be explained in an upcoming book called, "I'm Okay - You're Useless."

Melrose never got the players he wanted and had a running feud with General Manager Nick Beverly. Perhaps, things will be better this year. They couldn't be much worse.

And if they Kings get off to a slow start, Melrose will probably be fired before things get too far out of hand.

MANAGEMENT: Nick Beverley is out, Sam McMaster is in. He's been the GM of the Sudbury Wolves in the OHL the last six years.

McMaster's first deal is a curious one, giving up Luc Robitaille for Rick Tocchet. If both players are at their best it's not a bad deal because Tocchet can score and add toughness in a big way. But, his back problems may prevent that.

Robitaille is a proven scorer that a lot of teams would like to have, especially because he plays left wing.

Maybe he could have received more for him than one who might not be able to play at full effectiveness.

Wayne Gretzky, who has been accused of running the show in Los Angeles, seemed to make a concerted effort to remove himself from further speculation.

Wise move, he doesn't need it.

NEEDS: Character players who can lead by example. Toughness, more scoring from the forwards, and more defense from the defensemen.

POTENTIAL NEW FACES: RW Kevin Brown, 54-81-135 for Detroit (OHL); LW Keith Redmond; C Yanic Perreault, St. John's (AHL); RW Rob Brown, Kalamazoo (IHL); D Michel Petit, Calgary; RW Rick Tocchet, Pittsburgh.

McKENZIE'S BOTTOM LINE: It would be convenient to say the Los Angeles Kings will go as far as Wayne Gretzky takes them, but we know that not to be true.

If it were, the Kings would have made the playoffs last season on the strength of a productive year from the Great One, who won yet another Art Ross Trophy as NHL scoring champion.

No, the Kings have a number of problems that require attention and may be ill-suited to address them.

To give you an idea of the challenge facing new GM Sam McMaster, his mandate from the Kings' new owners was two-fold. One, make the team better. Two, cut the payroll.

The two don't necessarily have to be incongruous but it's not mean feat to get better and have to unload some high-priced talent.

There is hope, though.

The Kings lucked out at the entry draft by getting goaltender Jamie Storr. Even though he's only 19, don't count Storr out of the Kings' goaltending picture just yet. It's his initial goal to simply make the Kings, as a backup to veteran Kelly Hrudey, but in the bigger picture he sees himself as stealing the No. 1 job and leading coach Barry Melrose's team into the playoffs.

A flight of fancy from a naive youngster? Perhaps. But don't be surprised if Storr makes it happen.

In fairness, though, the Kings' problems last season had less to do with goaltending than anything else.

The young defence — led by Rob Blake, Alexei Zhitnik and Darryl Sydor — took a step back last season. It's imperative those three continue to make dramatic strides on their own personal learning curves. Of course, that's assuming the Kings were able to sign Blake to a new contract, which is part and parcel of the Kings' financial woes this season.

The other major problem is that Melrose-style hockey needs big, strong aggressive forwards to play it. Young ones would be nice, too. The Kings are anything but any of the above. The top scorers for the Kings last year were Gretzky, Jari Kurri and Luc Robitaille.

The latter was long tabbed as the player most likely to be traded — having considerable value on the open market. At this point is it's questionable whether the deal that sent him to Pittsburgh for 30-year old Rick Tocchet cashed in on that value. No doubt, Tocchet is Melrose's type of player, but whether he still has the crash and bang in him isn't certain. A steep price by any standards.

This deal not withstanding, McMaster is a good judge of talent. He'll do what he can to get Melrose the players he wants, but it will be difficult because of the organization's financial constraints.

A playoff spot isn't out of the question, but until we see how things shake down on the Blake contract and Tocchet's injury status, it's tough to pencil the Kings in as one of the top eight teams in the West.

DRAFT PICKS

Any number of NHL GMs will tell you on draft day that they couldn't believe their good fortune in getting the player they got. "Couldn't believe he was still available," they say.

Los Angeles GM Sam McMaster actually means it.

The Kings never expected that Owen Sound netminder Jamie Storr would still be there when they were selecting at No. 7 overall. The consensus was that Storr would go in the top five, if not to the teams that were drafting there then to another which would trade up to get a crack a potential franchise goaltender.

McMaster's master plan was to use the seventh pick to draft Brett Lindros and then trade to a number of interested teams, or consummate a trade on the floor allowing another team to use the seventh pick to get Lindros. All that went out the window when Storr was still there.

That Storr didn't go as high as expected tells you more about NHL conservatism than it does about the goaltender's pro prospects. It turned out to be a real plum pick for the Kings. Don't be surprised if Storr makes the Kings next fall and then wages a spirited battle to wrest away the No. 1 job from veteran Kelly Hrudey.

Getting a goaltender in the first round didn't do anything, though, to make the Kings a bigger or better team up front. Coach Barry Melrose has repeatedly expressed concern that his Kings are big or physical enough to play the style he demands. So McMaster went for pure toughness in the second round, taking Peterborough Pete enforcer Matt Johnson.

The question is this: Can Johnson be an everyday player in the NHL? There's no question he's a heavyweight scrapper, but to be truly effective in today's NHL, there has to be dimensions beyond that.

McMaster, the former Sudbury Wolves' GM, didn't stray too far home with many of his picks. Five of the Kings' eight selections were from the OHL and two of them, Luc Gagne and Andrew Dale, played for McMaster in Sudbury last season.

Another notable pick was ninth rounder Jan Nemecek, a Czech defenceman who was rated much higher than that by NHL Central Scouting.

1993-94 KEYS

KEY DEALS:

* obtained Marty McSorley and Jim Paek from Pittsburgh for Tomas Sandstrom and Shawn McEachern

* obtained Kevin Todd from Chicago for a 4th round draft pick

*obtained Rick Tocchet from Pittsburgh for Luc Robitaille

KEY INJURIES: No significant injuries, but Tony Granato missed 34 games with an assortment of ailments and suspensions.

KEY STAT: There's little left for Gretzky to accomplish individually now that he's become the all-time NHL leading goal scorer.

Gordie Howe disputes it, suggesting that WHA goals should be taken into account.

Yeah, right.

TOP TEN NHL GOAL SCORERS OF ALL TIME

1.	Wayne Gretzky	803
2.	Gordie Howe	801
3.	Marcel Dionne	731
4.	Phil Esposito	717
5.	Mike Gartner	617
6.	Bobby Hull	610
7.	Mike Bossy	573
8.	Guy Lafleur	560
9.	John Bucyk	556
10.	Jari Kurri	555

San Jose Sharks

It's not often you can do worse than a 24 point NHL season but the Sharks looked to be giving it a go when they came out of the gate with an 0-8-1 record. That put them on pace for nine points.

They finished with 82. The 58 point improvement was the biggest in NHL history. The BIGGEST.

How the heck did they do that? Five main reasons:

1. Arturs Irbe

2. Arturs Irbe

3. New coach Kevin Constantine

4. Improved play of young players; Improved play of veterans

5. OV line — Larionov, Makarov and Garpenlov

In the playoffs, the Sharks came pretty close to making it to the Western Conference finals. They pulled off a major upset by knocking Detroit out in the first round and took Toronto to seven games in the conference semi-finals. They were up 3-2 in that series and went to overtime in game six.

Don't laugh, they weren't that far away from a Stanley Cup victory. It would have been the biggest playoff upset in sports history. Bigger even than the 1969 Mets.

In the second half of the season, the Sharks had a record of 21-14-7. That pace over an entire season would put them up close to 100 points.

So, can we expect the Sharks to be one of the top teams in the league this year?

No. It was fun, but the party's over. We'll call you for the next one but it won't be this year.

For one thing, teams that make big strides like that in one season are often doomed to fall back down the next. For another, they ain't that good.

A lot of publications and prognosticators will be predicting big things for the Sharks this season. Not here.

1993-94 REGULAR SEASON AT A GLANCE

RECORD: 33-35-16

FINISH: 3rd in Pacific Division, 8th in Western Conference, 17th overall.

HOME: 19-13-10 (12th)

AWAY: 14-22-6 (19th)

OVERTIME: 2-1-16 (12th)

VS OWN DIVISION: 14-11-5

VS OTHER DIVISIONS: 19-24-11

VS OWN CONFERENCE: 25-22-9

VS OTHER CONFERENCE: 8-13-7

FIRST HALF RECORD: 12-21-9

SECOND HALF RECORD: 21-14-7

GOALS FOR: 252 (20th)

GOALS AGAINST: 265 (14th

TEAM PLUS/MINUS: -4

POWER PLAY: 16.0 (20th)

PENALTY KILLING: 78.6 (25th)

PENALTY MINUTES: 16.0 (1st)

1993-94 REGULAR SEASON LEADERS (WITH SAN JOSE ONLY)

GOALS: 30, Sergei Makarov

ASSISTS: 41, Todd Elik

POINTS: 68, Makarov

POWER PLAY GOALS: 10, Makarov

SHORTHANDED GOALS: 2, Igor Larionov

GAME WINNING GOALS: 5, Makarov

PLUS-MINUS: +20, Larionov

SHOTS: 193, Pat Falloon

PENALTY MINUTES: 222, Jeff Odgers

1993-94 PLAYOFFS AT A GLANCE

RESULTS: **Conference Quarterfinals -** defeated Detroit 4-3 **Conference Semifinals** - lost to Toronto 4-3

RECORD: 7-7

HOME: 4-2-0

AWAY: 3-5-0

GOALS FOR: 42, 3.0/game

GOALS AGAINST: 54, 3.8/game

OVERTIME: 0-1

POWER PLAY: 12.2% (11th)

PENALTY KILLING: 78.7% (11th)

PENALTY MINUTES: 16.0/game (4th)

1993-94 PLAYOFF LEADERS

GOALS: 8, Makarov

ASSISTS: 13, Larionov

POINTS: 18, Larionov

POWER PLAY GOALS: 3, Ulf Dahlen, Makarov

SHORTHANDED GOALS: 1, Rob Gaudreau, Tom Pederson

OVERTIME GOALS: None

GAME-WINNING GOALS: 2, Makarov, Johan Garpenlov

PENALTY MINUTES: 32, Jayson More

PLUS-MINUS: +4, Jeff Norton

SHOTS: 45, Elik

A LOOK AHEAD TO 1994-95

GOAL: Arturs Irbe set a record last season for the most minutes ever played by a goaltender in the NHL. As well, 74 games were the second most in league history.

Kind of a busy guy. And in most of those minutes and games he was nothing short of phenomenal. Bad games were few and far between.

Another incredible season won't be easy. It never is for any goaltender. No profound theories and statistics to show why, that's just the way it is. Jimmy Waite was the backup last season and did a poor job of it recording a 3-7-0 mark with a 4.30 goals against average. He has the credentials, but it probably didn't help only getting into action on rare occasions.

Wade Flaherty was the number one man in Kansas City.

DEFENCE: If Sandis Ozolinsh hadn't played 37 games the previous season, he might have been the rookie of the year. His 26 goals were second only to Al MacInnis; he played in the all-star game, scoring twice; and he finished the season at a plus 16.

He, along with defense partner Jeff Norton often accompanied the OV line to form an impressive five man offensive unit.

Ozolinsh is still only 22 years old, one of a youth dominated defense.

Another youngster, 19 year old Vlastimil Kroupa appears to have worked his way into a full time job after playing 14 playoff games last year.

Yet another kid is in the fray, Mike Rathje, the third overall selection in 1992, a 6-5, 205 behemoth, who is being brought along at his own pace. He played only one game in the playoffs but was in 47 during the regular season.

Michal Sykora, 21 years old, is another big guy at 6-4, 210, in the picture along with Tom Pederson, a 24 year old tiny defenseman at 5-9, 175,

who like most of the others is offensive¬minded.

Jayson More is also included in the mix and he's only 25. Shawn Cronin, noted tough guy, surprised with some excellent defensive play in the post-season last year, but he's a free agent and might not be back.

This has to be considered the defense group in the league with the most potential. The team's overall defensive style helped them out considerably last season and their mobility made them major contributors to the offense.

But, there are problems. Besides inexperience, few of them are an intimidating physical force. In size, yes, but not by the way they play.

If Arturs Irbe hadn't been such a rock behind them they would have suffered far more last season.

They could be in trouble this year. Probably not too far into the season, the Sharks will be looking for veteran stay-at¬home types who can give the young defense some stability and provide some physical punch.

They traded some of those, like Rob Zettler, Doug Zmolek and Mike Lalor towards the end of the season, however, so apparently it isn't worrying them too much.

FORWARD: Makarov will be 36 years old this season while Larionov turns 34. Both had great seasons last year, but they can't keep it up forever. The two of them, along with Garpenlov formed one of the better lines in the league.

When Larionov was out of the lineup with assorted injuries and illnesses, the Sharks had a record of 3-15-6. What's up with that? We're not talking Mario Lemieux here.

San Jose doesn't have a sniper up front. Makarov led the team with 30 goals but he's considered a playmaker first.

The next highest goal-scorer was Todd Elik, at 25. The Sharks were able to pick him up on waivers from Edmonton near the start of the season. A steal.

Ulf Dahlen came over from a trade with Dallas and was a force in the short time he was there, scoring six goals in 13 games, and adding six more in the playoffs.

Veterans Bob Errey and Gaetan Duchesne provide good defensive support from the left side, where Garpenlov and Ray Whitney also patrol.

At center, behind Larionov is Elik, Dale Craigwell, and Vyacheslav Butsayev, obtained from Philadelphia and scratched for almost every game with the Sharks. Jamie Baker was an unrestricted free agent and hadn't been signed back at press time.

The Sharks hope the newest center addition will be Victor Kozlov at 6-5, 225 pounds, the sixth player selected at the 1993 draft. He make take some time to adjust to the North American game.

At right wing, behind Makarov and Dahlen, is Rob Gaudreau and enforcer Jeff Odgers.

Possible newcomers include more Europeans in Andrei Nazarov and Alexander Cherbayev, both wingers.

SPECIAL TEAMS: Both are weak. The Sharks were fortunate that they were the least penalized team in the league last year because only Ottawa had a worse penalty killing percentage. San Jose had 105 fewer man-advantage penalties called against them than did Los Angeles, the leader.

There are no prospects for improvement in this area. The idea, apparently, will be to just not to take penalties.

COACHING: Before a game at Maple Leaf Gardens early in the season, a respected scout joked about the Shark pre-game warmup. He watched as they stood in circles or moved around in a set pattern, and just passed the puck to each other. "Looks like something out of pee-wee hockey," he laughed.

The snickers had died down considerably by playoff time. The Sharks were probably the best passing team in the league, something they proved with abundance in their playoff series against Toronto. The team also was one of the most disciplined in terms of their defensive system. And yes, one of the most boring.

Kevin Constantine, after two seasons in the IHL and one with the U.S. national Junior team, did an outstanding job and was second behind Jacques Lemaire in the Adams Trophy balloting for coach of the year.

MANAGEMENT: Vice-Presidents Dean Lombardi and Chuck Grillo share the office of General Manager. Lombardi is Director of Hockey Operations, while Grillo is Director of Player Personnel. Both are American born.

Time will tell if their committment to European players is genius or stupidity.

POTENTIAL NEW FACES: C Victor Kozlov, Russia; LW Andrei Nazarov, Kansas City; LW Alexander Cherbayev, Kansas City.

NEEDS: They probably don't think they need anything.

McKENZIE'S BOTTOM LINE: Kevin Constantine's club proved in its playoff win over Detroit and dramatic seven-game loss to Toronto that it's for real.

The Sharks are not a fluke.

They have a fine goaltender in Latvian Arturs Irbe.

They have an emerging young defence corps led by Sandis Ozolinsh and Vlastimil Kroupa, which will be augmented by big studs such as Michael Sykora and Mike Rathje.

Up front, they rely too heavily on their old Russians (Igor Larionov and Sergei Makarov) but that's only a temporary measure until the young Russians (Victor Kozlov, Andrei Nazarov and Alexandr Cherbaev) are ready to take over.

There is a chance that the Sharks, self satisfied with their remarkable achievement last spring, could suffer a setback this season. But Constantine, a hard driver behind the bench, should see to it that there's not letup. His challenge will be to obtain similar results — a playoff spot and then upset possibilities — while breaking in some of the Sharks' young talent, both on the blueline and up front.

The reason he's likely to succeed — even though both Los Angeles and Winnipeg, non-playoff teams last spring, will be improved and gunning for Shark — is that he'll continue to get outstanding mileage from veteran re-treads such Bob Errey, Jamie Baker and Ulf Dahlen, who is nothing less than the best corner man in the NHL.

A playoff spot is by no means guaranteed for the Sharks — they could easily slide to 10th or 11th in the conference — but they have a couple of edges over the competition. That is, momentum from last spring's playoff run and better-than-average goaltending from Irbe.

DRAFT PICKS

The Sharks, led by director of player personnel Chuck Grillo, continued their love affair with Europeans, taking four Russians and three Czechs amongst their 12 picks in '94.

But not before they took Regina Pats' left Jeff Friesen 11th overall.

Some NHL scouts believe Friesen is the most naturally talented player of all the 1994 draftees, but many teams professed to be scared off by a commitment level that doesn't always come close to his skill level.

Not the Sharks, a team loaded with blue-chip defensive talent that could desperately use some offensive firepower. It's early yet, but Pat Falloon, No. 2 overall in the Eric Lindros draft year, hasn't had the desired impact. Maybe, in time, Friesen will.

He certainly has the tools. He's a natural goal scorer and wildly creative when he has the puck.

The emphasis on forwards was obvious for the Sharks. Ten of their 12 picks were up front, with only one defenceman and one goaltender chosen. The one defenceman, Czech Angel Nikulov, is a close friend of Shark defenceman Vlastimil Kroupa, who played far beyond all expectations last season as an 18-year-old in the NHL. Grillo said Nikulov is a Kroupa clone.

1993-94 KEYS

KEY DEALS:

* Obtained Ulf Dahlen and conditional draft pick from Dallas for Doug Zmolek, and Mike Lalor.

* claimed Todd Elik on waivers from Edmonton

KEY INJURIES: Igor Larionov (19 games), Jayson More (26), Jeff Norton (20).

KEY STAT: The San Jose Sharks last year pulled off the biggest single season point increase in NHL history. These are the last season's biggest increases.

**BIGGEST POINT INCREASES
1993-94 SEASON**

	92-93	93-94	Increase
San Jose	24	82	58
NY Rangers	79	112	33
New Jersey	87	106	19
Tampa Bay	53	71	18
Dallas	82	97	15
Ottawa	24	37	13

St. Louis Blues

When you roll the dice, sometimes you win, sometimes you lose. St. Louis came out on the short end last season when GM Ron Caron performed a mid-season makeover of the team. They went from being a character type defensive team with one scoring line, to an offensive force, but lacking in character and defense.

The Blues were humiliated in four straight games in the first round of the playoffs by Dallas.

The transformation started when the Blues traded "the spine" of the team — Ron Sutter, Garth Butcher and Bob Bassen — to Quebec for holdout Steve Duchesne.

It continued with the signings of Peter Stastny and free agent with compensation, Petr Nedved.

The arbitrator awarded Vancouver Craig Janney for Nedved. That wouldn't have been so bad, but Janney refused to report and the Blues traded back for him, giving up Jeff Brown, Nathan Lafayette and Bret Hedican. Those three were instrumental in taking Vancouver to the Stanley Cup finals.

Oops, might have went a little too far. No matter, Caron just goes out and gets some more talent. During the summer, he traded for Al MacInnis, giving up Phil Housley who missed much of the season with injuries anyway.

Then he went out and got Scott Stevens. Or tried to. He signed him to an offer sheet, but New Jersey exercised their right to might to match.

Always lots of changes in St. Louis. Let's see now, what else will be different? Well, they will be playing in a new arena this season, the Kiel Centre. And they have a new uniform design.

What else, what else...Oh yeah, the Blues hired one of the best coaches in the history of the game and are now automatically one of the favorites to win the Stanley Cup.

In bizarre fashion, Mike Keenan, who also got the GM title, rolled into town after declaring himself a free agent when the Rangers were two days late with their bonus payment.

The whole thing stunk to high heavens, and Gary Bettman stepped in to teach everybody a lesson with fines, declaring conduct detrimental to the league. To help fix things, the Blues gave the Rangers Petr Nedved for Keenan, Doug Lidster and Esa Tikkanen.

A small price to pay for a legitimate shot at the Stanley Cup.

1993-94 REGULAR SEASON AT A GLANCE

RECORD: 40-33-11

FINISH: 4th in Central Division, 5th in Western Conference, 11th overall

HOME: 23-11-8 (6th)

AWAY: 17-22-3 (17th)

OVERTIME: 4-2-11 (7th)

VS OWN DIVISION: 12-13-5

VS OTHER DIVISIONS: 28-20-6

VS OWN CONFERENCE: 28-20-7

VS OTHER CONFERENCE: 12-13-4

FIRST HALF RECORD: 21-15-6

SECOND HALF RECORD: 19-18-5

GOALS FOR: 270 (17th)

GOALS AGAINST: 283 (18th)

TEAM PLUS/MINUS: -26 (20th-t)

POWER PLAY: 26.5 (8th)

PENALTY KILLING: 81.2% (14th)

PENALTY MINUTES: 19.8 (9th)

1993-94 REGULAR SEASON LEADERS

GOALS: 57, Brett Hull

ASSISTS: 68, Craig Janney

POINTS: 102, Brendan Shanahan

POWER PLAY GOALS: 25, Hull

SHORTHANDED GOALS: 7, Shanahan

GAME WINNING GOALS: 8, Shanahan

PLUS-MINUS: +6, Kevin Miller

SHOTS: 397, Shanahan

PENALTY MINUTES: 278, Kelly Chase

1993-94 PLAYOFFS AT A GLANCE

RESULTS: Conference Quarterfinals lost to Dallas 4-0

RECORD: 0-4

HOME: 0-2

AWAY: 0-2

GOALS FOR: 10, 2.5/game

GOALS AGAINST: 16, 4.0/game

OVERTIME: 0-1

POWER PLAY: 15.0 (8th)

PENALTY KILLING: 73.9 (14th)

PENALTY MINUTES: 20.3 (9th)

1993-94 PLAYOFF LEADERS

GOALS: 2, Phil Housley, Alexei Kasatonov, Hull

ASSISTS: 5, Shanahan

POINTS: 7, Shanahan

POWER PLAY GOALS: 2, Housley

SHORTHANDED GOALS: 1, Kevin Miller

OVERTIME GOALS: none

GAME-WINNING GOALS: none

PENALTY MINUTES: 12, Basil McRae, David Roberts

PLUS-MINUS: +6, Shanahan

SHOTS: 22, Hull

A LOOK AHEAD TO 1994-95

GOAL: The Blues were fortunate last season to have one of the best goaltenders in the NHL, otherwise it could have been a disaster. Curtis

Joseph faced an average of 35 shots a night. Only Los Angeles allowed more shots against.

Joseph still had one of the best save percentages in the league and appeared in 71 games, the most in his career.

Imagine how good he'll be when he gets some help from the other players, sure to come in the Keenan system. Maybe even a Vezina Trophy is in the cards.

He should be busy again this year, but he might get a little more rest. Jim Hrivnak didn't do the job as backup so the Blues signed Jon Casey, who fell out of favor with the Bruins and was offered a termination contract. He's used to a heavy workload himself, however, so it will be interesting to see how he handles appearing in only about 25 games.

DEFENCE: The Blues are set with Al MacInnis and Steve Duchesne manning the points on the power play. Can't do much better than that.

Other than those two, however, the only proven NHL defensemen left are Rick Zombo (a free agent with compensation), Murray Baron and Doug Lidster, obtained in the Keenan deal.

Daniel Laperriere will get a chance to stick around as will Jeff Batters and U.S. Olympian David Roberts.

No point getting into it much further. Changes under Keenan are a certainty.

FORWARD: Only two Blues forwards did any scoring of note last season: Brendan Shanahan and Brett Hull. Each surpassed the 50 goal plateau.

The only other one over 20 was Kevin Miller with 23. Craig Janney is the playmaker, and Peter Stastny still has some value in that regard. Petr Nedved, of course, was supposed to take over there but he was dealt to New York in the Keenan thing (lucky for him).

Esa Tikkanen, who came from the Rangers is a valuable defensive player who already knows what it takes to play the Keenan style.

So, what else do we have? Two of the three Russians still remain in Caron's great European experiment. Vitali Prokhorov scored 15 goals last season along with 25 points. To show how far the three have fallen in esteem, those numbers were considered outstanding.

Igor Korolev and Vitali Karamnov are the others. Caron predicted 30 goals out of two of them in their first season. In two years, the three of them together have scored a total of 38 goals.

Some of the silliness ended when Karamnov was offered a termination contract. He won't be back and the other two aren't long for this team either.

Like their scoring last season, the Blues pack all their aggressiveness into just a few players. Kelly Chase and Basil McRae can do it as well as anybody but they're only role players. Shanahan is too valuable to be spending so much time (211 PIM last year) in the penalty box.

Among others on the roster are Jim Montgomery, who showed value as a checking center last year and Philippe Bozon, who showed nothing.

There was speculation immediately after Keenan joined the team that Brett Hull would be traded, his style no match for the intensity of the new boss. Hull agreed with those sentiments, indicating a preference for Los Angeles so he could play with Wayne Gretzky.

If that's his attitude, good riddance. Who needs him? Winning hockey players are the kind that can't wait to play for the toughest coach in the game. The kind that will work hard every shift and don't have any qualms about it.

SPECIAL TEAMS: The power play was decent last year, ranking eighth, but they can move up to the top two or three. They have all the ingredients. Duchesne and MacInnis on the points are among the league's best, they have snipers in Hull and Shanahan, and a playmaker in Janney.

When down a man, the Blues go to the offensive. Shanahan led the league with seven short-handed markers. Even Hull, not your average penalty killer, had three while killing penalties.

COACHING: Keenan ranks up there among the greatest coaches of all-time. In nine years of coaching in the NHL, he has reached the finals four times, earning his first Stanley Cup last year. In six of his nine seasons, his team finished first in their division.

Keenan's actions can be bizarre at times, and there's no shortage of people saying he should have done this, or shouldn't have done that.

Even if he doesn't explain why he does something, or even if it appears he doesn't have a reason, there's no need to question the man. He's a hockey genius.

Bob Berry moves from head coach to assistant. Few would consider such an indignity, but he probably won't last long there anyway as other offers are likely to come. Getting the Blues to play as well as they did last season with only one line most of the time was a good accomplishment.

Berry moved into tenth place on the all-time games coached list last season. His 860 total is 54 behind Toe Blake, who is in ninth spot. He should start adding to it with some other team before too long.

MANAGEMENT: It was probably going to be Ron Caron's last season as GM anyway. At 64 years of age he was on the final year of his contract.

Always entertaining, the fiery Professor leaves an interesting legacy. Mind you, one that doesn't involve draft picks.

He never bothered building that way. Let someone else take chances on prospects that may or may not pan out. In 11 years as general manager, he's only had a first rounder three times, with ninth selection being the highest.

He let other teams develop the players and then went and got them as the need arose.

Caron himself had little else to prove, except maybe getting a Stanley Cup. He never missed the playoffs, and in seven of 11 years he advanced past the first round in the playoffs.

The Professor did things differently, but he at least did them, and usually quite well.

Mike Keenan wants certain types of players. He got them the hard way in New York last season, but it will be much easier now. Look for lots of trades, and lots of character players being added to the Blues.

POTENTIAL NEW FACES: D Daniel Laperriere, D Jeff Batters, D David Roberts, all of whom played a couple games with St. Louis last season. Also G Jon Casey, Boston; D Doug Lidster, NY Rangers; and LW Esa Tikkanen.

NEEDS: Nothing for long. Keenan will get the people he needs to win.

McKENZIE'S BOTTOM LINE: The Blues won't start the season with a lineup good enough to finish second in the West, but by the time GM-coach Mike Keenan is finished, they will have the right personnel in place.

Keenan is fortunate. He blows out of New York with his Stanley Cup ring and lands in a franchise that has the major building blocks in place to make a serious run at the Cup.

Start in goal with Curtis Joseph. CuJo, who has faced more shots than any other NHL goalie over the past three seasons, will benefit from a new Blue commitment to team defence. Keenan will insist on it.

The Blues came out way ahead on the Al MacInnis-for-Phil Housley swap. MacInnis is still one of the best three or four defencemen in the league and so long as you're not the Blues' bean counter, it's not your problem to figure out how they're going to pay all the high-priced talent.

With the demanding Keenan in place, it's going to be interesting to see how the Blues' players react. Brett Hull phoned and congratulated Keenan on his appointment, but did the Golden Brett really mean it?

Hull is good pals with Chicago's Jeremy Roenick and the former used to scoff at what the latter had to go through when Keenan was with the Hawks. Hull, in his own way, is competitive and a much harder worker (especially off the ice) than he lets on. But he's also a bit of a free spirit and that could clash with Keenan, who is less dogmatic than he was but still awfully demanding.

It will be interesting, too, to see how players like Craig Janney, Petr Nedved and Steve Duchesne, all regarded as somewhat soft players, react to Keenan.

Keenan will weed out those who can't hack him and replace them with the gritty performers the Blues were sadly lacking in last spring's playoff run.

The one intangible, though, that could work against Keenan's success in St. Louis is the issue of loyalty. Keenan has always used it as a touchstone of sorts to unite his teams, but after the unsavory manner in which he bolted the Rangers, Iron Mike would do well to choose his words carefully with the Blues. The players aren't fools, after all, even if these ones in St. Louis lack the commitment to play gritty team defence.

By the time all is said and done, though, the Blues under Keenan will be right there in the thick of the race.

DRAFT PICKS

That sound you heard emanating from the Blues' draft table was snoring.

St. Louis never had a pick until No. 68 overall, in the third round. The Blues are still paying the mortgage on their signing of Scott Stevens (the first time) from the Washington Capitals. And their second-round pick was in the hands of the Vancouver Canucks as part of the Petr Nedved compensation/trade debacle.

When the Blues finally got around to drafting, the strategy was simple — go for strength up the middle. They took four centres, three defencemen and one goalie with their eight picks in rounds three through 11.

1993-94 KEYS

KEY DEALS:

* obtained Steve Duchesne and Denis Chasse from Quebec for Garth Butcher, Ron Sutter and Bob Bassen

* signed free agent Petr Nedved

* lost Craig Janney to Vancouver as compensation for signing Nedved

* signed free agent Peter Stastny

* obtained Craig Janney (who never left St. Louis) from Vancouver for Jeff Brown, Bret Hedican and Nathan Lafayette.

* obtained Alexei Kasatonov from Anaheim for Maxim Bets and sixth round pick in 1995

Post Season

* obtained Al MacInnis from Calgary for Phil Housley.

* obtained Mike Keenan, Esa Tikkanen and Doug Lidster from NY Rangers for Petr Nedved.

KEY INJURIES: Phil Housley (58 games), Basil McRae (39).

KEY STAT: The St. Louis Blues were outshot and outplayed so often last year, that being tied after a period seemed to give them incentive.

"Look guys, we played terrible and we're still tied. Let's not waste the opportunity."

The accompanying table shows the top records of teams tied after the first and second periods. The Blues are the only team on both lists.

BEST RECORDS WHEN TIED AFTER ONE PERIOD

	Record	Winning Percentage
ST. LOUIS	19-8-1	.696
Detroit	14-7-0	.667
NY Rangers	14-7-4	.640
Toronto	19-10-5	.632
San Jose	10-5-9	.604

BEST RECORDS WHEN TIED AFTER TWO PERIODS

Quebec	10-3-1	.750
ST. LOUIS	12-5-4	.667
New Jersey	9-3-7	.658
Dallas	9-3-7	.658
Calgary	5-2-7	.607

Toronto Maple Leafs

Hockey fans in Toronto sure got spoiled quickly. After years and years of suffering, one good season under Pat Burns and Cliff Fletcher and they expect it every time.

Make that two good seasons. Ninety-nine points, and then 98 last year. Plus, they're the only team to make it to the final four the last two years in a row.

In the playoffs, Toronto got past Chicago and San Jose (barely) and then were clearly outclassed by Vancouver in the conference finals.

But, instead of a great accomplishment to get that far (like it was considered the previous year) it was somewhat of a disappointment. Hey, we did that one already. Let's do something new.

Over the summer, changes were made, including one blockbuster deal, with Wendel Clark going to Quebec for Mats Sundin.

By some of the reaction in Toronto, you'd think the Leafs had given up Wayne Gretzky. A little reality check might be in order. In the six seasons prior to last year, Clark was injured so often he didn't reach the 20 goal plateau even

once. Last year he came through with 46 goals so Fletcher was smart enough to realize his value would probably never be this high on the open market again.

Sure, Clark was the "heart and soul" of the Maple Leafs - when he played, which wasn't very often. After his two first seasons, he was in only 317 of 528 games, a 60 percent participation rate.

No doubt, he's a superior hitter and scrapper, but they were also parts of his game that were slowed by necessity in recent years.

In Mats Sundin, they get somebody who has played 320 of a possible 324 games over his four year NHL career. He's had seasons, in order, of 59, 76, 114 and 85 points. Clark had 76 this past season, a career high, surpassing his next best of only 60 points.

Plus, and this is a big plus, Sundin is only 23 years old and hasn't even reached his prime. Clark turns 28 a month into the season, and he's an old 28.

In reality, the trade was a steal. Toronto fans don't see it yet because Clark was so popular, but eventually they'll come around.

1993-94 REGULAR SEASON AT A GLANCE

RECORD: 43-29-12

FINISH: 2nd in Central Division, 2nd in Western Conference and 5th overall

HOME: 23-15-4 (9th)

AWAY: 20-14-8 (5th)

OVERTIME: 4-1-12 (3rd)

VS OWN DIVISION: 18-8-4

VS OTHER DIVISIONS: 25-21-8

VS OWN CONFERENCE: 27-19-8

VS OTHER CONFERENCE: 16-10-4

FIRST HALF RECORD: 21-14-7

SECOND HALF RECORD: 22-15-5

GOALS FOR: 280 (13th)

GOALS AGAINST: 243 (6th)

TEAM PLUS/MINUS: +23 (7th)

POWER PLAY: 19.2% (12th)

PENALTY KILLING: 81.9% (11th)

PENALTY MINUTES: 22.3/game (20th)

1993-94 REGULAR SEASON LEADERS

GOALS: 53, Dave Andreychuk

ASSISTS: 84, Doug Gilmour

POINTS: 111, Gilmour

POWER PLAY GOALS: 21, Andreychuk, Wendel Clark

SHORTHANDED GOALS: 5, Andreychuk

GAME WINNING GOALS: 8, Clark, Andreychuk

PLUS-MINUS: +33, Sylvain Lefebvre

SHOTS: 333, Andreychuk

PENALTY MINUTES: 189, Rob Pearson

1993-94 PLAYOFFS AT A GLANCE

RESULTS: Conference Quarterfinals - defeated Chicago 4-2 **Conference Semi-Finals** - defeated San Jose 4-3 **Conference Finals** - lost to Vancouver 4-1

RECORD: 9-9

HOME: 7-2

AWAY: 2-7

GOALS FOR: 2.8/game

GOALS AGAINST: 2.6/game

OVERTIME: 3-2

POWER PLAY: 29.7% (1st)

PENALTY KILLING: 84.9% (6th)

PENALTY MINUTES: 20.8/game (11th)

1993-94 PLAYOFF LEADERS

GOALS: 9, Clark

ASSISTS: 22, Gilmour

POINTS: 28, Gilmour

POWER PLAY GOALS: 6, Dimitri Mironov

SHORTHANDED GOALS: 2, Mark Osborne

OVERTIME GOALS: 1, Todd Gill, Mike Gartner, Peter Zezel

GAME-WINNING GOALS: 3, Gartner

Penalty Minutes: 52, Osborne

PLUS-MINUS: +3, Gartner, Gilmour

SHOTS: 72, Clark

A LOOK AHEAD TO 1994-95

GOAL: Felix Potvin had some stretches last season when he seemed to lose his concentration. When that happens, he's just an average NHL goalie. Otherwise, he's sensational. Still only 23 years old, he will be one of the best goaltenders in the league for many years to come.

Damian Rhodes did everything you could expect from a backup goaltender, and more. He won his first seven NHL decisions, and finished the season with a 2.55 GAA in 22 games.

DEFENCE: Some of the younger players will get an opportunity now that Sylvain Lefebvre has been traded and Bob Rouse has been lost to free agency.

Kenny Jonsson is an almost sure bet for one of those spots and is expected to play the point on the power play. The reviews have been high for the Swede, who was voted best defenseman at the World Junior Championships.

U.S. Olympian, Matt Martin is another expected to join the defense corps. He played 12 games for Toronto last season and didn't look out of place.

David Harlock, considered a Sylvain Lefevbre clone, who played last year with the Canadian Olympic team, will also get a shot.

It's also time for Drake Berehowsky to make his move. The offensive rearguard showed very little last year after making an impression the season before. Perhaps a regular spot on the blueline without having to worry about every mistake will help him considerably. If he can show something he'll be out on the power play.

The most improved player last season was Dimitri Mironov. After looking like a sluggo much of the previous year, he came into his own and fit in well, both offensively and defensively. He makes mistakes that 28 year olds shouldn't make, like trying to stickhandle the puck out of his end when he's the last man, but he's still adapting to the North American game and doing it fairly well.

Todd Gill may be the steadiest defenseman on the team now that Lefebvre has left. Prone to giveaways before Pat Burns came on the scene, he doesn't do that nearly as often anymore, although he does have his lapses and is a fairly frequent visitor to the coach's doghouse.

Garth Butcher will be a welcome addition. He gives the team toughness, something they have in short supply. He goes from being one of the most-hated opponents to one who should be a big fan favourite in Toronto.

Thirty-three year old Jamie Macoun can still do the job but it will be tougher this year. He was paired with Lefebvre much of last season, making for a pretty good defensive duo. This year, he'll probably be asked to help one of the younger defensemen.

The transformation from veteran, stay-at-home types to youthful offensive players is on. Teams around the league didn't forecheck much last season, but when they did they found the Toronto defense could cough up the puck with the best of them.

But, they were among the best when the other team had the puck. This year, they'll be better offensively, but now there are question marks defensively.

FORWARD: Someone once asked somebody how was it that Doug Gilmour could give a 100% effort each and every time he stepped on the ice.

The person answered, "It's simple, the guy's not human." He may be right. His play since joining the Maple Leafs has been out of this world. All last season, the team looked for a second line center. John Cullen was that man early, showing a lot of imagination with the puck and making his line tick. He had nine points in the team's first eight games and 16 in their first 15. Linemates, Rob Pearson and Mark Osborne both were playing well too, piling up the points. All three suffered injuries, however, and none were able to regain the touch. Osborne retained his value later in the season when he moved onto a checking line, but the other two never regained form. None will be back with the team this year, unless Osborne signs as a free agent.

The Leafs may regret giving up on Pearson. He clearly wasn't one of Burns favorite players, and while he was aggressive and showed a sniper's touch at times, he would often do a lot of dumb things on the ice and take stupid penalties. But, don't be surprised if things come together for him and he pots a lot of goals for Washington.

Mike Ridley will satisfy their search for another center, over the short term. The 31 year old is coming off a 26 goal, 70 point season for Washington. He can contribute on the power play and the penalty killing unit.

Also at center is: Peter Zezel, who headed up the top checking line late in the season; Mike Eastwood, a decent role player who always gave a full effort; and Alexei Kudashov who looked outstanding at times. He proved that looks aren't everything, however, when he could manage just one point in 25 games.

The left side is headed up by Dave Andreychuk, who scored 53 goals last season and just missed by one, for the second year in a row, of reaching the 100 point mark. He set a team record in goals and assists for a left winger and his 16 game point streak was the longest of the year in the NHL. Andreychuk goes through mysterious slumps, though, and during the playoffs he was AWOL, almost completely a non-factor.

Also on the left wing is Kent Manderville who has developed into a valuable commodity. He's not going to fight much, but he uses his size to advantage, crashing and banging when the spirit moves him. Look for him to show a sizeable point increase this season.

Crashing and banging always suits Bill Berg. He led the team in hits almost nightly, and we're not just talking little love taps. He drives his opponents through the boards or in open ice, almost always cleanly. He may be the best hitting forward in the league.

Eric Lacroix will get a shot over there as well, but probably Ken Baumgartner will be suiting up every night for the fourth line to inject some muscle. With Clark and Pearson gone, there isn't much toughness up front anymore.

Behind Sundin on the right wing (unless he plays center), is Mike

Gartner, free agent signee Mike Craig, Nikolai Borschevsky, and perhaps David Sacco.

Gartner looked good when he joined the team from the Rangers, using his tremendous speed to hit everything in sight. His stock dropped rapidly, however, as did his hitting and scoring. That's no knock against Gartner who has had a great career, but it has to end sometime and he turns 35 this season.

Borschevsky had an injury plagued season but two years ago had 34 goals, so he obviously has some value. The problem with the 5-9, 180 pounder (he's listed at that but is smaller) is that he's one of the most timid players in the league. There's some question of whether or not he should be playing in the NHL.

Free agent Mike Craig may be a more valuable addition than the Leafs anticipate. They already know about his feistiness, but even though he hasn't shown it in the past, he could be ready to break out as a goal-scorer.

Toronto still appears to be soft up front. Unless they get some bigger, tougher guys other teams are going to push them around and they won't be able to do anything about it.

SPECIAL TEAMS: The power play was up and down last season, at or near the top on occasion. They finished in 12th spot. There are lots of defensemen who can handle the supporting roles, but they need a quarterback. They're hoping Jonsson will fit the bill.

The penalty killing was good too, if not spectacular. You could always find Macoun and Lefebvre out there when down a man, so it will be interesting to see if they can compensate for Lefebvre's absence.

COACHING: You'd have a hard time finding fault with the job Pat Burns has done for the Maple Leafs. He's more a motivator than a tactician, but he does the former very well. If he doesn't like what a player is doing he sits him in the press box or on the bench. They often respond to that type of treatment by coming back with inspired efforts.

He did show a curious habit of speaking out in the media about some injured players, with the inference being that they were dogging it. That certainly didn't win him any friends among those perceived as guilty parties.

Maybe it's just another motivational technique. Burns isn't trying to win friends anyway, he's trying to win hockey games. So far, so good.

MANAGEMENT: You sometimes get the impression that Cliff Fletcher, the soft-spoken savior of the Maple Leafs is beyond making mistakes.

But, hey, the guy traded Brett Hull part way through his first NHL season, so he's not perfect.

Awfully close though. Assistant GM Bill Watters gives them two intelligent men running the show. If and when he wants, Watters will make a good GM of some other club in the league.

POTENTIAL NEW FACES: D Kenny Jonsson, Sweden; C Mats Sundin, Quebec; D Garth Butcher, Quebec; D Matt Martin, U.S. Olympic team; D David Harlock, Canadian Olympic team; Mike Craig, Dallas.

NEEDS: More aggressiveness from the forwards, a quarterback for the power play, a couple young defensemen to step up and show they belong in the NHL.

McKENZIE'S BOTTOM LINE: The only team that has gone to the Final Four in back to back years has undergone a dramatic transformation.

Last season's critical flaw — no depth at centre behind team leader Doug Gilmour — has been addressed in a big way. Mats Sundin, over from Quebec, gives the Leafs a potential superstar and the best part is he's still just a (23-year-old) pup. Throw in the very effective Mike Ridley from Washington and the Leafs suddenly have an excellent 1-2-3 punch up the middle.

But they paid a steep price to get it. Team captain Wendel Clark's goals and guts, especially in playoff warfare will be missed, as will Sylvain Lefebvre's steadiness on the blueline. Lefebvre may well have been the NHL's best defensive defenceman.

The departure of free agent Bob Rouse complicates matters for coach Pat Burns, whose immediate challenge is to develop new chemistry.

The Leafs aren't as strong on defence as they would like to be and they lack toughness, too. Goal-scoring from the wings could also be better. But the Sundin trade secures a decent long-term future for the franchise once Gilmour is gone.

It's up to GM Cliff Fletcher to plug the gaps as best as he can and it's up to Burns to get players who might not otherwise think defence or exhibit Clark-like playoff gusto naturally.

Don't underestimate Burns' ability to get young players playing and contributing immediately and don't forget that having Sundin in the lineup is going to free up Gilmour from intense checking on a lot more nights.

The new-look Leafs, as long as netminder Felix Potvin and new captain Gilmour come through, will be right back where they were a year ago, although an adjustment period will be required early on.

DRAFT PICKS

Forget the Wendel Clark-Mats Sundin blockbuster for a moment. What the Maple Leafs did at the 1994 draft was move from the 22nd pick overall to the 16th pick overall. And what did they have to show for it?

Only one of the two top-rated goaltenders, Eric Fichaud, in the entire draft and veteran centre Mike Ridley. Not bad. Not bad at all.

Leaf GM Cliff Fletcher, because of the Clark-Sundin blockbuster, parlayed No. 22 into the Nordiques' No. 10 pick. Under ideal circumstances, Fletcher would have liked to take power forward Brett Lindros with that pick. But when the Nordiques peddled No. 9 to the Islanders so they could take Lindros, Fletcher realized he'd been "submarined."

No problem for the wily veteran GM. He quickly peddled the pick to someone who wanted it — Washington, so it could draft Kamloops defenceman

Nolan Baumgartner — and got back Ridley, an effective and useful player, especially on a team lacking depth at centre, and the 16th overall selection.

Then Fletcher took Fichaud, a clone of Leaf goaltender Felix Potvin. There are some, including the Leafs' late chief scout Pierre Dorion, who ranked Fichaud ahead of top-rated Jamie Storr.

In any case, the Leafs picked up an excellent long-range goaltending prospect plus a solid two-way centre.

In the second round, the Leafs settled on a speedy winger with some scoring potential, Sean Haggerty of the Detroit Jr. Red Wings. And when big Swedish winger Fredrik Modin was still available in the third round — the Leafs had no third-round pick this year — Fletcher promptly made a deal with the Islanders to get one.

Two late-round Leaf picks have some intersting bloodlines. Sixth-rounder Kam White is the son of former NHL defenceman Bill White and left winger Rob Butler is the son of former Leaf Jerry Butler.

1993-94 KEYS

KEY DEALS:

* obtained Mike Gartner from NY Rangers for Glenn Anderson, 1994 4th round pick and Scott Malone.

Post Season:

* obtained Garth Butcher, Mats Sundin, Todd Warriner and 10th pick in 1994 draft from from Quebec for Wendel Clark, Sylvain Lefebvre, Landon Wilson and 22nd pick in 1994 draft.

* obtained Mike Ridley and 16th pick in 1994 draft from Washington for Rob Pearson and 10th overall pick.

* signed free agent Mike Craig from Dallas.

KEY INJURIES: Wendel Clark (18 games), Nikolai Borschevsky (36), John Cullen (21), Todd Gill (39), Peter Zezel (43), Bob Rouse (21).

KEY STAT: It was a streaky year for the Maple Leafs. They went through stretches where they were unbeatable, and others where they couldn't beat the worst teams in the league.

The accompanying table shows how two of the hot spells were among the best last season.

LONGEST TEAM STREAKS

1993-94 Consecutive Wins

Team	Date	Games
TORONTO	Oct. 7 - Oct. 28	10
New Jersey	Oct. 6 - Oct. 23	7
NY Rangers	Oct. 30 - Nov. 13	7
San Jose	Mar. 24 - Apr. 5	7

Consecutive Undefeated

NY Rangers	Oct. 24 - Nov. 24	14
TORONTO	Jan. 6 - Feb. 1	11
Montreal	Feb. 23 - Mar. 19	11
TORONTO	Oct. 7 - Oct. 28	10

Vancouver Canucks

Those Crazy Canucks. And their crazy season. It started with Petr Nedved, whose salary demands were out of whack with reality, according to Vancouver. A free agent with compensation, the Canucks tried to work out a deal with other teams, but found his salary demands were out of whack with reality all over the league. They had an agreement with the Rangers but bonus clauses attempted by Nedved's agent, Tony Kondel, such as $3,500 for an assist on a short-handed goal or $3,500 for a goal in the second period, stretched the imagination too far for the Rangers and the deal was off.

Finally, St. Louis signed him, after he had played for Canada in the Olympics.

Then more weirdness. Unable to agree on compensation, it went to an arbitrator who awarded Craig Janney to Vancouver. But, Janney refused to report and was traded back to St. Louis for three good players who were instrumental in their playoff drive.

But, that wasn't the strangest thing that happened to Vancouver last season. It was making it to the Stanley Cup finals after finishing the regular season at just one game over .500, needing the last game of the year just to accomplish that.

And it became evident as the playoffs wore on that they were indeed worthy of such an honour. Nobody would have considered it a fluke had they won the Stanley Cup.

After beating Calgary in seven games, the last three in overtime, Vancouver showed what it takes to be successful in the playoffs. They had size, speed, determination, solid defense, toughness, intimidation, great leadership from captain Trevor Linden, an impact type player in Bure, and perhaps most importantly of all, outstanding goaltending from Kirk McLean.

A couple inches here or there versus Calgary in any one of the overtimes and we wouldn't be speaking nearly so highly of them, however.

We've seen it before. An upstart team comes up big and does some heavy damage in the playoffs. It doesn't often lead to any continued success, but it was nice for them while it lasted.

1993-94 SEASON AT A GLANCE

RECORD: 41-40-3

FINISH: 2nd in Pacific Division, 7th in Western Conference, 14th overall

HOME: 20-19-3 (16th)

AWAY: 21-21-0 (11th)

OVERTIME: 5-4-3 (9th)

VS OWN DIVISION: 17-14-1

VS OTHER DIVISIONS: 24-26-2

VS OWN CONFERENCE: 30-24-2

VS OTHER CONFERENCE: 11-16-1

FIRST HALF RECORD: 21-21-0

SECOND HALF RECORD: 20-19-3

GOALS FOR: 279 (14th)

GOALS AGAINST: 276 (17th)

TEAM PLUS/MINUS: +4 (15th-t)

POWER PLAY: 18.8% (14th)

PENALTY KILLING: 81.7% (12th)

PENALTY MINUTES: 22.9/game (22nd)

1993-94 REGULAR SEASON LEADERS (WITH VANCOUVER ONLY)

GOALS: 60, Pavel Bure

ASSISTS: 47, Bure (Jeff Brown 52 overall)

POINTS: 107, Bure

POWER PLAY GOALS: 25, Bure

SHORTHANDED GOALS: 4, Bure

GAME WINNING GOALS: 9, Bure

PLUS-MINUS: +15, Geoff Courtnall

SHOTS: 374, Bure

PENALTY MINUTES: 271, Gino Odjick

1993-94 PLAYOFFS AT A GLANCE

RESULTS: Conference Quarterfinals - defeated Calgary 4-3 **Conference Semifinals -** defeated Dallas 4-1 **Conference Finals -** defeated Toronto 4-1 **Finals -** lost to NY Rangers 4-3

RECORD: 15-9

HOME: 7-5

AWAY: 8-4

GOALS FOR: 3.2/game

GOALS AGAINST: 2.5/game

OVERTIME: 5-1

POWER PLAY: 16.4% (7th)

PENALTY KILLING: 82.5% (9th)

PENALTY MINUTES: 18.2/game (7th)

1993-94 PLAYOFF LEADERS

GOALS: 16, Bure

ASSISTS: 15, Bure

POINTS: 31, Bure

POWER PLAY GOALS: 5, Trevor Linden

SHORTHANDED GOALS: 1, Linden, Geoff Courtnall

OVERTIME GOALS: 1, five players tied

GAME-WINNING GOALS: 3, Courtnall

PENALTY MINUTES: 56, Sergio Momesso

PLUS-MINUS: +13, Bret Hedican, Nathan Lafayette

SHOTS: 101, Bure

A LOOK AHEAD TO 1994-95

GOAL: It's impossible to say enough about the job Kirk McLean did for the Canucks in the playoffs last season.

Statistically, he had four shutouts, one more than during the regular season, and posted a sparkling 2.38 GAA and a .926 save percentage. But, you can't measure his full contribution with statistics.

McLean had just an average regular season, actually finishing with a losing record, but that's acceptable if you're going to be a money goaltender who comes through in the playoffs.

More was expected out of backup Kay Whitmore, such as he was able to provide the previous season. No matter, he's a capable backup who can bounce back. Also waiting in the wings is highly touted Mike Fountain who played 70 games for Hamilton in the AHL.

DEFENSE: The Canucks are loaded at this position. Maybe over-loaded. They have nine NHL caliber defensemen, and others who could be there if they had the opportunity.

Jyrki Lumme and Jeff Brown dominate most of the power play time.

Lumme was probably the best all-round defenseman on the team last season.

Brown had 66 points from the blueline, 41 on the power play. Curiously, he had to bide his time when he first got to Vancouver. He wasn't put on the power play right away, the Canucks preferring to stick with Jiri Slegr, who ended up not playing any games at all in the playoffs.

There is a host of good defensive defensmen in Gerald Diduck, Dana Murzyn, Dave Babych, and Brian Glynn, a valuable addition they were able to pick up on waivers from Ottawa of all teams.

Bret Hedican may be the fastest defenseman in the NHL. He hasn't used any of it for offense yet, and maybe never will, but he's still young at 24.

With so many ahead of him, Adrian Plavsic had to find a comfortable seat in the press box. He teases with bursts of talent on occasion, but not often enough yet. He's still young too, however, at only 24.

That leaves Yevgeny (John) Namestnikov in the wings, with some more young talent on the way in Jassen Cullimore and Brent Tully.

There's not enough room for everybody, but it's not a bad situation to be in. Most NHL teams wouldn't mind having the same problem.

FORWARD: What's the big fuss about looking for a center all the time? There's nothing wrong with Trevor Linden there, Cliff Ronning might be small but he scores, newcomer Nathan Lafayette looked good in the playoffs and did some scoring as well, and John McIntyre is about all you need in a fourth line center.

Another possibility is Mike Peca, a 50 goal scorer in junior. Murray Craven, who played on the wing for the Canucks is also a natural centreman.

Okay, so there's not a lot of size or toughness, but what do they think wingers are for?

After Eric Lindros there aren't a lot of tough centers in the league anyway.

That's not the position to find them.

On left wing is oft-injured Greg Adams, the dependable Sergio Momesso, Craven sometimes, Geoff Courtnall sometimes, and two toughniks in Gino Odjick and Shawn Antoski.

On right wing is Pavel Bure; Martin Gelinas, a surprise success as a waiver pick-up from Quebec; Craven or Courtnall; Tim Hunter and Jose Charbonneau.

Hunter deserves a lot of credit for his play, especially in the playoffs. He was an intimidating force who played it so much smarter and more disciplined than most would have thought possible. He even absorbed a beating from Rob Pearson, whom he could have pummeled if he wanted, just to help his team.

The fourth line of Antonski (or Odjick), McIntyre in the middle and Hunter on the right side deserves a lot of credit for their playoff performance. They were good enough to give the other lines more rest, good defensively, disciplined and with their aggressiveness helped set things up for the Canucks' other lines.

Some of the forwards are getting on in years. Greg Adams is 31, Courtnall 32, and Craven is 30. An injection of youth in the near future will be needed.

That doesn't seem to be a big worry either, though. The main concern is center. Eleven centers and Pavel Bure would make everybody happy and we wouldn't have to hear anymore about it.

SPECIAL TEAMS: The Canuck powerplay was number one last season — on the road. At home, they were 24th.

What's up with that? The Canuck penalty killing was 3rd on the road and 24th at home.

Another wacky stat. Despite all this great special team play on the road they still finished only at .500 away from home. And in Vancouver, they were one game over .500.

This year? Who the heck knows. Power play and penalty-killing will be somewhere around the middle of the pack.

COACHING/MANAGEMENT: Pat Quinn has given up the coaching reins. Oops, not so fast. He was just kidding. As of this writing, Quinn is still the man behind the bench. And why not? Great job with the team last year.

As for the GM position, he seems to have a good grasp of talent that other teams can't see. He picked up four key performers for the team off the waiver wire — Gelinas, Glynn, McIntyre and Hunter. The Craig Janney deal where they got Jeff Brown, Bret Hedican and Nathan Lafayette was also a winner.

NEEDS: We hear they need a center.

POTENTIAL NEW FACES: D John Namestnikov, Hamilton; D Scott Walker, Hamilton; D Jassen Cullimore, Hamilton; C Mike Peca, Ottawa (OHL); D Brent Tully, Peterborough (OHL); C Dan Kesa, Hamilton.

McKENZIE'S BOTTOM LINE: Their trip to the Stanley Cup final notwithstanding, the Canucks should be the top team in the Pacific Division almost by acclamation.

The Calgary Flames, minus Mike Vernon and Al MacInnis, are not, on paper anyway, going to be as good as they were a year ago. And unless the Canucks fall into the same sort of doldrums that affected the Cup finalist Los Angeles Kings two years ago, Vancouver should be the class of Pacific Division and a regular-season contender to push the best of the Central, too.

Netminder Kirk McLean should use last spring's playoff heroics as a launching pad for his personal improvement plan.

And the Petr Nedved trade the Canucks fell into with St. Louis has bolstered a defence that seemed to be flagging. Veteran Jeff Brown showed in the playoffs he's a much better player than he's ever been given credit for. And Brett Hedican overcame a seeming lack of hockey sense to be an important part of the Canucks' defensive unit.

The Russian Rocket Pavel Bure, if he plays with any consistency at all, has a good shot at a 70- or 80-goal season and Hart Trophy consideration. Trevor Linden's maturation as the team leader will continue.

The only pitfall could be too much self satisfaction at having achieved beyond all expectations last spring. That, and getting used to a new coach if Pat Quinn followed through on his quasi-promise to step down.

If Quinn quit as coach, assistant Rick Ley was the natural successor, which will guarantee continuity. But if it's Ley, is he as respected and as liked by the players as Quinn was? Probably not.

Nevertheless, it's difficult to pick the Canucks for anything but first in the Pacific.

DRAFT PICKS

Once the Canucks made Swedish defenceman Mattias Ohlund their first-round pick, they didn't stray too far from home.

Second-rounder Robb Gordon, a pure offensive centre, played just up the road in Powell River in the British Columbia Junior League. Including Powell, eight of the Canucks' 11 picks played hockey last season in the WHL or a western tier two league.

The only excpetions were Ohlund, the strong two-way defenceman in the first round, Quebec League scoring champion Yannick Dube in the fifth round and Russian Yuri Kuznetsov in the seventh.

Ohlund could be on the Canuck scene quickly, since his agent, Mike Barnett, pre-negotiated the players' release from Swedish club team Pitea.

Gordon is likely destined for U.S. college hockey for awhile although Tacoma of the WHL was to make a strong bid to get the slick centre in its lineup.

Dube is certainly an intriguing pick. He was passed over in each of the last two drafts. He starred for Canada at the 1994 world junior championships and led Laval to a Memorial Cup finalist appearance. He's small, but he could be the rare item who is fast and skilled enough to compensate for his lack of physical stature.

1993-94 KEYS

KEY DEALS:

* obtained Jimmy Carson from Los Angeles for Dixon Ward and future considerations.

* claimed Martin Gelinas on waivers from Quebec

* claimed Brian Glynn on waivers from Ottawa

* acquired Craig Janney and 2nd round choice in 1994 draft as compensation for St. Louis signing Petr Nedved.

* obtained Jeff Brown, Bret Hedican and Nathan Lafayette from St. Louis for Craig Janney

KEY INJURIES: Greg Adams (16 games), Gerald Diduck (25).

KEY STAT: All that playoff experience. You would think a team that makes it to the finals one year would know what it takes to do it again the next.

But over the last ten years, not one of the Stanley Cup finals losers has made it back that far the following season. Worse, one didn't even make the playoffs, and five got bounced by their very first opponent. Three others made it to the second round and just one made it to the conference finals before bowing out.

Mind you, the season before, the Edmonton Oilers lost in the finals and then came back to win the Stanley Cup, but the stats show it doesn't happen very often.

STANLEY CUP LOSER - FOLLOWING SEASON

1992-93	Los Angeles	failed to make playoffs
1991-92	Chicago	knocked out in first round
1990-91	Minnesota	knocked out in first round
1989-90	Boston	lost conference championships
1988-89	Montreal	lost division final
1987-88	Boston	lost division final
1986-87	Philadelphia	knocked out in first round
1985-86	Calgary	knocked out in first round
1984-85	Philadelphia	knocked out in first round
1983-84	NY Islanders	lost division final

Winnipeg Jets

The big news in Winnipeg last season was the crash landing of the Jets.

The second biggest news was the firing of GM Mike Smith, the man responsible for the first biggest news.

Smith is a great success at some things, maybe more important things, like education. If managing a hockey team is his only failure, he's well ahead of the game.

And it was a failure, totally and completely. In five years at the helm, he accomplished absolutely nothing. Oh, one year they finished five games over .500. Whoopee. And he never won a single playoff series.

Smith tried to build Team Europe. When it collapsed in his face, people blamed it on the Europeans. In the politically correct nineties that made them racists, a convenient term for those with a difficult time grasping reality.

A good point is made by those who suggest that teams also fail with mostly Canadian lineups, and people don't give the reason as too many Canadians.

But, that's because they're in the majority. If a team in Sweden loaded up with Canadians (and were allowed to) then the success or failure of that team would be based on that fact. If somebody tried to play a team of Canadians in the NHL that were 5'9" and shorter, the same thing.

If Smith's project had been a success, guess who would have been given the credit. Yeah, the Europeans. Smith would have been lauded for his foresight and ingenuity.

What's the opposite of foresight and ingenuity? Doesn't matter because race is involved and it can't be spoken out loud.

Do people think there really isn't a difference between European and Canadian hockey players?

If there were no names on the sweaters and all the helmets were the same, any serious hockey fan could pick out the Europeans. They're the ones with the fancy skating and stickhandling.

Everything's nicey-nicey if you stop right there. But, point out that they generally don't have the same brand of intensity, toughness or haven't grown up with the same defensive skills, and man, you've stepped way over the line.

Doesn't matter if it's true or not, you can't say it. After being fired, Smith said his biggest mistake was trading Dave Ellett.

Dave Ellett? Get real. Some suggest perhaps he was ahead of his time. Based on the Dave Ellett comment, it could be that he was just in another time zone.

The man chose to build a team made up of mostly Europeans. You can't avoid that reality. Hey, wait a minute...what do you call it when somebody favors one group over another strictly because of their birthplace? Hmm....

1993-94 REGULAR SEASON AT A GLANCE

RECORD: 24-51-9

FINISH: 6th in Central Division, 12th in Western Conference, 25th overall

HOME: 15-23-4 (22nd)

AWAY: 9-28-5 (25th)

OVERTIME: 1-5-9 (25th)

VS OWN DIVISION: 10-17-3

VS OTHER DIVISIONS: 14-34-6

VS OWN CONFERENCE: 13-35-6

VS OTHER CONFERENCE: 11-16-3

FIRST HALF RECORD: 15-22-5

SECOND HALF RECORD: 9-29-4

GOALS FOR: 245 (21st)

GOALS AGAINST: 344 (25th)

TEAM PLUS/MINUS: -90 (25th)

POWER PLAY: 19.4% (11th)

PENALTY KILLING: 79.6% (23rd)

PENALTY MINUTES: 25.5/game (26th)

1993-94 REGULAR SEASON LEADERS

GOALS: 41, Keith Tkachuk

ASSISTS: 45, Alexei Zhamnov

POINTS: 81, Tkachuk

POWER PLAY GOALS: 22, Tkachuk

SHORTHANDED GOALS: 5, Nelson Emerson

GAME WINNING GOALS: 6, Emerson

PLUS-MINUS: 0, four players tied

SHOTS: 282, Emerson

PENALTY MINUTES: 347, Tie Domi

A LOOK AHEAD TO 1994-95

GOAL: Tim Cheveldae was never a bad goaltender, he was just in the wrong nets at the wrong time in Detroit. He may find the pressure less intense in Winnipeg, at least until they come close to being winners.

He's not going to be a first team all-star or even a second teamer, but he'll get the job done.

Departed Bob Essensa did an outstanding job most of the time for the Jets, considering how often he was a target for a shooting gallery.

Backups are Michael O'Neill and Stephane Beauregard. Their combined record last season was 0-13-2.

It hasn't been a situation in Winnipeg where a goaltender could be judged fairly. Wait until there's some protection in front of them and then we'll talk.

DEFENCE: It's a mess, but steps are being taken to rectify the situation. This year it will be tough enough to make opposing forwards at least think twice about dipsy-doodling by them.

Neil Wilkinson joins late season addition Dave Manson, and holdovers Igor Ulanov, Stephane Quintal, and Dean Kennedy, making them a much stronger force in their own end.

Teppo Numminen is supposed to supply the offense and quarterback the power play. He had 23 points in 53 games last season, only eight of those points even strength. In six seasons, his point high is 43, so he's not exactly a Phil Housley.

Others battling for jobs will be Wayne McBean, Darryl Shannon and a host of Europeans who are going to have to show more than the norm in this atmosphere to stick.

FORWARD: A top line of Keith Tkachuk on the left, Alexei Zhamnov in the middle and Teemu Selanne on the right is projected.

Tkachuk developed into one of the league's premier power forwards last season. He does a little bit of everything, all of them well. Forty-one goals and 81 points, 22 power play goals and 255 penalty minutes.

Zhamnov, if healthy could project to around 100 points playing with Tkachuk and Selanne. In fact, they could be one of the top lines in the league.

Selanne didn't come anywhere near the 76 goals he earned as a rookie. He had just 25 and was suffering from the sophomore jinx well before severing his Achilles Tendon and sitting out 33 games.

He'll be back. You don't score 76 goals by accident. Nelson Emerson also had an outstanding season with 33 goals and 74 points. He'll toil on the right side along with pickup Sheldon Kennedy from Detroit who plays with a lot of spirit but has had his share of trouble off the ice. Also on the right side is Tie Domi, one of the best enforcers in the league and a pretty good skater who can contribute in more ways than just with his fists.

On left wing behind Tkachuk, is: Darrin Shannon, coming off a decent season and a dynamite second half when he scored 16 of his 21 goals; valuable fourth-liner Kris King, and possibly Russ Romaniuk.

The center position will be handled by Zhamnov, Thomas Steen, Dallas Drake, Luciano Borsato, checker Randy Gilhen and Mike Eagles.

SPECIAL TEAMS: Thanks to Tkachuk, the Jets power play was decent last year, finishing 12th overall. With Selanne back to normal and Zhamnov healthy, it could make for an outstanding power play.

They could use somebody to man the points, however. Numminen will take care of one of them much of the time, and maybe Manson, who has performed the duties in the past.

The penalty killing ranked 23rd last year, but will improve this season. They've added toughness and good defensive defensemen.

COACHING/MANAGEMENT: When Sergei Bautin was traded to Detroit in the Essensa-Cheveldae deal, he couldn't play right away with that team because he was in such poor condition. He couldn't even handle the practises.

Does that say something about John Paddock or Sergei Bautin? Many thought Paddock might be in over his head taking over the GM reins along with his coaching duties, but so far so good.

Much of his time has been spent trading away Europeans from the great spoiled Mike Smith experiment. He's added toughness and competitiveness. Already they're a better team.

That's one of the good things about being in his position. The team has nowhere to go but up, so when they do he'll get the credit.

POTENTIAL NEW FACES: D Neil Wilkinson, Chicago; RW Sheldon Kennedy, Detroit.

NEEDS: Most of them are being taken care of with the addition of character players who will make the team more competitive. Otherwise, a little bit of everything at each position.

McKENZIE'S BOTTOM LINE: One always suspected that coach John Paddock didn't have a Jet team to his liking, but when he became the GM

after Mike Smith was fired, the suspicions were confirmed.

The first thing Paddock started doing was de-Euroizing the Jets. In his trade to get Tim Cheveldae and Sheldon Kennedy from Detroit, Paddock shipped out Russian defenceman Sergei Bautin.

He traded Russian Yan Kaminsky to the New York Islanders for Wayne McBean.

He acquired tough hombre Dave Manson from Edmonton and sent packing Russian defender Boris Mironov and top Swedish prospect Mats Lindgren.

Don't get Paddock wrong. He has nothing against Europeans. He just doesn't want too many of them, and the ones he wants are superstar or star material — like Teemu Selanne, Alexei Zhamnov or Teppo Numminen.

The Jets have one of the most impressive non-playoff rosters ever.

As long as Selanne can come to full health after the torn Achilles tendon, the Jets have a game-breaking winger who plays more than a one-dimensional scoring style. Keith Tkachuk gives Paddock one of the premier power forwards in the game, a rare blend of toughness and talent. Zhamnov, Nelson Emerson and veteran Thomas Steen give the Jets plenty of depth and talent up front. There's no shortage of role players either, with the likes of Darrin Shannon, Kris King, Mike Eagles and Tie Domi, to name a few.

Paddock's thrust as GM has been to rebuild the defence. He's counting on Manson and Numminen to lead the way and make this Jet squad a much more fearsome squad than it has been.

Cheveldae will give the Jets' adequate regular-season goaltending. His well documented playoff woes in Detroit won't be a factor in Winnipeg until the Jets first make the playoffs. He should be good enough over 84 games to give them a fighting chance.

If you look at this team on paper, it's difficult to imagine them not making the playoffs. But it's also possible the goaltending and defence may not be as good as the Jets think it is.

Either way, the Jets will be in the hunt for a playoff spot. There are just no guarantees they'll get it.

DRAFT PICKS

For a team that was without a first-round pick (because of the Dave Manson deal with Edmonton), the Jets came away with a pretty fair prospect in defenceman Deron Quint.

The Seattle Thunderbird rookie was tabbed as likely to be taken in the first round, but fell all the way to No. 30 overall, where the Jets made their first selection of the day.

Quint is an excellent rushing defenceman with great physical tools. He has to learn to use his teammates better and show that he's capable of playing in heavy pro traffic. But the young American is well worth the risk of a second rounder. His upside is high.

Otherwise, the Jets' draft was notable for another reason. Eight of the 11 picks, including the first seven, originated from teams in the Canadian Hockey League. That was in stark contrast to the Jets' recent drafting trends under former GM Mike Smith, who believed the best prospects for the Jets were from Europe, primarily Russia.

New GM John Paddock figured otherwise this time around.

The real crux of the Jets' draft, though, is the decision to trade for Manson. He had better turn out to be everything Paddock hopes he'll be, because the price was high. Not only did the Jets have to surrender one of the top prospects from this year's draft (No. 4 overall), they gave up 1993 first-rounder Mats Lindgren as well.

It will be well worth monitoring the progress of Lindgren and Jason Bonsignore, the player the Oilers picked with the Jets' No. 4 selection.

1993-94 KEYS

KEY DEALS:

* obtained Dave Manson and 6th round 1994 draft pick from Edmonton for Boris Mironov, 1st and 4th round picks in 1994 draft and right to Mats Lindgren.

Post Season:

* obtained Neil Wilkinson from Chicago for a 1995 third round pick

* obtained Sheldon Kennedy from Detroit for 1995 third round pick.

KEY INJURIES: Teemu Selanne (33 games), Teppo Numminen (27), Alexei Zhamnov (17), Mike Eagles (21).

KEY STAT:

Almost all teams had goal scoring drops last season when defensive hockey took over the game. Interesting to see that many of the teams that relied heavily on offense in 1992-93 are the teams that took the biggest falls in goal scoring and point production.

Quebec, Pittsburgh and Vancouver were ranked second, third and fourth respectively in goals scored in 1992-93. All three teams are on both lists below.

BIGGEST DROPS IN GOALS SCORED

	1992-93	1993-94	Drop
WINNIPEG	322	245	-77
Quebec	351	277	-74
Pittsburgh	367	299	-68
Vancouver	346	279	-67
Hartford	284	227	-57

BIGGEST DROP IN POINT PRODUCTION

	1992-93	1993-94	Drop
WINNIPEG	87	57	-30
Quebec	104	76	-28
Chicago	106	87	-19
Pittsburgh	119	101	-18
Vancouver	101	85	-16

Ultimate Pool Picks

First, a little recap. Bob McKenzie, who wrote last year's Hockey Annual, doesn't participate in hockey pools and admitted calling in a consultant. McKenzie had input, and rightly so, because few know the game and the players as well.

Let me just say this. The consultant guy was some smart dude. Good looking, too.

Let's go through the categories, and rest assured we wouldn't be bothering if there wasn't a measure of success.

In the "10 Players Who Won't Equal Last Season's Totals" category, we were dead right on nine of them. Most weren't even close. The miss was Garry Galley of Philadelphia, who improved from 60 to 70 points.

Another successful category was "10 Players Who Will Improve On Last Season's Totals." Seven out of ten right, with one of the misses being a player injured much of the year.

Very little success on break-out players, however. Keith Primeau fit the bill, and Rob Pearson and Brad May to some degree early in the season. Others had varying levels of progress, while a couple, like Patrick Poulin and Drake Berehowsky flopped badly.

The "sleeper" category had a couple good selections. Alexei Zhitnik, John MacLean, Sandis Ozolinsh, Corey Millen and Bryan Smolinski all were mentioned and all came through.

There are more predictions this year. No consultant though. Too bad. I'm telling you, that guy was a wiz. Modest, too.

The player's list ranks them in order of expected performance. The categories are self-explanatory in most cases, but a guide to their relevance is included.

POWER PLAY POINTS

There would be no such thing as a 100 point scorer in the NHL if it weren't for the power play. Last year, for example, Sergei Fedorov led all scorers at even strength with 81 points. Jaromir Jagr was second at 70, and in rounding out the top ten you get down to players in the fifties.

Those numbers are even more pronounced for defensemen. Most of the top scoring rearguards earned more than half their points with the man advantage. The leader, Brian Leetch, had 67 percent of his points on the power play.

Just getting on the power play makes all the difference. Look at Lyle Odelein with Montreal last season. An established non-scorer, he went a little wacky when he started getting time with the man advantage. In three NHL seasons prior to last year he had point outputs of 2, 8 and 16. Then, he jumped to 40. The difference? Nineteen power play points.

It won't be as easy for him this year because the Canadiens acquired Yves Racine in the off-season, but the example shows the importance of a team's depth chart. Odelein would never have been given the opportunity had he played with the Rangers or any other team rich with offensive defensemen.

The same goes for forwards. You want your players inhabiting the number one unit. Sometimes that's more difficult to do on strong teams because there are others in line for that time. So, oddly enough, if two players are of equal ability, often you want the one playing for the weaker team.

Another thing to consider when using the player rankings is that if there are two players who have around the same number of points, it's better to take the one with fewer from the power play. Players get moved on and off power play units, so one who we know will still score at even strength is a more valuable commodity.

As well, some power plays don't work as well from one year to the next.

Quebec scored 34 fewer man-advantage goals last season than the year before. That affects the points of a number of players. If it picks up this season, and it might with a new coach and Wendel Clark and Peter Forsberg aboard, then individual point totals increase significantly.

AGE

The peak age for NHL players is between 24 and 28. That's an average. Plenty of good scoring before and after for many, but the younger ones can be inconsistent and when a player hits the not-so-magic age of 30, you start rolling the dice.

When a player appears to be losing it, he can be gone quickly. Patience wears thinner in relation to birth certificates. The thinking changes. When he goes into a slump, people start whispering that his career could be winding down. The oldster doesn't have the same time frame to work out slumps as does the younger guy.

Poor teams with older players starting thinking about next year. They're quicker to dump the older guy and bring in the youth.

The ages listed in the player rankings are as of October 1, the starting date of the NHL season.

INJURY STATUS

"A" players miss very few games. They're the ironmen of the league or at least have been for a number of years. Steve Larmer, Jeremy Roenick and Mark Recchi are a few examples.

"B" players are average or haven't been around long enough to be classified. They're injury status is not a consideration when picking them.

"C" guys are injury prone or have established injuries that make them risky picks. Mario Lemieux, Wendel Clark and Pat Flatley are a few of those.

INDICATOR

The indicators show the likelihood of a player increasing his point production considerably (U), staying around the same (E), decreasing considerably (D), increasing gradually (GU) or decreasing gradually (GD).

The indicator is based on a player's projected points over 84 games as opposed to actual totals. For example, it would be ridiculous to grade Pat LaFontaine of Buffalo, who only played in 16 games. His totals project to 95 points over 84 games and that's what his indicator is based upon. In some cases, however, injuries have to be considered. If Mario Lemieux were to play 84 games, he would be the leading scorer, no contest. But, he won't. Even the total predicted for him (120) is very optimistic.

Most of a player's ranking is based on where he fits on the team depth chart - first line, second line, third line, fourth line, fighting for a job, top power play unit, etc.

That means his abilities are often a reflection of his teammates abilities, or the style of play the coach prefers.

Something to keep in mind is that players with "U" or "D" beside their name are the most speculative in nature. Other pool players aren't likely to judge them the same way so you can adjust your selection process accordingly. "U" players can be selected later than listed, while "D" players may still be worth picking higher if they're available.

Many of the indicators also reflect general principles about scoring that have been studied over the years. A couple examples: rookies with big point totals often suffer the sophomore jinx the following season (it's not just a myth); a player who is going to be a top point getter often has his breakout season in his third or fourth year; someone who all of a sudden has a high point total, after eight or nine years in the league, often reverts to form the following season; someone who had a poor season after a number of good ones, especially if he's younger, also often reverts to form.

A number of other things were done to help determine the rankings. A depth chart was constructed to determine where an individual fits on the team; the history, and consistency of each player was checked over his career; playoff performances for younger players from last year, which could be telling us a bigger role is planned for them; and first and second half points were checked for each player. That helps determine if a young player is coming on, an older player is starting to fade, or if his role changed in the latter part of the season.

Good luck. But, hey, be careful out there. There's lots of pool sharks around.

10 POTENTIAL SLEEPERS

OWEN NOLAN, Quebec Nordiques: Nolan played just six games last season because of injury. He's not going to be such a valuable commodity at the draft table, but remember, he had two 70 plus point seasons to his credit before last year and he's still only 23 years old.

ROB BROWN, Los Angeles Kings: A 115 point scorer with Pittsburgh he 1988-90, he sunk slowly into oblivion as team after team became frustrated and gave up on him. Don't ask Brown to play defense because he doesn't know the meaning of the word. But score points? On Los Angeles? Could be a good fit. He got into just one game with Dallas last year, but led the IHL in scoring with 155 points for Kalamazoo and was named the league's most valuable player. As long as the Kings just want the free agent signee to score, he could have a bundle.

PATRICK POULIN, Chicago Blackhawks: Two years ago, Poulin was projected as a future all-star left-winger. Last season, he looked like anything but. The guy is only 21, though, don't give up on him yet. He might be worth a shot in the late rounds of your draft.

PHILLIPE BOUCHER, Buffalo Sabres: The Sabres badly need someone to step up and become a power play quarterback. Boucher could be their man. Or maybe not.

ROB PEARSON, Washington Capitals: The Maple Leafs didn't think much of him, but he showed flashes last year of becoming a good sniper. Not much on pure talent and doesn't use his head all the time, but he's got an excellent shot and a nose for the net. A good start and an injury free season could be the key for him.

KENNY JONSSON, Toronto Maple Leafs: Highly touted rookies aren't normally considered sleepers, but Jonsson isn't known as well as the Radek Bonks, etc. His services are badly needed in Toronto on the power play. It's his job to lose. If he shows something, a 50 point season isn't out of the question.

RAY FERRARO, NY Islanders: Ferraro had a bad year. He's had them before and rebounded in a big way. Maybe he can do it again.

DALE HUNTER, Washington Capitals: With suspensions and injuries, Hunter only earned 38 points, less than half the 79 he earned the previous season. The problem is that Hunter is 34 years old. One more good season? Maybe.

JIM DOWD, New Jersey Devils: Fifteen points in 15 regular season games and eight points in 19 playoff contests. He won't be on many draft lists, so he is an excellent late round sleeper pick. As an added bonus, the team would like him to succeed because he was born in New Jersey.

PETER FORSBERG, Quebec Nordiques: We have to put him somewhere because he's going to be a big scorer in the NHL. He stands a good chance of being the rookie of the year, and a Selanne type inaugural season isn't out of the question. A hundred points? Don't bet the farm on it, but it's a possibility.

10 PLAYERS WHO WON'T EQUAL LAST SEASON'S TOTALS

BOB CORKUM, Mighty Ducks of Anaheim: Once the Ducks get some scorers on board, like Paul Kariya and Valeri Karpov, Corkum will return to his normal game, which is concentrating on keeping the other teams from scoring.

MICHAEL NYLANDER, Calgary Flames: With the Flames so deep at centre and so deep in scoring, Nylander doesn't bring enough to the party to justify a lot of ice time. Not known for playing both ways, he'll drive King nuts. Nylander barely played at all in the playoffs.

NEAL BROTEN, Dallas Stars: A good comeback season with 52 points, but the jig is almost up for Broten, who turns 35 this year.

BOB KUDELSKI, Florida Panthers: His scoring dropped when he moved from Ottawa to the more defensive-minded Florida.

LYLE ODELEIN, Montreal Canadiens: Had a nice run of points because he got on the power play, but the Canadiens obtained power play specialist Yves Racine from Philadelphia in the off-season. Racine and Schneider should get the bulk of point time on the power play, pushing Odelein down a notch.

MIKE GARTNER, Toronto Maple Leafs: Age is catching up to him, finally. He turns 35 this year. He can still skate like the wind, but the scoring touch is slowing down.

VALERI KAMENSKY, Quebec Nordiques: He could have been a contender. Instead he played like a pretender, underachieving with 65 points. Now, his number one line opportunities are gone with Wendel Clark on the scene.

SERGEI ZUBOV, New York Rangers: Guess what? Most everybody will suffer with the loss of Mike Keenan. They're an old team and they'll no longer be driven. A lazy Zubov is still a good Zubov but not a great Zubov.

DOUG BROWN, Pittsburgh Penguins: Twenty-one points better than your career high at age 30 is not an omen of things to come.

DEREK PLANTE, Buffalo Sabres: Too bad, after such a fine season and putting the team ahead of a previous desire to join the U.S. Olympic club. The problem is that Pat LaFontaine will be back, reducing Plante's role. He had 26 power play points last season. Many of those revert to LaFontaine.

10 PLAYERS WHO WILL IMPROVE UPON LAST SEASON'S TOTALS

CHRIS PRONGER, Hartford Whalers: It wasn't exactly a banner season for the highly-touted rookie, on or off the ice. A year can be a big difference for a 19 year old. There's nobody else on the Whalers to carry the offensive load from the defense position. He's the man and it's time to start showing it.

KIRK MULLER, Montreal Canadiens: Last season was just an off year. He was bothered by injuries, but he's still only 28 and a big rebound season is likely.

SHAWN MCEACHERN, Pittsburgh Penguins: He had 21 points last season for Los Angeles and 21 for Pittsburgh. The difference was he accumulated those totals in 22 fewer games for the Penguins after he was traded back to them.

CLAUDE LEMIEUX, New Jersey Devils: Personal problems pertaining to his marriage were a big factor in Lemieux's drop from 81 points to 44. If he can put those behind him, he should return to a level more fitting his abilities.

TEEMU SELANNE, Winnipeg Jets: You don't score 76 goals and 132 points by accident. He only played 51 games last year because of injury and only scored 54 points, but the sophemore jinx is finished with, and he should move back up to elite type numbers.

TONY AMONTE, Chicago Blackhawks: It was an off year for Amonte with just 17 goals and 42 points, after earning 35-34-69 and 33-43-76, in his first two NHL seasons. A full year on the right side of Jeremy Roenick is cure for almost any scoring woes.

MIKE RICCI, Quebec Nordiques: The NHL's most traded player last season (on paper anyway) had only 51 points after earning 78 the season before. He probably moves down the depth chart in Quebec at center with Joe Sakic and probably newcomer Peter Forsberg ahead of him. But, that increases the likelihood of a trade so Quebec can get a quarterback for their powerplay. If he gets traded, look for him to have an excellent season.

TONY GRANATO, Los Angeles Kings: Just seven goals after three seasons of 30, 39 and 37? Granato should just forget about last year. Pretend it didn't happen. All of it, including the stick swinging part.

MICHAL PIVONKA, Washington Capitals: He slumped to just 51 points last season after averaging 76 over the previous three seasons. Back up to the 70 point range.

PETER BONDRA, Washington Capital: Another Capital slumper, he fell from 85 to just 43. A return to form, somewhere between the two, is in order.

A POOLSTER'S GUIDE TO THE COMING SEASON

NAME	TEAM	92/93 GP	PTS	PP PTS	AGE	INJ	IND
100-PLUS POTENTIAL POINTS							
LINDROS	PHI	65	97	27	21	C	U
LAFONTAINE	BUF	16	18	5	29	B	E
LEMIEUX	PIT	22	37	15	28	C	E
RECCHI	PHI	84	107	36	26	A	E
BURE	VAN	76	107	43	23	B	E
ROENICK	CHI	84	107	41	24	A	E
OATES	BOS	77	112	45	32	B	E
FEDOROV	DET	82	120	28	24	B	GD
SHANAHAN	STL	81	102	42	25	B	E
MODANO	DAL	76	93	39	24	B	GU
YZERMAN	DET	58	82	24	29	B	GD
TURGEON,P	NYI	69	94	32	25	B	E
BRIND'AMOUR	PHI	84	96	31	24	A	E
GILMOUR	TOR	83	111	40	31	A	GD
JAGR	PIT	80	99	29	22	B	E
SAKIC	QUE	84	92	33	25	B	GU
SELANNE	WPG	51	54	23	24	B	U
POTENTIAL 75-99 POINTS							
GRETZKY	LA	81	130	61	33	B	D
NEDVED	STL	19	20	6	22	B	U
MOGILNY	BUF	66	79	39	25	C	U
ROBITAILLE	A	83	86	40	28	A	U
LEETCH	NYR	84	79	53	26	B	U
STEVENS,K	PIT	83	88	41	29	B	GU
HULL	STL	81	97	40	30	B	E
NIEUWENDYK	CGY	64	75	28	28	B	GU
ROBERTS	CGY	73	84	29	28	B	E
MACINNIS	STL	75	82	46	31	B	E
SUNDIN	TOR	84	85	27	23	A	GU
REICHEL	CGY	84	93	34	23	B	E
JUNEAU	WSH	74	85	34	26	B	E
SHEPPARD	DET	82	93	34	28	B	E
HOUSLEY	CGY	26	22	11	30	B	U
NEELY	BOS	39	74	27	29	C	GD
DAMPHOUSSE	MTL	84	91	37	26	A	E
FLEURY	CGY	83	85	28	26	A	E
SANDERSON	HFD	82	67	24	22	B	U
MULLER	MTL	76	57	23	28	A	U
PRIMEAU	DET	78	73	14	22	B	GU
TKACHUK	WPG	84	81	38	22	A	E
JANNEY	STL	69	84	40	27	B	GD
FRANCIS	PIT	82	93	41	31	B	GD
BOURQUE	BOS	72	91	52	33	B	GD
MACLEAN	NJ	80	70	19	29	B	GU
FORSBERG	QUE	-	-	-	21	B	-
MURPHY,J	CHI	81	70	26	26	A	GU
ARNOTT	EDM	78	68	23	19	B	GU
VERBEEK	HFD	84	75	25	30	A	E
KOVALEV	NYR	76	56	13	21	B	U
HAWERCHUK	BUF	1	86	41	31	A	GD
COURTNALL,R	DAL	84	80	21	29	B	E
EMERSON	WPG	83	74	29	27	B	E
MAY	BUF	84	45	12	22	B	U
DUCHESNE,S	STL	36	31	16	29	A	E
RICCI	QUE	83	51	18	22	B	U
NOLAN	QUE	6	4	0	23	C	-
GAGNER	DAL	76	61	19	29	B	GU
BONK	OTT	-	-	-	18	B	-
MESSIER	NYR	76	84	36	33	B	D
GRAVES	NYR	84	79	28	26	A	E
KOZLOV	DET	77	73	19	22	B	E
CASSELS	HFD	79	58	26	25	B	U
BELLOWS	MTL	77	71	27	30	B	E
FERRARO	NYI	82	53	12	30	B	U
RICHER	NJ	80	72	12	28	B	E
KING	NYI	78	70	26	27	B	E
BROWN,R	LA	1	0	0	26	B	-
POTENTIAL 50-74 POINTS							
ZHAMNOV	WPG	61	71	29	24	C	GD
NIEDERMAYER,S	NJ	81	46	14	21	B	U
ZUBOV	NYR	78	89	49	24	B	D
CLARK	QUE	64	76	32	27	C	GD
ANDREYCHUK	TOR	83	99	44	31	A	D
HOGUE	NYI	83	69	18	27	B	E
DAHLEN	SJ	78	69	38	27	B	E
YASHIN	OTT	83	79	27	20	B	E
SMOLINSKI	BOS	83	51	8	22	B	U
BLAKE	LA	84	68	33	24	B	E
MURPHY,L	PIT	84	73	31	33	A	E
PEAKE	WSH	49	29	9	20	B	U
LINDEN	VAN	84	61	10	24	A	GU
WEIGHT	EDM	84	74	28	23	B	E
THOMAS	NYI	78	75	30	31	B	GD
KARIYA	ANA	-	-	-	-	-	-
GRANATO	LA	50	21	2	30	B	U
COFFEY	DET	80	77	36	33	B	GD
O'NEILL	HFD	-	-	-	-	-	-
LEMIEUX,C	NJ	79	44	12	29	B	U
BRADLEY	TB	78	64	21	29	B	E
TURGEON,S	OTT	47	26	13	29	C	U
DOWD	NJ	15	15	7	25	B	-

NAME	TEAM	92/93		PP	AGE	INJ	IND
		GP	PTS	PTS		STATUS	
AMONTE	CHI	79	42	13	24	B	U
HATCHER,K	WSH	72	40	19	28	B	U
STRAKA	PIT	84	64	4	22	B	E
MCEACHERN	PIT	76	42	3	25	B	U
OZOLINSH	SJ	81	64	17	22	B	E
RACINE	MTL	67	52	32	25	B	E
KONOWALCHUK	WSH	62	26	4	21	B	U
RENBERG	PHI	83	82	23	22	B	D
STASTNY	STL	17	16	8	38	B	GD
LARMER	NYR	68	60	21	33	A	GD
MAKAROV	SJ	80	68	21	36	B	E
BELANGER	FLA	70	50	23	25	B	U
RONNING	VAN	76	68	28	29	B	E
BROWN,J	VAN	74	66	34	28	B	E
STEVENS,S	NJ	83	78	25	30	B	GD
DRAKE	WPG	62	40	7	25	B	GU
COURTNALL,G	VAN	82	70	29	32	B	GD
YAKE	ANA	82	51	15	25	B	GU
BURRIDGE	WSH	78	42	13	28	C	U
KAMENSKY	QUE	76	65	14	28	C	GD
LIDSTROM	DET	84	56	18	24	A	E
WHITNEY	SJ	61	40	9	22	B	GU
LARIONOV	SJ	60	56	16	33	B	E
GALLEY	PHI	81	70	35	31	B	GD
ZALAPSKI	CGY	69	47	21	26	B	E
MALAKHOV	NYI	76	57	27	26	B	E
BARNES	FLA	77	47	16	23	B	U
FALLOON	SJ	83	53	12	22	B	GU
KOVALENKO	QUE	58	33	11	23	B	U
MULLEN,J	PIT	84	70	13	37	B	GD
SIMPSON	BUF	22	16	6	27	C	E
TURCOTTE	HFD	32	19	5	26	B	U
TOCCHET	PIT	51	40	16	30	C	E
CIGER	EDM	84	57	18	24	B	E
DAIGLE	OTT	84	51	14	19	B	U
GARPENLOV	SJ	80	53	15	26	B	GU
AUDETTE	BUF	77	59	28	25	B	E
PRONGER	HFD	81	30	13	19	B	U
SACCO	ANA	84	37	8	25	B	U
RIDLEY	TOR	81	70	22	31	A	GD
SYDOR	LA	84	35	10	22	A	U
KLIMA	TB	75	55	22	29	B	E
BERANEK	PHI	80	49	9	24	B	GU
SUTER	CHI	41	18	13	30	B	U
SHANNON,DN	WPG	77	58	18	24	B	E
MELLANBY	FLA	80	60	24	28	B	E
LECLAIR	MTL	74	43	0	25	B	GU
CHELIOS	CHI	76	60	33	32	B	E

NAME	TEAM	92/93		PP	AGE	INJ	IND
		GP	PTS	PTS		STATUS	
WALZ	CGY	53	38	9	24	B	GU
TUCKER	TB	66	40	30	7	C	E
KUDELSKI	FLA	86	70	30	30	B	D
IAFRATE	BOS	79	58	25	28	B	E
PIVONKA	WSH	82	50	15	28	B	E
RANHEIM	HFD	82	27	0	28	B	U
KEANE	MTL	80	40	17	27	D	CU
DIONNE	MTL	74	45	10	24	B	GU
ZELEPUKIN	NJ	82	57	12	25	B	E
NIEDERMAYER,R	FLA	65	26	12	19	B	U
NORTON	SJ	64	40	11	28	C	E
MCINNIS	NYI	81	56	8	23	B	E
PEARSON,ROB	WSH	67	30	4	23	B	U
ROLSTON	NJ	-	-	-	-	-	-
CHIASSON	CGY	82	46	17	27	B	E
GRATTON	TB	84	42	16	19	B	GU
NASLUND,M	PIT	71	11	1	21	B	U
CULLEN	F/A	53	30	6	30	B	E
JOSEPH	TB	76	31	18	25	B	U
HOULDER	ANA	80	39	17	27	B	U
ADAMS	VAN	68	37	10	31	C	GU
KHRISTICH	WSH	83	58	15	25	B	E
LUMME	VAN	83	55	16	28	B	E
ELYNUIK	OTT	67	28	7	26	B	U
DONATO	BOS	84	54	13	25	A	E
POULIN,P	CHI	67	28	3	21	B	U
CICCARELLI	DET	66	57	20	34	C	D
BONDRA	WSH	69	43	10	26	B	E
SCHNEIDER	MTL	75	52	27	25	B	E
CORSON	EDM	64	54	21	28	B	GD
COLE	TB	81	43	15	27	B	GU
TIKKANEN	NYR	83	54	21	29	B	E
GREEN	NYI	83	40	5	23	B	GU
DAWE	BUF	32	13	5	21	B	U
KURRI	LA	81	77	39	34	B	D
TVERDOSKY	ANA	-	-	-	-	B	-
FLATLEY	NYI	64	42	4	30	C	E
CRAVEN	VAN	78	55	14	30	B	E

49 POINTS OR LESS

NAME	TEAM	GP	PTS	PP PTS	AGE	INJ	IND
MIRONOV	TOR	76	36	18	28	B	U
COTE	WSH	84	51	14	28	B	E
WESLEY	BOS	81	58	39	25	B	GD
KLATT	DAL	61	38	9	23	B	E
SEMENOV	ANA	49	30	11	32	C	GD
SILLINGER	DET	62	29	4	23	B	GU
MURRAY	BOS	81	31	0	21	B	U
JONSSON	TOR	-	-	-	19	B	-
LEACH	BOS	42	15	3	28	B	U

NAME	TEAM	92/93 GP	92/93 PTS	PP PTS	AGE	INJ STATUS	IND STATUS
ZHITNIK	LA	81	52	29	21	B	E
HATCHER	DAL	83	31	7	22	B	U
YUSHKEVICH	PHI	75	30	4	22	B	U
HILL	OTT	68	27	14	23	B	U
ELIK	SJ	79	66	30	28	B	D
ZAMUNER	TB	59	12	0	25	B	U
LAFAYETTE	VAN	49	7	1	21	B	U
KHYMLEV	BUF	72	58	28	30	B	D
PLANTE	BUF	77	56	26	24	B	GD
NYLANDER	CGY	73	55	11	21	B	D
KRON	HFD	77	50	7	27	B	E
MILLER,KEV	STL	74	48	13	29	B	E
LEBEAU	ANA	66	26	10	26	B	GU
PEARSON	EDM	72	37	6	24	B	GU
CHORSKE	NJ	76	41	1	28	B	E
RUCINSKY	QUE	60	32	9	23	B	GU
GARTNER	TOR	81	64	20	34	A	D
CRAIG	DAL	72	37	12	23	B	GU
KRAVCHUK	EDM	81	50	24	28	B	E
CAVALLINI	DAL	74	44	16	27	B	E
TINORDI	DAL	61	24	10	28	C	E
DIPIETRO	MTL	70	33	6	24	B	E
GAUDREAU	SJ	84	35	15	23	B	GU
MANSON	WPG	70	21	6	27	B	U
MANDERVILLE	TOR	67	16	0	23	B	U
HUNTER,D	WSH	52	38	7	34	B	D
SWEENEY,T	ANA	78	43	11	27	B	E
BOUCHER	BUF	38	14	8	21	B	U
TODD	LA	47	22	6	26	B	E
CHAMBERS	TB	66	34	18	27	B	E
CREIGHTON	TB	53	20	4	29	B	GU
KRUPP	QUE	41	21	7	29	B	E
MATTEAU	NYR	77	38	4	25	B	E
YSEBAERT	CHI	71	35	12	28	B	GU
BODGER	BUF	75	39	24	28	C	E
VALK	ANA	78	45	8	26	B	E
MCPHEE	DAL	79	35	1	34	B	E
CARSON	HFD	59	28	9	26	B	E
RICE	EDM	63	32	10	23	B	GU
JONES,K	WSH	68	35	9	25	B	E
SEMAK	NJ	54	29	6	28	B	E
NUMMINEN	WPG	57	23	13	26	B	GU
CZERKAWSKI	BOS	4	3	1	22	B	-
KISIO	CGY	51	30	11	35	C	E
HILL	OTT	68	27	14	24	B	GU
DONNELLY	LA	81	42	9	29	B	E
JOVANOVSKI	FLA	-	-	-	-	-	-
DRUCE	LA	55	31	1	28	B	E

NAME	TEAM	92/93 GP	92/93 PTS	PP PTS	AGE	INJ STATUS	IND STATUS
MURPHY,G	FLA	84	43	28	27	B	E
DRIVER	NJ	66	32	17	32	B	E
YOUNG	QUE	76	51	17	27	B	GD
TITOV	CGY	76	45	10	28	B	GD
BONK	ANA	-	-	-	-	-	-
JOHANSSON	WSH	84	42	16	27	B	E
WOOD	BUF	84	38	4	30	A	E
NEMCHINOV	NYR	76	49	7	30	B	E
SHANTZ	CHI	52	16	1	20	B	E
SKRUDLAND	FLA	79	40	0	31	C	E
GUERIN	NJ	81	44	9	22	B	E
LOMAKIN	FLA	76	47	16	30	B	D
PETROV	MTL	55	27	0	23	B	E
NICHOLLS	FA	61	46	11	33	B	GD
SMEHLIK	BUF	84	41	10	24	B	E
ELLETT	TOR	68	43	29	30	B	GD
DINEEN	PHI	71	42	9	30	B	E
NOONAN	NYR	76	41	19	28	B	E
BRUNET	MTL	71	30	0	26	B	E
KOZLOV, VICTOR	SJ	-	-	-	19	B	-
ERREY	SJ	64	30	11	30	B	E
STUMPEL	BOS	59	23	3	22	B	U
BROTEN,N	DAL	79	52	11	34	B	D
MCSORLEY	LA	65	31	13	31	B	E
LAPOINTE	QUE	59	28	1	25	B	E
DALGARNO	NYI	73	30	4	27	B	E
CORKUM	ANA	76	51	6	26	B	D
SUTTER,B	CHI	73	38	6	32	B	E
SWEENEY,B	BUF	60	25	5	30	B	E
RUUTTU	CHI	54	29	7	30	B	E
LEDYARD	DAL	84	46	26	32	B	GD
GELINAS	VAN	64	28	5	24	B	E
JOHNSON,G	DET	52	17	2	23	B	GU
STADJUHAR	EDM	-	-	-	19	B	-
MACIVER	OTT	53	23	13	30	C	E
HOLIK	NJ	70	33	3	23	B	E
KARPOV	ANA	-	-	-	-	-	-
LAPOINTE,M	DET	50	16	2	21	B	GU
MILLER,KEL	WSH	84	39	1	31	A	E
SLANEY	WSH	47	16	7	22	B	U
BEREHOWSKY	TOR	49	10	8	22	B	U
BEERS	EDM	82	43	24	27	B	GD
FEDYK	PHI	72	38	7	27	B	E
VAN ALLEN	ANA	80	33	8	27	B	E
LAMB	PHI	85	36	11	30	C	E
STEEN	WPG	76	51	18	34	B	E
MILLEN	NJ	78	50	11	30	B	D
SLEGR	VAN	78	38	20	23	B	E

NAME	TEAM	92/93		PP	AGE	INJ	IND
		GP	PTS	PTS		STATUS	
SAVARD	TB	74	46	13	33	B	D
PROKHOROV	STL	55	25	3	27	B	E
FRASER	QUE	60	37	7	25	B	GD
WEINRICH	CHI	62	28	13	27	B	E
GILCHRIST	DAL	76	31	4	27	B	E
ZEZEL	TOR	41	16	0	29	B	E
BUTSAYEV	SJ	59	23	5	23	B	E
BRISEBOIS	MTL	53	23	9	23	B	E
KONSTANTINOV	DET	80	33	4	27	B	E
CARPENTER	NJ	76	33	1	31	B	E
PEDERSON,TOM	SJ	4	25	12	23	B	E
BROWN,D	PIT	77	55	3	30	B	D
DOURIS	ANA	74	34	6	28	B	GD
EVASON	DAL	80	44	11	30	B	GD
PATRICK	CGY	68	35	18	31	C	E
PRESLEY	BUF	65	25	1	29	C	E
GRAHAM	CHI	67	33	1	35	B	GD
LOWRY	FLA	80	37	9	29	B	GD

NAME	TEAM	92/93		PP	AGE	INJ	IND
		GP	PTS	PTS		STATUS	
OLAUSSON	EDM	73	35	21	27	B	E
HALLER	PHI	68	13	4	23	B	U
BABYCH	VAN	73	32	8	33	B	E
DESJARDINS	MTL	84	35	16	25	B	E
KRYGIER	WSH	66	30	1	28	B	E
MCLLWAIN	OTT	66	43	5	27	B	D
SMITH,S	CHI	57	27	11	31	B	E
MIRONOV	EDM	79	31	20	22	B	E
SIMON	BUF	15	1	1	22	B	U
ODELEIN	MTL	79	40	19	26	B	D
FITZGERALD	FLA	83	32	3	26	B	E
HULL,J	FLA	69	26	0	25	B	E
BOZON	STL	80	25	0	27	B	E
BENNING	FLA	73	30	13	28	B	E
QUINTAL	WPG	81	26	6	25	B	E
CARBONNEAU	MTL	79	38	0	34	B	GD
HUGHES	BOS	77	24	1	28	B	E
SVOBODA	BUF	60	16	10	28	C	E

Townsend's Grab Bag

10 BEST GOALS AGAINST AVERAGES (Minimum 1200 minutes)

1. Dominik Hasek   Buf.   1.95
2. Martin Brodeur   N.J.   2.40
3. Patrick Roy   Mtl.   2.50
4. John Vanbiesbrouck   Fla.   2.53
5. Mike Richter   NYR   2.57
6. Damian Rhodes   Tor.   2.62
7. Darcy Wakaluk   Dal.   2.64
8. Ed Belfour   Chi.   2.67
9. Daren Puppa   TB   2.71
10. Chris Terreri   N.J.   2.72

10 WORST GOALS AGAINST AVERAGES (Minimum 1200 minutes)

1. Craig Billington   Ott.   4.59
2. Darrin Madeley   Ott.   4.36
3. Tommy Soderstrom   Phi.   4.01
4. Grant Fuhr   Buf.   3.68
5. Kelly Hrudey   L.A.   3.68
6. Tim Cheveldae   Det./Wpg   3.64
7. Bob Essensa   Wpg./Det   3.60
8. Kay Whitmore   Van.   3.53
9. Bill Ranford   Edm.   3.48
10. Stephane Fiset   Que.   3.39

TOP 10 GOALIES YOU'D WANT IF THE PLAYOFFS STARTED TOMORROW

1. Patrick Roy   Mtl.
2. Bill Ranford   Edm.
3. John Vanbiesbrouck   Fla.
4. Dominik Hasek   Buf.
5. Mike Richter   NYR
6. Felix Potvin   Tor.
7. Curtis Joseph   St.L.
8. Kirk McLean   Van.
9. Ed Belfour   Chi.
10. Mike Vernon   Det.

THE TEN BEST COACHES

1. Mike Keenan   St.L.
2. Roger Neilson   Fla.

3. John Muckler   Buf.

4. Jacques Lemaire   N.J.

5. Pat Burns   Tor.

6. Dave King   Cgy.

7. Bob Gainey   Dal.

8. Scotty Bowman   Det.

9. Pat Quinn   Van.

10. Kevin Constantine   S.J.

10 FUTURE HALL OF FAMERS CURRENTLY PLAYING IN THE NHL

1. Wayne Gretzky
2. Mario Lemieux
3. Ray Bourque
4. Patrick Roy
5. Mike Gartner
6. Brian Trottier
7. Mark Messier
8. Jari Kurri
9. Paul Coffey
10. Denis Savard

10 BEST GENERAL MANAGERS

1. Cliff Fletcher   Tor.
2. Harry Sinden   Bos.
3. Serge Savard   Mtl.
4. David Poile   Wsh.
5. Mike Keenan   St.L.
6. Craig Patrick   Pit.
7. Glen Sather   Edm.
8. Bob Clarke   Phi.

9. Pat Quinn   Van.
10. Neil Smith   NYR

TOP GOAL SCORERS

1. Pavel Bure	Van.	60
2. Brett Hull	St.L.	57
3. Sergei Fedorov	Det.	56
4. Dave Andreychuk	Tor.	53
5. Brendan Shanahan	St.L.	52
Ray Sheppard	Det.	52
Adam Graves	NYR	52
8. Cam Neely	Bos.	50
Mike Modano	Dal.	50
10.Wendel Clark	Tor.	46
Jeremy Roenick	Chi.	46

10 TOP ASSIST SCORERS

1. Wayne Gretzky	L.A.	92
2. Doug Gilmour	Tor.	84
3. Adam Oates	Bos.	80
4. Sergei Zubov	NYR	77
5. Ray Bourque	Bos.	71
6. Craig Janney	St.L.	68
7. Jaromir Jagr	St.L.	67
Mark Recchi	Phi.	67
9. Joe Juneau	Bos.-Wsh.	66
Ron Francis	Pit.	66

10 TOP POINT SCORERS

1. Wayne Gretzky	L.A.	130
2. Sergei Fedorov	Det.	120

3. Adam Oates	Bos.	112		Kevin Stevens	Pit.	41
4. Doug Gilmour	Tor.	111		Jeremy Roenick	Chi.	41
5. Pavel Bure	Van.	107		Dale Hawerchuk	Buf.	41
Jeremy Roenick	Chi.	107		Ron Francis	Pit.	41
Mark Recchi	Phi.	107		Jeff Brown	St.L-Van	41
8. Brendan Shanahan	St.L.	102				
9. Dave Andreychuk	Tor.	99				
Jaromir Jagr	Pit.	99				

MOST EVEN STRENGTH POINTS

1. Sergei Fedorov	Det.	81
2. Jaromir Jagr	Pit.	70
3. Mark Recchi	Phi.	69
4. Eric Lindros	Phi.	67
5. Doug Gilmour	Tor.	66
6. Wayne Gretzky	L.A.	62
Rod Brind'Amour	Phi.	62
Adam Oates	Bos.	62
9. Martin Straka	Pit.	60
10. Mikael Renberg	Phi.	59
Russ Courtnall	Dal.	59
Jeremy Roenick	Chi.	59

10 MOST POWER PLAY GOALS

1. Pavel Bure	Van.	25
Brett Hull	St.L.	25
3. Luc Robitaille	L.A.	24
Jeremy Roenick	Chi.	24
5. Keith Tkachuk	Wpg.	22
6. Wendel Clark	Tor.	21
Dave Andreychuk	Tor.	21
Kevin Stevens	Tor.	21
9. Cam Neely	Bos.	20
Adam Graves	NYR	20

MOST POWER PLAY POINTS

1. Wayne Gretzky	L.A.	61
2. Brian Leetch	NYR	53
3. Ray Bourque	Bos.	52
4. Sergei Zubov	NYR	49
5. Al MacInnis	Cgy.	46
6. Adam Oates	Bos.	45
7. Dave Andreychuk	Tor.	44
8. Pavel Bure	Van.	43
9. Brendan Shanahan	St.L.	42
10. Brett Hull	St.L.	41

10 MOST SHORT-HANDED POINTS

1. Sergei Fedorov	Det.	11
2. Mark Messier	NYR	9
3. Brendan Shanahan	St.L.	8
Dave Hannan	Buf.	8
5. Wayne Presley	Buf.	7
Jeremy Roenick	Chi.	7
Pierre Turgeon	NYI	7
Wayne Gretzky	L.A.	7
Jari Kurri	L.A.	7
Jyrki Lumme	Van.	7

TOP TEN MOST PENALIZED PLAYERS

1. Tie Domi	Wpg.	347
2. Shane Churla	Dal.	333
3. Warren Rychel	L.A.	322
4. Craig Berube	Wsh.	305
5. Kelly Chase	St.L.	278
6. Lyle Odelein	Mtl.	276
7. Bob Probert	Det.	275
8. Rob Ray	Buf.	274
9 Todd Ewen	Ana.	272
Marc Potvin	Hfd.	272

TOP TEN LEAST PENALIZED PLAYERS (Minimum 70 games)

1. Zdeno Ciger	Edm.	8
Robert Kron	Hfd.	8
3. Ulf Dahlen	S.J.	10
4. Scott Young	Que.	14
5. Jesse Belanger	Fla.	16
Igor Kravchuk	Edm.	16
Stephane Richer	N.J.	16
8. Doug Brown	Pit.	18
Bob Corkum	Ana.	18
Joe Sakic	Que.	18

TOP TEN IN GAME WINNING GOALS

1. Cam Neely	Bos.	13
2. Sergei Fedorov	Det.	10
Vincent Damphousse	Mtl.	10
4. Eric Lindros	Phi.	9
Pavel Bure	Van.	9
Stephane Richer	N.J.	9
Joe Mullen	Pit.	9
Joe Sakic	Que.	9
9. Dave Andreychuk	Tor.	8
Wendel Clark	Tor.	8

TOP TEN POINT SCORING DEFENSEMEN

1. Ray Bourque	Bos.	91
2. Sergei Zubov	NYR	89
3. Al MacInnis	Cgy.	82
4. Brian Leetch	NYR	79
5. Scott Stevens	NJ	78
6. Paul Coffey	Det.	77
7. Larry Murphy	Pit.	73
8. Garry Galley	Phi.	70
9. Rob Blake	L.A.	68
10. Jeff Brown	StL-Van	66

TOP TEN ROOKIE POINT SCORERS

1. Mikael Renberg	Phi.	82
2. Alexei Yashin	Ott.	79
3. Jason Arnott	Edm.	68
4. Derek Plante	Buf.	56
5. Bryan Smolinski	Bos.	51
Alexandre Daigle	Ott.	51
7. Jesse Belanger	Fla.	50
8. Chris Gratton	TB	42
9. Iain Fraser	Que.	37
10. Boris Mironov	Wpg-Edm	31

TOP TEN SHOTS

1. Brendan Shanahan	St.L.	397
2. Brett Hull	St.L.	392
3. Ray Bourque	Bos.	386
4. Pavel Bure	Van.	374
5. Sergei Fedorov	Det.	337
6. Dave Andreychuk	Tor.	333
7. Brian Leetch	NYR	328
8. Al MacInnis	Cgy.	324
9. Rob Blake	L.A.	304
10. Al Iafrate	Wsh-Bos	299

TOP 10 FEWEST SHOTS (Minimum 70 games)

1. Dave Brown	Phi.	16
2. Mick Vukota	NYI	26
3. Doug Zmolek	SJ-Dal	32
4. Jim McKenzie	Hfd-Dal-Pit	33
5. Stu Grimson	Ana.	34
Rob Ray	Buf.	34
7. Keith Acton	Wsh-NYI	35
8. Dean Kennedy	Wpg.	38
9. Sandy McCarthy	Cgy.	39
10. Dave Hannan	Buf.	40

10 BEST PLUS/MINUS RECORDS

1. Scott Stevens	N.J.	+53
2. Sergei Fedorov	Det.	+48
3. Nicklas Lidstrom	Det.	+43
4. Frank Musil	Cgy.	+38
5. Gary Roberts	Cgy.	+37
6. Valeri Zelepukin	N.J.	+36
7. Al MacInnis	Cgy.	+35
8. Keith Primeau	Det.	+34
Scott Niedermayer	N.J.	+34
10. Sylvain Lefebvre	Tor.	+33

10 WORST PLUS/MINUS RECORDS

1. Gord Dineen	Ott.	-52
2. Darren Rumble	Ott.	-50
3. Alexei Yashin	Ott.	-49
4. Alexandre Daigle	Ott.	-45
5. Mark Lamb	Ott-Phi	-44
6. Andrew McBain	Ott.	-41
7. Brad Shaw	Ott.	-41
8. Dave McLlwain	Ott.	-40
9. Thomas Steen	Wpg.	-38
10. Nelson Emerson	Wpg.	-38

10 BEST FACEOFF MEN

1. Brent Sutter	Chi.
2. Peter Zezel	Tor.
3. Joel Otto	Cgy.
4. Ron Sutter	Phi.
5. Craig MacTavish	Phi.
6. Ron Francis	Pit.
7. Mike Eastwood	Tor.
8. Adam Oates	Bos.
9. Trevor Linden	Van.
10. Sergei Fedorov	Det.

10 POSSIBLE CHRIS BERMANISMS

Steve (Dunk) Duchesne

Maxim (Place Your) Bets

Adam (Sow Your Wild) Oates

Tim (Muddy) Watters

Mike (Peachy) Keane

John (Chocolate) LeClair

Darren (Let's Get Ready To) Rumble

Tony (Peppermint) Twist

Jason (Wild and) Wooley

Doug (You've got to carry that) Weight

TOP TEN WORST SCORERS

		Gms	Pts
1. Herb Raglan	Ott.	29	0
2. Joe Day	NYI	24	0
3. Bryan Erickson	Wpg.	16	0
4. Jamie Huscroft	Bos.	36	1
5. Greg Smyth	Fla-Tor-Chi	61	2
6. Mike Needham	Pit-Dal	30	1
7. Andrew McKim	Bos.	29	1
8. Todd Harkins	Hfd.	28	1
9. Brian Curran	Wsh.	26	1
10. Alexei Kudashov	Tor.	25	1

TOP FIRST HALF POINT SCORERS (After his team had played 42 games)

1. Wayne Gretzky	L.A.	75
2. Sergei Fedorov	Det.	74
3. Mark Recchi	Phi.	56
4. Joe Sakic	Que.	53

Mike Modano	Dal.	53
6. Brett Hull	St.L.	52
Luc Robitaille	L.A.	52
8. Dave Andreychuk	Tor.	51
Doug Gilmour	Tor.	51
Craig Janney	St.L.	51
Jeremy Roenick	Chi.	51
Alexei Zhamnov	Wpg.	51

TOP TEN SECOND HALF POINT SCORERS

1. Pavel Bure	Van.	65
2. Eric Lindros	Phi.	62
3. Doug Gilmour	Tor.	60
4. Steve Yzerman	Det.	58
5. Adam Oates	Bos.	57
6. Rod Brind'Amour	Phi.	56
Jeremy Roenick	Chi.	56
8. Wayne Gretzky	L.A.	55
9. Robert Reichel	Cgy.	54
10. Vincent Damphousse	Mtl.	53
Brett Hull	St.L.	53

1993-94 Complete Season Stats

ANAHEIM MIGHTY DUCKS

POS	NO	PLAYER	GP	G	A	PTS	+/-	PIM	PP	SH	GW	GT	S	PCTG
C	25	TERRY YAKE	82	21	31	52	2	44	5	0	2	0	188	11.2
R	20	BOB CORKUM	76	23	28	51	4	18	3	3	0	1	180	12.8
L	18	GARRY VALK	78	18	27	45	8	100	4	1	5	0	165	10.9
L	8	TIM SWEENEY	78	16	27	43	3	49	6	1	2	0	114	14.0
D	23	BILL HOULDER	80	14	25	39	18-	40	3	0	3	0	187	7.5
R	14	JOE SACCO	84	19	18	37	11-	61	3	1	2	1	206	9.2
L	16	PETER DOURIS	74	12	22	34	5-	21	1	0	1	0	142	8.5
C	22	SHAUN VAN ALLEN	80	8	25	33	0	64	2	2	1	0	104	7.7
C	19	ANATOLI SEMENOV	49	11	19	30	4-	12	4	0	2	0	103	10.7
D	6	SEAN HILL	68	7	20	27	12-	78	2	1	1	0	165	4.2
C	47	STEPHAN LEBEAU	56	15	11	26	4-	22	6	0	3	1	98	15.3
C	21	*PATRIK CARNBACK	73	12	11	23	8-	54	3	0	2	0	81	14.8
D	2	BOBBY DOLLAS	77	9	11	20	20	55	1	0	1	0	121	7.4
D	4	DAVID WILLIAMS	56	5	15	20	8	42	2	0	0	0	74	6.8
L	24	TROY LONEY	62	13	6	19	5-	88	6	0	1	0	93	14.0
R	36	TODD EWEN	76	9	9	18	7-	272	0	0	2	0	59	15.3
D	39	DON MCSWEEN	32	3	9	12	4	39	1	0	2	0	43	7.0
R	17	*STEVEN KING	36	8	3	11	7-	44	3	0	1	0	50	16.0
D	29	RANDY LADOUCEUR	81	1	9	10	7	74	0	0	0	0	66	1.5
C	10	JARROD SKALDE	20	5	4	9	3-	10	2	0	2	0	25	20.0
D	3	MARK FERNER	50	3	5	8	16-	30	0	0	0	0	44	6.8
R	48	*JOHN LILLEY	13	1	6	7	1	8	0	0	1	0	20	5.0
L	32	STU GRIMSON	77	1	5	6	6-	199	0	0	0	0	34	2.9
D	44	MYLES O'CONNOR	5	0	1	1	0	6	0	0	0	0	7	.0
C	26	ROBIN BAWA	12	0	1	1	3-	7	0	0	0	0	1	.0
C	45	*SCOTT MCKAY	1	0	0	0	0	0	0	0	0	0	1	.0
L	27	LONNIE LOACH	3	0	0	0	2-	2	0	0	0	0	8	.0
D	34	ANATOLI FEDOTOV	3	0	0	0	1-	0	0	0	0	0	1	.0

POS	NO	PLAYER	GP	G	A	PTS	+/-	PIM	PP	SH	GW	GT	S	PCTG
L	43	*MAXIM BETS	3	0	0	0	3-	0	0	0	0	0	1	.0
R	33	JIM THOMSON	6	0	0	0	0	5	0	0	0	0	1	.0
G	31	GUY HEBERT	52	0	0	0	0	2	0	0	0	0	0	.0

BOSTON BRUINS

POS	NO	PLAYER	GP	G	A	PTS	+/-	PIM	PP	SH	GW	GT	S	PCTG
C	12	ADAM OATES	77	32	80	112	10	45	16	2	3	0	197	16.2
D	77	RAY BOURQUE	72	20	80	112	10	45	16	2	3	0	197	16.2
R	8	CAM NEELY	49	50	24	74	12	54	20	0	13	1	185	27.0
D	43	AL IAFRATE	79	15	43	58	16	163	6	0	4	0	299	5.0
D	26	GLEN WESLEY	81	14	44	58	1	64	6	1	1	1	265	5.3
C	21	TED DONATO	84	22	32	54	0	59	9	2	1	1	158	13.9
C	20	*BRYAN SMOLINSKI	83	31	20	51	4	82	4	3	5	0	179	17.3
R	44	GLEN MURRAY	81	18	13	31	1-	48	0	0	4	2	1 4	15.8
R	22	*JOZEF STUMPEL	59	8	15	23	4	14	0	0	1	0	62	12.9
L	17	DAVE REID	83	6	17	232	10	25	0	2	1	0	145	4.1
R	23	STEPHEN HEINZE	77	10	11	21	2-	32	0	2	1	0	183	5.5
D	32	DON SWEENEY	75	6	15	21	29	50	1	2	2	0	136	4.4
L	10	DMITRI KVARTALNOV	39	12	7	19	9-	10	4	0	0	0	68	17.6
R	27	STEPHEN LEACH	42	5	10	15	10-	74	1	0	1	1	89	5.6
R	33	DAN MAROIS	22	7	3	10	4-	18	3	0	0	0	32	21.9
D	34	DAVID SHAW	55	1	9	10	11-	85	0	0	0	0	107	0.9
D	25	PAUL STANTON	71	3	7	10	7-	54	1	0	1	0	136	2.2
C	16	*CAMERON STEWART	57	3	6	9	6-	66	0	0	1	0	55	5.5
D	6	GLEN FEATHERSTONE	58	1	8	9	5-	152	0	0	1	0	55	1.8
D	14	GORDIE ROBERTS	59	1	6	7	13-	40	0	0	0	0	19	5.3
L	48	*FRED KNIPSCHEER	11	3	2	5	3	14	0	0	1	0	15	20.0
R	19	*MARIUSZ CZERKAWSKI	4	2	1	3	2-	0	1	0	0	0	11	18.2
R	11	*SERGEI ZHOLTOK	24	2	1	3	7-	2	1	0	0	0	25	8.0
G	30	JON CASEY	57	0	2	2	0	14	0	0	0	0	0	0.0
L	56	DARREN BANKS	4	0	1	1	0	9	0	0	0	0	3	0.0
D	29	*JOHN GRUDEN	7	0	1	1	3-	2	0	0	0	0	8	0.0
G	37	VINCENT RIENDEAU	26	0	1	1	0	0	0	0	0	0	0	0.0
C	45	*ANDREW MCKIM	29	0	1	1	10-	4	0	0	0	0	22	0.0
D	28	JAMIE HUSCROFT	36	0	1	1	2-	144	0	0	0	0	13	0.0
D	28	MIKHAIL TATARINOV	2	0	0	0	0	2	0	0	0	0	4	0.0
C	29	JON MORRIS	4	0	0	0	2-	0	0	0	0	0	3	0.0
D	36	JIM WIEMER	4	0	0	0	3-	2	0	0	0	0	8	0.0
L	13	GRIGORI PANTELEEV	10	0	0	0	2-	0	0	0	0	0	8	0.0
G	39	JOHN BLUE	18	0	0	0	0	7	0	0	0	0	0	0.0

BUFFALO SABRES

POS	NO	PLAYER	GP	G	A	PTS	+/-	PIM	PP	SH	GW	GT	S	PCTG
C	10	DALE HAWERCHUK	81	35	51	86	10	91	13	1	7	0	227	15.4
R	89	ALEXANDER MOGILNY	66	32	47	79	8	22	17	0	7	1	258	12.4
R	28	DONALD AUDETTE	88	29	30	59	2	41	16	1	4	0	207	14.0
L	13	YURI KHMYLEV	72	27	31	58	13	49	11	0	4	0	171	15.8
C	26	*DEREK PLANTE	77	21	35	56	4	24	8	1	2	0	147	14.3
L	27	BRAD MAY	84	18	27	45	6-	171	3	0	3	0	166	10.8
D	42	RICHARD SMEHLIK	84	14	27	41	22	69	3	3	1	1	106	13.2
D	8	DOUG BODGER	75	7	32	39	8	76	5	1	1	0	144	4.9
L	19	RANDY WOOD	84	22	16	38	11	71	2	2	5	0	161	13.7
R	18	WAYNE PRESLEY	65	17	8	25	18	103	1	5	1	0	93	18.3
C	20	BOB SWEENEY	60	11	14	25	3	94	3	3	1	0	76	14.5
D	41	KEN SUTTON	78	4	20	24	6-	71	1	0	0	0	95	4.2
C	14	DAVE HANNAN	83	6	15	21	10	53	0	3	1	0	40	15.0
C	16	PAT LAFONTAINE	16	5	13	18	4-	2	1	0	0	0	40	12.5
L	22	CRAIG SIMPSON	22	8	8	16	3-	8	2	0	2	0	28	28.6
D	7	PETR SVOBODA	60	2	14	16	11	89	1	0	0	0	80	2.5
D	4	*PHILIPPE BOUCHER	38	6	8	14	1-	29	4	0	1	0	67	9.0
D	5	CRAIG MUNI	82	2	12	14	31	66	0	1	2	0	45	4.4
L	43	*JASON DAWE	32	6	7	13	1	12	3	0	1	0	35	17.1
D	24	RANDY MOLLER	78	2	11	13	5-	154	0	0	0	0	77	2.6
L	32	ROB RAY	82	3	4	7	2	274	0	0	0	0	34	8.8
L	36	*MATTHEW BARNABY	35	2	4	6	7-	106	1	0	0	0	13	15.4
C	40	JAMES BLACK	15	2	3	5	4-	2	2	0	0	0	18	11.1
R	21	*SCOTT THOMAS	32	2	2	4	6-	8	1	0	0	0	26	7.7
L	15	*SERGEI PETRENKO	14	0	4	4	3-	0	0	0	0	0	7	.0
G	31	GRANT FUHR	32	0	4	4	0	16	0	0	0	0	0	0
G	39	DOMINIK HASEK	58	0	3	3	0	6	0	0	0	0	0	.0
C	17	*TODD SIMON	15	0	1	1	3-	0	0	0	0	0	14	.0
D	33	*MARK ASTLEY	1	0	0	0	1-	0	0	0	0	0	2	.0
L	44	*DOUG MACDONALD	4	0	0	0	2-	0	0	0	0	0	3	.0
D	29	*DENIS TSYGUROV	8	0	0	0	1-	8	0	0	0	0	3	.0

CALGARY FLAMES

POS	NO	PLAYER	GP	G	A	PTS	+/-	PIM	PP	SH	GW	GT	S	PCTG
C	26	ROBERT REICHEL	84	40	553	93	20	58	14	0	6	0	249	16.1
R	14	THEOREN FLEURY	83	40	45	85	30	186	16	1	6	0	278	14.4
L	10	GARY ROBERTS	73	41	43	84	37	145	12	3	5	1	202	20.3
D	2	AL MACINNIS	75	28	54	82	35	95	12	1	5	0	324	8.6
C	25	JOE NIEUWENDYK	64	36	39	75	19	51	14	1	7	1	191	18.8
C	92	MICHAEL NYLANDER	73	13	42	55	8	30	4	0	1	2	95	13.7
D	33	ZARLEY ZALAPSKI	69	10	37	47	6-	74	1	0	1	0	156	6.4

POS	NO	PLAYER	GP	G	A	PTS	+/-	PIM	PP	SH	GW	GT	S	PCTG
C	13	GERMAN TITOV	76	27	18	45	20	28	8	3	2	0	153	17.6
C	17	WES WALZ	53	11	27	38	20	16	1	0	0	0	79	13.9
D	6	JAMES PATRICK	68	10	25	35	5-	40	5	1	2	1	91	11.0
C	11	KELLY KISIO	51	7	23	30	6-	28	1	0	1	0	62	11.3
R	22	RONNIE STERN	71	9	20	29	6	243	0	1	3	0	105	8.6
C	29	JOEL OTTO	81	11	12	23	17-	92	3	1	1	0	108	10.2
D	7	MICHEL PETIT	63	2	21	23	5	110	0	0	0	0	103	1.9
D	39	DAN KECZMER	69	1	21	22	8-	60	0	0	0	0	116	.9
D	18	TRENT YAWNEY	58	6	15	21	21	60	1	1	1	1	62	9.7
D	5	CHRIS DAHLQUIST	77	1	11	12	5	52	0	0	0	0	57	108
L	12	PAUL KRUSE	68	3	8	11	6-	185	0	0	0	0	52	5.8
R	15	*SANDY MCCARTHY	79	5	5	10	3-	173	0	0	0	0	39	12.8
C	32	MIKE SULLIVAN	45	4	5	9	1-	10	0	2	1	0	48	8.3
D	3	FRANK MUSIL	75	1	8	9	38	50	0	0	0	0	65	1.5
D	21	BRAD SCHLEGEL	26	1	6	7	4-	4	0	0	0	0	24	4.2
C	42	GUY LAROSE	17	1	3	4	5-	14	0	0	0	0	12	8.3
G	37	*TREVOR KIDD	31	0	4	4	0	4	0	0	0	0	0	.0
L	19	*VESA VIITAKOSKI	8	1	2	3	0	0	1	0	0	0	18	6.7
D	36	*LEONARD ESAU	6	0	3	3	1-	7	0	0	0	0	4	.0
D	4	KEVIN DAHL	33	0	3	3	2-	23	0	0	0	0	20	.0
R	23	GREG PASLAWSKI	15	2	0	2	4-	2	0	0	1	0	13	15.4
L	19	*DAVID HAAS	2	1	1	2	2	7	0	0	0	0	3	33.3
D	34	BRAD MILLER	8	0	1	1	2-	14	0	0	0	0	2	.0
D	6	LEE NORWOOD	16	0	1	1	3	16	0	0	0	0	10	.0
G	31	*JASON MUZZATTI	1	0	0	0	0	0	0	0	0	0	0	.0
C	16	MARK FREER	2	0	0	0	0	4	0	0	0	0	0	.0
D	38	PETER AHOLA	2	0	0	0	0	0	0	0	0	0	1	.0
C	33	*DAVID STRUCH	4	0	0	0	2-	4	0	0	0	0	3	.0
D	34	*KEVIN WORTMAN	5	0	0	0	1	2	0	0	0	0	2	.0
G	1	*ANDREI TREFILOV	11	0	0	0	0	4	0	0	0	0	0	.0
G	30	MIKE VERNON	48	0	0	0	0	14	0	0	0	0	0	.0

CHICAGO BLACKHAWKS

POS	NO	PLAYER	GP	G	A	PTS	+/-	PIM	PP	SH	GW	GT	S	PCTG
C	28	JEREMY ROENICK	84	46	61	107	21	125	24	5	5	1	281	16.4
R	17	JOE MURPHY	81	31	39	70	1	111	7	4	4	0	222	14.0
D	7	CHRIS CHELIOS	46	16	44	60	12	212	7	1	2	0	219	7.3
R	10	TONY AMONT	79	17	25	42	0	37	4	0	4	0	195	8.7
C	12	BRENT SUTTER	73	9	29	38	17	43	3	2	0	0	127	7.1
L	14	PAUL YSEBAERT	71	14	24	35	7-	26	3	0	1	0	151	9.3

POS	NO	PLAYER	GP	G	A	PTS	+/-	PIM	PP	SH	GW	GT	S	PCTG
R	33	DIRK GRAHAM	67	15	18	33	13	45	0	2	5	0	122	12.3
L	16	MICHEL GOULET	56	15	14	30	1	26	3	0	6	0	120	13.3
C	22	CHRISTIAN RUUTTU	54	9	20	29	4-	68	1	1	1	0	96	9.4
L	44	PATRICK POULIN	67	14	14	28	8-	51	2	0	3	0	96	14.6
D	2	ERIC WEINRICH	62	4	24	28	1	33	2	0	2	0	115	3.5
D	5	STEVE SMITH	57	5	22	27	5-	174	1	0	1	0	89	5.6
R	15	RICH SUTTER	83	12	14	26	8-	108	0	0	2	0	122	9.8
L	19	RANDY CUNNEYWORTH	79	13	11	24	1-	100	0	1	2	0	154	8.4
D	20	GARY SUTER	41	6	12	18	12-	38	4	1	0	0	86	7.0
C	11	*JEFF SHANTZ	52	3	13	16	14-	39	0	0	0	0	37	10.8
D	4	KEITH CARNEY	37	4	8	12	14	39	0	0	0	0	37	10.9
D	23	NEIL WILKINSON	72	3	9	12	2	116	1	0	0	0	72	4.2
C	32	*STEVE DUBINSKY	27	2	6	8	1	16	0	0	0	0	20	10.0
D	8	CAM RUSSELL	67	1	7	8	10	200	0	0	0	0	41	2.4
R	29	DARIN KIMBLE	65	4	2	6	2	133	0	0	0	0	17	23.5
D	6	ROBERT DIRK	71	2	3	5	18	131	0	0	0	0	42	4.8
G	30	ED BELFOUR	70	0	4	4	0	61	0	0	0	0	0	.0
R	25	DAVE CHRISTIAN	9	0	3	3	0	0	0	0	0	0	6	.0
D	3	GREG SMYTH	61	1	1	2	4-	183	0	0	0	0	36	2.8
R	55	*SERGEI KRIVOKRASOV	9	1	0	1	2-	4	0	0	0	0	7	14.3
D	58	*IVAN DROPPA	12	0	1	1	2	12	0	0	0	0	13	.0
G	31	JEFF HACKETT	22	0	1	1	0	2	0	0	0	0	0	.0
G	50	*CHRISTIAN SOUCY	1	0	0	0	0	0	0	0	0	0	0	.0
L	34	TONY HORACEK	7	0	0	0	1	53	0	0	0	0	2	.0

DETROIT RED WINGS

POS	NO	PLAYER	GP	G	A	PTS	+/-	PIM	PP	SH	GW	GT	S	PCTG
C	91	SERGEI FEDOROV	82	56	64	120	48	34	13	4	10	0	337	16.6
R	26	RAY SHEPPARD	82	52	41	93	13	26	19	0	5	0	260	20.0
C	19	STEVE YZERMAN	58	24	58	82	11	36	7	3	3	1	217	11.1
D	77	PAUL COFFEY	80	14	63	77	28	106	5	0	3	0	278	5.0
C	13	VYACHESLAV KOZLOV	77	34	39	73	27	50	8	2	6	0	202	16.8
L	55	KEITH PRIMEAU	78	31	42	73	34	173	7	3	4	2	155	20.0
R	22	DINO CICCARELLI	66	28	29	57	10	73	12	0	1	2	153	18.3
D	5	NICKLAS LIDSTROM	84	10	46	56	43	26	4	0	3	0	200	5.0
D	3	STEVE CHIASSON	82	13	33	46	18	122	4	1	2	0	238	5.5
D	16	VLAD. KNOSTANTINOV	80	12	21	33	30	138	1	3	3	0	97	12.4
C	12	MIKE SILLINGER	62	8	21	29	2	10	0	1	1	0	91	8.8
R	25	*DARREN MCCARTY	67	9	17	26	12	181	0	0	2	0	81	11.1
D	4	MARK HOWE	44	4	20	24	16	8	1	0	0	0	72	5.6
L	11	SHAWN BURR	51	10	12	22	12	31	0	1	1	0	64	15.6

POS	NO	PLAYER	GP	G	A	PTS	+/-	PIM	PP	SH	GW	GT	S	PCTG
R	24	BOB PROBERT	66	7	10	17	1-	275	1	0	0	0	105	6.7
C	23	*GREG JOHNSON	52	6	11	17	7-	22	1	1	0	0	48	12.5
R	20	*MARTIN LAPOINTE	50	8	8	16	7	55	2	0	0	0	45	17.8
R	15	SHELDON KENNEDY	61	6	7	13	2-	30	0	1	0	0	60	10.0
C	33	KRIS DRAPER	39	5	8	13	11	31	0	1	0	0	55	9.1
C	27	*MICAH AIVAZOFF	59	4	4	8	1-	38	0	0	0	0	52	7.7
D	2	TERRY CARKNER	68	1	6	7	13	130	0	0	0	0	32	3.1
D	29	SERGEI BAUTIN	60	0	7	7	12-	78	0	0	0	0	39	.0
D	21	BOB HALKIDIS	28	1	4	5	1-	93	0	0	0	0	35	2.9
D	38	*JASON YORK	7	1	2	3	0	2	0	0	0	0	9	11.1
G	35	BOB ESSENSA	69	0	2	2	0	6	0	0	0	0	0	.0
C	38	*TIM TAYLOR	1	1	0	1	1-	0	0	0	0	0	4	25.0
D	29	*AARON WARD	5	1	0	1	2	4	0	0	0	0	3	33.3
L	34	STEVE MALTAIS	4	0	1	1	1-	0	0	0	0	0	2	.0
L	18	MARK PEDERSON	2	0	0	0	4-	2	0	0	0	0	0	.0
G	31	PETER ING	3	0	0	0	0	0	0	0	0	0	0	.0
D	44	*GORD KRUPPKE	9	0	0	0	4-	12	0	0	0	0	5	.0
G	30	*CHRIS OSGOOD	41	0	0	0	0	2	0	0	0	0	0	.0

EDMONTON OILERS

POS	NO	PLAYER	GP	G	A	PTS	+/-	PIM	PP	SH	GW	GT	S	PCTG
C	39	DOUG WEIGHT	84	24	50	74	22-	47	4	1	1	0	188	12.8
C	7	*JASON ARNOTT	78	33	35	68	1	104	10	0	4	1	194	17.0
R	8	ZDENO CIGER	84	22	35	57	44-	8	8	0	1	2	158	13.9
L	9	SHAYNE CORSON	64	25	29	54	8-	118	11	0	3	1	181	14.6
D	21	IGOR KRAVCHUK	81	12	38	50	12-	16	5	0	2	0	197	6.1
D	2	BOB BEERS	82	11	32	43	22-	86	6	0	0	1	187	5.9
L	33	SCOTT PEARSON	72	19	18	37	4-	165	3	0	7	0	160	11.9
D	15	FREDRIKOLAUSSON	73	11	24	35	7-	30	7	0	1	0	126	8.7
R	12	STEVEN RICE	63	17	15	32	10-	36	6	0	1	1	129	13.2
D	30	*BORIS MIRONOV	79	7	24	31	33-	110	5	0	0	1	145	4.8
D	10	ILYA BYAKIN	44	8	20	28	3-	30	6	0	3	0	51	15.7
C	37	*DEAN MCAMMOND	45	6	21	27	12	16	2	0	0	0	52	11.5
C	25	MIKE STAPLETON	81	12	13	25	5-	46	4	0	0	1	102	11.8
R	16	KELLY BUCHBERGER	84	3	18	21	20-	199	0	0	0	0	93	3.2
R	18	*KIRK MALTBY	69	11	8	19	2-	84	0	1	1	0	89	12.4
L	23	VLADIMIR VUJTEK	40	4	15	19	7-	14	1	0	0	0	66	6.1
L	34	*BRENT GRIEVE	27	13	5	18	4	21	4	0	0	1	54	24.1
C	17	SCOTT THORNTON	61	4	7	11	15-	104	0	0	0	0	65	6.2
L	29	LOUIE DEBRUSK	48	4	6	10	9-	185	0	0	0	0	27	14.8
D	35	*ADAM BENNETT	48	3	6	9	8-	49	1	0	0	0	57	5.3

POS	NO	PLAYER	GP	G	A	PTS	+/-	PIM	PP	SH	GW	GT	S	PCTG
L	27	*PETER WHITE	26	3	5	8	1	2	0	0	0	0	18	18.6
C	26	SHJON PODEIN	28	3	5	8	3	8	0	0	0	0	26	11.5
D	22	LUKE RICHARDSON	69	2	6	8	13-	131	0	0	0	0	92	2.2
R	28	*ROMAN OKSIUTA	10	1	2	3	1-	4	0	0	0	0	18	5.6
D	6	IAN HERBERS	22	0	2	2	6-	32	0	0	0	0	16	.0
G	30	BILL RANFORD	71	0	2	2	0	2	0	0	0	0	0	.0
C	36	*TODD MARCHANT 4	4	0	1	1	2-	2	0	0	0	0	0	.0
D	32	GORDON MARK	12	0	1	1	2-	43	0	0	0	0	8	.0
G	1	WAYNE COWLEY	1	0	0	0	0	0	0	0	0	0	0	.0
R	20	*JOZEF CIERNY	1	0	0	0	1-	0	0	0	0	0	0	.0
D	20	JEFF CHYCHRUN	2	0	0	0	1	0	0	0	0	0	2	.0
D	34	*DARCY MARTINI	2	0	0	0	1-	0	0	0	0	0	0	.0
L	20	*BRADLEY ZAVISHZ	2	0	0	0	2-	0	0	0	0	0	1	.0
L	20	*MARK LAFORGE	5	0	0	0	2-	21	0	0	0	0	0	.0
C	19	*TYLER WRIGHT	5	0	0	0	3-	4	0	0	0	0	2	.0
R	34	ALEXANDER KERCH	5	0	0	0	8-	2	0	0	0	0	4	.0
G	31	*FRED BRAITHWAITE	19	0	0	0	0	0	0	0	0	0	0	.0

FLORIDA PANTHERS

POS	NO	PLAYER	GP	G	A	PTS	+/-	PIM	PP	SH	GW	GT	S	PCTG
R	22	BOB KUDELSKI	86	40	30	70	33-	24	17	0	3	1	251	15.9
R	27	SCOTT MELLANBY	80	30	30	60	0	149	17	0	4	1	204	14.7
C	26	*JESSE BELANGER	70	17	33	50	4-	16	11	0	3	1	104	16.3
C	14	STU BARNES	77	23	24	47	4	38	8	1	3	0	172	13.4
L	19	ANDREI LOMAKIN	76	19	28	47	1	26	3	0	2	0	139	13.7
D	5	GORD MURPHY	84	14	29	43	11-	71	9	0	2	3	172	8.1
C	20	BRIAN SKRUDLAND	79	15	25	40	13	136	0	2	1	0	110	13.6
L	10	DAVE LOWRY	80	15	22	37	4-	64	3	0	3	1	122	12.3
R	21	TOM FITZGERALD	83	18	14	32	3-	54	0	3	1	0	144	12.5
D	7	BRIAN BENNING	73	6	24	30	7-	107	2	0	0	0	112	5.4
L	18	MIKE HOUGH	78	6	23	29	3	62	0	1	1	0	106	5.7
R	12	JODY HULL	69	13	13	26	6	8	0	1	5	1	100	13.0
C	44	*ROB NIEDERMAYER	65	9	17	26	11-	51	3	0	2	0	67	13.4
L	11	BILL LINDSAY	84	6	6	12	2-	97	0	0	0	0	90	6.7
D	4	KEITH BROWN	51	4	8	12	11	60	1	0	0	0	52	7.7
D	24	BRENT SEVERYN	67	4	7	11	1-	156	1	0	1	0	93	4.3
D	2	JOE CIRELLA	63	1	9	10	8	99	0	0	0	0	63	1.6
R	17	MIKE FOLIGNO	43	4	5	9	7	53	0	0	0	0	35	11.4
D	25	GEOFF SMITH	77	1	8	9	13-	50	0	0	0	0	35	11.4
L	23	JEFF DANIELS	70	3	5	8	1-	20	0	0	1	0	52	5.8
D	6	PETER ANDERSSON	16	2	2	4	8-	2	0	1	1	0	21	9.5

POS	NO	PLAYER	GP	G	A	PTS	+/-	PIM	PP	SH	GW	GT	S	PCTG
D	3	*PAUL LAUS	39	2	0	2	9	109	0	0	1	0	15	13.3
L	28	*PATRICK LEBEAU	4	1	1	2	0	4	1	0	0	0	4	25.0
G	30	MARK FITZPATRICK	28	0	2	2	0	4	0	0	0	0	0	.0
R	9	JAMIE LEACH	2	1	0	1	2-	0	0	0	0	0	2	50.0
D	41	STEPHANE RICHER	2	0	1	1	1-	0	0	0	0	0	3	.0
L	29	JEFF GREENLAW	4	0	1	1	1-	2	0	0	0	0	6	.0
D	8	DALLAS EAKINS	1	0	0	0	0	0	0	0	0	0	2	.0
C	16	*LEN BARRIE	2	0	0	0	2-	0	0	0	0	0	0	.0
G	33	ELDON REDDICK	2	0	0	0	0	0	0	0	0	0	0	.0
R	15	*DOUG BARRAULT	2	0	0	0	2-	0	0	0	0	0	2	.0
G	34	JOHN VANBIESBROUCK	57	0	0	0	0	38	0	0	0	0	0	.0

HARTFORD WHALERS

POS	NO	PLAYER	GP	G	A	PTS	+/-	PIM	PP	SH	GW	GT	S	PCTG
R	16	PAT VERBEEK	84	37	38	75	15-	177	15	1	3	1	226	16.4
C	8	GEOFF SANDERSON	82	41	26	67	13-	42	15	1	6	2	266	15.4
C	21	ANDREW CASSELS	79	16	42	58	21-	37	8	1	3	0	126	12.7
C	18	ROBERT KRON	77	24	26	50	0	8	2	1	3	0	194	12.4
D	44	*CHRIS PRONGER	81	5	25	30	3-	113	2	0	0	0	174	2.9
L	26	BRIAN PROPP	65	12	17	29	3	44	3	1	2	0	108	11.1
L	23	JOCELYN LEMIEUX	82	18	9	27	3-	82	0	0	2	1	151	11.9
L	14	PAUL RANHEIM	82	10	17	27	18-	22	0	2	2	0	131	7.6
D	5	ALEXANDER GODYNYUK	69	3	19	22	13	75	0	0	1	0	110	2.7
D	4	FRANTISEK KUCERA	76	5	16	21	3-	48	3	0	0	0	122	4.1
C	89	DARREN TURCOTTE	32	4	15	19	13-	17	0	0	0	0	60	6.7
C	17	*TED DRURY	50	6	12	18	15-	36	0	1	1	1	80	7.5
D	6	ADAM BURT	63	1	17	18	4-	75	0	0	0	0	91	1.1
L	24	*JIM STORM	68	6	10	16	4	27	1	0	0	0	84	7.1
C	32	IGOR CHIBIREV	37	4	11	15	7	2	0	0	1	0	30	13.3
D	27	BRYAN MARCHMENT	55	4	11	15	14-	166	0	1	1	0	92	4.3
C	22	MARK JANSSENS	84	2	10	12	13-	137	0	0	0	0	52	3.8
C	39	ROBERT PETROVICKY	33	6	5	11	1-	39	1	0	0	0	33	18.2
R	14	JIM SANDLAK	27	6	2	8	6	32	2	0	1	0	32	18.8
D	10	BRAD MCCRIMMON	65	1	5	6	7-	72	0	0	0	0	39	2.6
L	20	*KEVIN SMYTH	21	3	2	5	1-	10	0	0	0	0	8	37.5
R	29	MARC POTVIN	54	2	3	5	8-	272	0	0	0	0	26	7.7
D	33	*TED CROWLEY	21	1	2	3	1-	10	1	0	0	0	28	3.6
D	45	JOHN STEVENS	9	0	3	3	4	4	0	0	0	0	3	.0
D	25	BOB MCGILL	33	0	3	3	7-	46	0	0	0	0	14	.0
R	15	*TODD HARKINS	28	1	0	1	4-	49	0	0	0	0	15	6.7
G	35	JEFF REESE	20	0	1	1	0	0	0	0	0	0	0	.0

POS	NO	PLAYER	GP	G	A	PTS	+/-	PIM	PP	SH	GW	GT	S	PCTG
C	28	MIKE TOMLAK	1	0	0	0	0	0	0	0	0	0	2	.0
G	35	*MIKE LENARDUZZI	1	0	0	0	0	0	0	0	0	0	0	0.0
L	11	YVON CORRIVEAU	3	0	0	0	0	00	0	0	0	0	0	0.0
G	31	MARIO GOSSELIN	7	0	0	0	0	0	0	0	0	0	0	0.0
D	41	ALLEN PEDERSEN	7	0	0	0	0	1-	9	0	0	0	1	.0
G	40	FRANK PIETRANGELO	19	0	0	0	00	2	0	0	0	0	0	0.0
G	1	SEAN BURKE	47	0	0	0	0	16	0	0	0	0	0	.0

LOS ANGELES KINGS

POS	NO	PLAYER	GP	G	A	PTS	+/-	PIM	PP	SH	GW	GT	S	PCTG
C	99	WAYNE GRETZKY	81	38	92	130	25-	20	14	4	0	1	233	16.3
L	20	LUC ROBITAILLE	83	44	42	86	20-	86	24	0	3	0	267	16.5
L	17	JARI KURRI	81	31	46	77	24-	48	14	4	3	1	198	15.7
D	4	ROB BLAKE	84	20	48	68	7-	137	7	0	6	0	304	6.6
D	2	ALEXEI ZHITNIK	81	12	40	52	11-	101	11	0	1	1	227	5.3
L	11	MIKE DONNELLY	81	21	21	42	2	34	4	2	3	0	177	11.9
D	25	DARRYL SYDOR	84	8	27	35	9-	94	1	0	0	0	146	5.5
R	19	JOHN DRUCE	55	14	17	31	16	50	1	1	0	0	104	13.5
D	33	MARTY MCSORLEY	65	7	24	31	12-	194	1	0	1	1	160	4.4
L	15	PAT CONACHER	77	15	13	28	0	71	0	3	1	0	98	15.3
C	12	KEVIN TODD	47	8	14	22	3-	24	4	0	1	0	65	12.3
L	21	TONY GRANATO	50	7	14	21	2-	150	2	0	0	0	117	6.0
L	10	WARREN RYCHEL	80	10	9	19	19-	322	0	0	3	0	105	3.5
C	13	*ROBERTLANG	32	9	10	19	7	10	0	0	0	0	41	22.0
D	22	CHARLIE HUDDY	79	5	13	18	4	71	1	0	0	0	134	3.7
R	9	DIXON WARD	67	12	3	15	22-	82	4	0	1	0	90	13.3
D	5	TIM WATTERS	60	1	9	10	11-	67	0	1	0	0	38	2.6
D	29	DONALD DUFRESNE	60	2	6	8	7-	58	0	0	0	0	56	3.6
D	6	DOUG HOUDA	61	2	6	8	19-	188	0	0	0	0	32	6.3
R	18	DAVE TAYLOR	33	4	3	7	1-	28	0	1	2	0	39	10.3
C	14	GARY SHUCHUK	56	3	4	7	8-	30	0	0	1	0	55	5.5
D	42	DOMINIC LAVOIE	8	3	3	6	2-	2	2	0	1	0	21	14.3
D	7	JIM PAEK	59	1	5	6	8-	18	0	0	0	0	35	2.9
C	26	BRIAN MCREYNOLDS	20	1	3	4	2-	4	0	0	0	0	10	10.0
D	24	MARK HARDY	16	0	3	3	5-	27	0	0	0	0	8	.0
L	37	*DAN CURRIE	5	1	1	2	1-	0	0	0	0	0	12	8.3
L	23	PHILIP CROWE	31	0	2	2	4	77	0	0	0	0	5	.0
L	45	*KEITH REDMOND	12	1	0	1	3-	20	0	0	0	0	9	11.1
D	3	BRENT THOMPSON	24	1	0	1	1-	81	0	0	0	0	9	11.1
D	50	BOB JAY	3	0	1	1	2-	0	0	0	0	0	2	.0
C	28	*GUY LEVEQUE	5	0	1	1	1	2	0	0	0	0	3	.0

POS	NO	PLAYER	GP	G	A	PTS	+/-	PIM	PP	SH	GW	GT	S	PCTG
C	8	ROB MURPHY	8	0	1	1	3-	22	0	0	0	0	4	.0
G	32	KELLY HRUDEY	64	0	1	1	0	6	0	0	0	0	0	.0
G	41	*DAVID GOVERDE	1	0	0	0	0	0	0	0	0	0	0	.0
D	51	*JUSTIN HOCKING	1	0	0	0	0	0	0	0	0	0	0	.0
G	1	RICK KNICKLE	4	0	0	0	0	0	0	0	0	0	0	.0
L	27	DAVE THOMLINSON	7	0	0	0	6-	21	0	0	0	0	6	.0
G	35	ROBB STAUBER	22	0	0	0	0	18	0	0	0	0	0	.0

MONTREAL CANADIENS

POS	NO	PLAYER	GP	G	A	PTS	+/-	PIM	PP	SH	GW	GT	S	PCTG
L	25	VINCENT DAMPHOUSSE	84	40	51	91	0	75	13	0	10	1	274	14.6
L	23	BRIAN BELLOWS	77	33	38	71	9	36	13	0	2	1	251	13.1
L	11	KIRK MULLER	76	23	34	57	1-	96	9	2	3	0	168	13.7
D	27	MATT SCHNEIDER	75	20	32	52	15	62	11	0	4	0	193	10.4
R	12	MIKE KEANE	80	16	30	46	6	119	6	2	2	1	129	12.4
L	45	GILBERT DIONNE	75	19	26	45	9-	31	3	0	5	2	162	11.7
C	17	JOHN LECLAIR	74	19	24	43	18	32	1	0	1	0	153	2.4
D	24	LYLE ODELEIN	79	11	29	40	8	276	6	0	2	0	116	9.5
C	21	GUY CHARBONNEAU	79	14	24	38	16	48	0	0	1	0	120	11.7
D	28	ERIC DESJARDINS	84	12	23	35	1-	97	6	1	3	0	193	6.2
C	15	PAUL DI PIETRO	70	13	20	33	2-	37	2	0	0	0	115	11.3
L	22	BENOIT BRUNET	71	10	20	30	14	20	0	3	1	0	92	10.9
R	6	*OLEG PETROV	55	12	15	27	7	2	1	0	1	1	107	11.2
D	43	PATRICE BRISEBOIS	53	2	21	23	5	63	1	0	0	0	71	2.8
R	26	GARY LEEMAN	31	4	11	15	5	17	0	0	0	0	53	7.5
R	31	ED RONAN	61	6	8	14	3	42	0	0	1	0	49	12.2
D	34	*PETER POPOVIC	47	2	12	14	10	26	1	0	0	0	58	3.4
D	48	J.J. DAIGNEAULT	68	2	12	14	16	73	0	0	1	0	61	3.3
D	14	KEVIN HALLER	68	4	9	13	3	118	0	0	1	0	72	5.6
C	8	RON WILSON	48	2	10	12	2-	12	0	0	0	0	39	5.1
L	20	*PIERRE SEVIGNY	43	4	5	9	6	42	1	0	1	0	19	21.1
L	35	*DONALD BRASHEAR	14	2	2	4	0	34	0	0	0	0	15	13.3
D	5	*CHRISTIAN PROULX	7	1	2	3	0	20	0	0	0	0	11	9.1
D	44	BRYAN FOGARTY	13	1	2	3	4-	10	0	0	0	0	22	4.5
L	32	MARIO ROBERGE	28	1	2	3	2-	55	0	0	0	0	5	20
C	49	*BRIAN SAVAGE	3	1	0	1	0	0	0	0	0	0	3	33.3
C	46	*CRAIG FERGUSON	2	0	1	1	1	0	0	0	0	0	0	.0
G	33	PATRICK ROY	68	0	1	1	0	30	0	0	0	0	0	.0
R	42	*LINDSAY VALLIS	1	0	0	0	0	0	0	0	0	0	0	.0
R	30	*TURNER STEVENSON	2	0	0	0	2-	2	0	0	0	0	0.0	0.
L	36	GERRY FLEMING	5	0	0	0	4-	25	0	0	0	0	4	.0

POS	NO	PLAYER	GP	G	A	PTS	+/-	PIM	PP	SH	GW	GT	S	PCTG
G	40	*LES KUNTAR	6	0	0	0	0	2	0	0	0	0	0	.0
G	37	ANDRE RACICOT	11	0	0	0	0	0	0	0		0	0	.0
G	1	RON TUGNUTT	36	0	0	0	0	2	0	0	0	0	0	0.0

NEW JERSEY DEVILS

POS	NO	PLAYER	GP	G	A	PTS	+/-	PIM	PP	SH	GW	GT	S	PCTG
D	4	SCOTT STEVENS	83	18	60	78	53	112	5	1	4	0	215	8.4
R	44	STEPHANE RICHER	80	36	36	72	31	16	7	3	9	3	217	16.6
R	15	JOHN MACLEAN	80	37	33	80	30	95	8	0	4	0	277	13.4
L	25	VALERI ZELEPUKIN	82	26	31	57	36	70	8	0	0	0	155	16.8
C	10	COREY MILLEN	78	20	30	50	24	52	4	0	3	1	132	15.2
C	9	BERNIE NICHOLLS	61	19	27	46	24	86	3	0	1	1	142	13.4
D	27	SCOTT NIEDERMAYER	81	10	36	46	34	42	5	0	2	1	134	7.4
R	12	BILL GUERIN	81	25	19	44	14	101	2	0	3	0	195	12.9
R	22	CLAUDE LEMIEUX	79	18	26	44	13	86	5	0	5	0	181	9.9
L	17	TOM CHORSKE	76	21	20	41	14	32	1	1	4	0	131	16.0
L	16	BOBBY HOLIK	70	13	20	33	28	72	2	0	3	0	130	10.0
L	19	BOB CARPENTER	76	10	23	33	7	51	0	2	1	0	125	8.0
D	23	BRUCE DRIVER	66	8	24	32	29	63	3	1	0	1	109	7.3
C	20	ALEXANDER SEMAK	54	12	17	29	6	22	2	2	2	0	88	13.6
R	21	RANDY MCKAY	78	12	15	27	24	244	0	0	1	1	77	15.6
L	8	MIKE PELUSO	69	4	16	20	19	238	0	0	0	0	44	9.1
D	6	TOMMY ALBELIN	62	2	17	19	20	36	1	0	1	0	62	3.2
D	5	*JAROSLAV MODRY	41	2	15	17	10	18	2	0	0	0	35	5.7
C	11	*JIM DOWD	15	5	10	15	8	0	2	0	0	0	26	19.2
D	2	VIACHESLAV FETISOV	52	1	14	15	14	30	0	0	0	0	36	2.8
R	24	*DAVID EMMA	15	5	5	10	0	2	1	0	2	0	14	20.8
D	3	KEN DANEYKO	78	1	9	10	27	176	0	0	1	0	60	1.7
D	26	*JASON SMITH	41	0	5	5	7	43	0	0	0	0	47	.0
G	31	CHRIS TERRERI	44	0	2	2	0	4	0	0	0	0	0	.0
R	14	*BEN HANKINSON	13	1	0	1	0	23	0	0	1	0	14	7.1
R	18	SCOTT PELLERIN	1	0	0	0	0	2	0	0	0	0	0	.0
G	1	PETER SIDORKIEVICZ	3	0	0	0	0	0	0	0	0	0	0	.0
G	30	*MARTIN BRODEUR	47	0	0	0	0	2	0	0	0	0	0	.0

NEW YORK ISLANDERS

POS	NO	PLAYER	GP	G	A	PTS	+/-	PIM	PP	SH	GW	GT	S	PCTG
C	77	PIERRE TURGEON	69	38	56	94	14	18	10	4	6	0	254	15.0
L	32	STEVE THOMAS	78	42	33	75	9-	139	17	0	5	2	249	16.9
L	27	DEREK KING	78	30	40	70	18	59	10	0	7	1	171	17.5

POS	NO	PLAYER	GP	G	A	PTS	+/-	PIM	PP	SH	GW	GT	S	PCTG
C	33	BENOIT HOGUE	83	36	33	69	7-	73	9	5	3	0	218	16.5
D	23	VLADIMIR MALAKHOV	76	10	47	57	29	80	4	0	2	0	235	4.3
C	18	MARTY MCINNIS	81	25	31	56	31	24	3	5	3	1	136	18.4
C	20	RAY FERRARO	82	21	32	53	1	83	5	0	3	3	136	15.4
R	26	PATRICK FLATLEY	64	12	30	42	12	40	2	1	2	0	112	10.7
C	39	TRAVIS GREEN	83	18	22	40	16	44	1	0	2	1	164	11.0
D	28	TOM KURVERS	66	9	31	40	7	47	5	0	1	0	141	6.4
R	15	BRAD DALGARNO	73	11	19	30	14	62	3	0	1	0	97	11.3
D	4	UWE KRUPP	41	7	14	21	11	30	3	0	0	0	82	8.5
L	25	DAVE VOLEK	32	5	9	14	0	10	2	0	1	0	56	8.9
D	7	SCOTT LACHANCE	74	3	11	14	5-	70	0	0	1	0	59	5.1
D	37	DENNIS VASKE	65	2	11	13	21	76	0	0	0	0	71	2.8
D	11	DARIUS KASPARAITIS	76	1	10	11	6-	142	0	0	0	0	81	1.2
C	24	KEITH ACTON	77	2	7	9	5-	71	0	0	0	0	35	5.7
L	8	DAVID MALEY	56	0	6	6	7-	104	0	0	0	0	23	.0
D	47	RICHARD PILON	28	1	4	5	4-	75	0	0	0	0	20	5.0
R	12	MICK VUKOTA	72	3	1	4	5-	237	0	0	0	0	26	11.5
D	2	CHRIS LUONGO	17	1	3	4	1-	13	0	0	0	0	16	6.3
D	3	DEAN CHYNOWETH	39	0	4	4	3	122	0	0	0	0	26	.0
L	17	*YAN KAMINSKY	24	2	1	3	5	4	0	0	0	0	23	8.7
G	72	RON HEXTALL	65	0	3	3	0	52	0	0	0	0	0	.0
C	10	CLAUDE LOISELLE	17	1	1	2	2-	49	0	0	0	0	14	7.1
L	9	DAVE CHYZOWSKI	3	1	0	1	1-	4	0	0	0	0	4	25.0
R	34	*DAN PLANTE	12	0	1	1	2-	4	0	0	0	0	9	.0
G	29	*JAMIE MCLENNAN	22	0	1	1	0	6	0	0	0	0	0	.0
C	14	*SCOTT SCISSONS	1	0	0	0	0	0	0	0	0	0	0	.0
C	38	*DEREK ARMSTRONG	1	0	0	0	0	0	0	0	0	0	2	.0
L	38	*JASON SIMON	4	0	0	0	0	34	0	0	0	0	0	.0
L	68	*ZIGMUND PALFFY	5	0	0	0	6-	0	0	0	0	0	5	.0
L	17	*STEVE JUNKER	5	0	0	0	0	0	0	0	0	0	2	.0
G	35	TOM DRAPER	7	0	0	0	0	0	0	0	0	0	0	.0
L	14	JOE DAY	24	0	0	0	7-	30	0	0	0	0	16	.0

NEW YORK RANGERS

POS	NO	PLAYER	GP	G	A	PTS	+/-	PIM	PP	SH	GW	GT	S	PCTG
D	21	SERGEI ZUBOV	78	12	77	89	20	39	9	0	1	0	222	5.4
C	11	MARK MESSIER	76	26	58	84	25	76	6	2	5	0	216	12.0
L	9	ADAM GRAVES	84	52	27	79	27	127	20	4	4	1	291	17.9
D	2	BRIAN LEETCH	84	23	56	79	28	67	17	1	4	0	328	7.0
R	28	STEVE LARMER	68	21	39	60	14	41	6	1	7	0	146	14.4
C	27	ALEXEI KOVALEV	76	23	33	56	18	154	7	0	3	0	184	12.5

POS	NO	PLAYER	GP	G	A	PTS	+/-	PIM	PP	SH	GW	GT	S	PCTG
L	10	ESA TIKKANEN	83	22	32	54	5	114	5	3	4	0	257	8.6
C	13	SERGEI NEMCHINOV	76	22	27	49	13	36	4	0	6	0	144	15.3
R	36	GLENN ANDERSON	85	21	20	41	5-	62	7	0	3	0	149	14.1
R	16	BRIAN NOONAN	76	18	23	41	7	69	10	0	6	1	160	11.3
L	32	STEPHANE MATTEAU	77	19	19	38	15	57	3	0	1	1	135	14.1
C	14	CRAIG MACTAVISH	78	20	12	32	14-	91	1	0	2	1	122	16.4
D	4	KEVIN LOWE	71	5	14	19	4	70	0	0	1	0	50	10.0
D	25	*A. KARPOVTSEV	67	3	15	18	12	58	1	0	1	0	78	3.8
D	23	JEFF BEUKEBOOM	68	8	8	16	18	170	1	0	0	0	58	13.8
L	17	GREG GILBERT	76	4	11	15	3-	29	1	0	0	1	64	6.3
C	15	MIKE HUDSON	48	4	7	11	5-	47	0	0	1	0	48	8.3
D	24	JAY WELLS	79	2	7	9	4	110	0	0	0	0	64	3.1
C	12	ED OLCZYK	37	3	5	8	1-	28	0	0	1	0	40	7.5
L	19	NICK KYPREOS	56	3	5	8	16-	139	0	0	1	0	34	8.8
R	26	JOEY KOCUR	71	2	1	3	9-	129	0	0	0	0	43	4.7
L	18	MIKE HARTMAN	35	1	1	2	5-	70	0	0	0	0	19	5.3
D	8	*JOBY MESSIER	4	0	2	2	1-	0	0	0	0	0	7	.0
D	5	*MATTIAS NORSTROM	9	0	2	2	0	6	0	0	0	0	3	.0
D	6	DOUG LIDSTER	34	0	2	2	12-	33	0	0	0	0	25	.0
R	16	JIM HILLER	2	0	0	0	1	7	0	0	0	0	0	.0
L	32	*DAN LACROIX	4	0	0	0	0	0	0	0	0	0	0	.0
G	35	MIKE RICHTER	68	0	0	0	0	2	0	0	0	0	0	.0

OTTAWA SENATORS

POS	NO	PLAYER	GP	G	A	PTS	+/-	PIM	PP	SH	GW	GT	S	PCTG
C	19	*ALEXEI YASHIN	83	30	49	79	49-	22	11	2	3	0	232	12.9
C	91	*ALEXANDER DAIGLE	84	20	31	51	45-	40	4	0	2	0	168	11.9
C	17	DAVE MCLLWAIN	66	17	26	43	40-	48	1	1	1	0	115	14.8
L	61	SYLVAIN TURGEON	47	11	15	26	25-	52	7	0	2	2	116	9.5
L	18	TROY MALLETTE	82	7	16	23	33-	166	0	0	0	0	100	7.0
D	4	BRAD SHAW	66	4	19	23	41-	59	1	0	0	0	113	3.5
D	22	NORM MACIVER	53	3	20	23	26-	26	0	0	0	0	88	3.4
D	6	GORD DINEEN	77	0	21	21	52-	89	0	0	0	0	62	.0
R	11	EVGENY DAVYDOV	61	7	13	20	9-	46	1	0	0	1	66	10.6
R	20	ANDREW MCBAIN	55	11	8	19	41-	64	8	0	0	0	91	12.1
C	26	*SCOTT LEVINE	62	8	11	19	26-	162	4	0	1	0	77	10.4
C	15	DAVID ARCHIBALD	33	10	8	18	7-	14	2	0	1	0	65	15.4
C	38	VLADIMIR RUZICKA	42	5	13	18	21-	14	4	0	0	1	64	7.8
D	5	KERRY HUFFMAN	62	4	14	18	28-	40	2	1	0	1	112	3.6
D	34	DARREN RUMBLE	70	6	9	15	50-	116	0	0	0	0	95	6.3
D	7	DAN QUINN	13	7	0	7	0	6	2	0	3	0	31	22.6

POS	NO	PLAYER	GP	G	A	PTS	+/-	PIM	PP	SH	GW	GT	S	PCTG
R	16	BRAD LAUER	30	2	5	7	15-	6	0	1	0	0	45	4.4
D	21	DENNIS VIAL	55	2	5	7	9-	214	0	0	0	0	37	5.4
L	27	PHIL BOURQUE	27	2	4	6	4-	8	0	2	0	0	21	9.5
C	33	TROY MURRAY	27	2	4	6	2	10	0	1	0	0	21	9.5
C	11	JARMO KEKALAINEN	28	1	5	6	8-	14	0	0	0	0	18	5.6
R	24	ROBERT BURAKOWSKY	23	2	3	5	7-	6	0	0	0	0	40	5.0
D	55	*DIMITRI FILIMONOV	30	1	4	5	10-	18	0	0	0	0	15	6.7
C	9	*DEREK MAYER	17	2	2	4	16-	8	1	0	0	0	29	6.9
L	28	BILL HUARD	63	2	2	4	19-	162	0	0	0	0	24	8.3
L	23	CLAUDE BOIVIN	41	2	1	3	17-	95	0	0	0	0	17	11.8
D	27	HANK LAMMENS	27	1	2	3	20-	22	0	0	0	0	6	16.7
L	10	DARCY LOEWEN	44	0	3	3	11-	52	0	0	0	0	39	.0
L	78	*PAVOL DEMITRA	12	1	1	2	7-	4	1	0	0	0	10	10.0
D	24	STEVE KONROYD	27	0	2	2	3-	12	0	0	0	0	21	.0
D	3	KENT PAYNTER	9	0	1	1	6-	8	0	0	0	0	8	.0
D	29	*FRANCOIS LEROUX	23	0	1	1	4-	70	0	0	0	0	8	.0
G	32	DANIEL BERTHIAUME	1	0	0	0	0	0	0	0	0	0	0	.0
D	2	KEVIN MACDONALD	1	0	0	0	0	2	0	0	0	0	2	.0
L	25	*CHAD PENNEY	3	0	0	0	2-	2	0	0	0	0	2	.0
R	33	*GREG PANKEWICZ	3	0	0	0	1-	2	0	0	0	0	3	.0
G	35	MARK LAFOREST	5	0	0	0	0	0	0	0	0	0	0	.0
D	5	*RADEK HAMR	7	0	0	0	10-	0	0	0	0	0	5	.0
L	9	*ANDY SCHNEIDER	10	0	0	0	6-	15	0	0	0	0	4	.0
L	12	GRAEME TOWNSHEND	14	0	0	0	7-	9	0	0	0	0	5	.0
R	25	HERB RAGLAN	29	0	0	0	13-	52	0	0	0	0	13	.0
G	30	*DARRIN MADELEY	32	0	0	0	0	0	0	0	0	0	0	.0
G	1	CRAIG BILLINGTON	63	0	0	0	0	8	0	0	0	0	1	.0

PHILADELPHIA FLYERS

POS	NO	PLAYER	GP	G	A	PTS	+/-	PIM	PP	SH	GW	GT	S	PCTG
R	8	MARK RECCHI	84	40	67	107	2-	46	11	0	5	0	217	18.4
C	88	ERIC LINDROS	65	44	53	97	16	103	13	2	9	1	197	22.3
17	17	ROD BRIND'AMOUR	84	35	62	97	9-	85	14	1	4	0	230	15.2
L	19	*MIKAEL RENBERG	83	38	44	82	8	36	9	0	1	0	195	19.5
D	3	GARRY GALLEY	81	10	60	70	11-	91	5	1	0	1	186	5.4
D	29	YVES RACINE	67	9	43	52	11-	48	5	1	1	1	142	6.3
L	42	JOSEF BERANEK	80	28	21	49	2-	85	6	0	2	0	182	15.4
R	11	KEVIN DINEEN	71	19	23	42	9-	113	5	1	2	1	156	12.2
R	18	BRENT FEDYK	72	20	18	38	14-	74	5	0	1	0	104	19.2
C	22	MARK LAMB	85	12	24	36	44-	72	4	1	2	0	124	9.7
D	2	DIMITRI YUSHKEVICH	75	5	25	31	8-	86	1	0	2	0	136	3.7

POS	NO	PLAYER	GP	G	A	PTS	+/-	PIM	PP	SH	GW	GT	S	PCTG
C	20	ROB DIMAIO	53	11	12	23	4-	46	2	0	2	0	81	13.6
C	14	DAVE TIPPETT	73	4	11	15	20-	38	0	2	1	0	45	8.9
C	36	*ANDRE FAUST	37	8	5	13	1-	10	0	0	1	0	33	24.2
D	25	JEFF FINLEY	55	1	8	9	16	24	0	0	0	0	43	2.3
R	15	ALLAN CONROY	62	4	3	7	12-	65	0	1	0	0	40	10.0
D	26	ROB ZETTLER	75	0	7	7	26-	134	0	0	0	0	55	.0
D	28	*JASON BOWEN	56	1	5	6	12	87	0	0	1	0	50	2.0
R	21	DAVE BROWN	71	1	4	5	12-	137	0	0	0	0	16	6.3
D	24	*BOB WILKIE	10	1	3	4	2-	8	0	0	0	0	10	10.0
D	27	RYAN MCGILL	50	1	3	4	5-	112	0	0	0	0	53	1.9
D	23	*STEWART MALGUNAS	67	1	3	4	2	86	0	0	0	0	54	1.9
D	41	*MILOS HOLAN	8	1	1	2	4-	4	1	0	0	0	26	3.8
R	32	CHRIS WINNES	4	0	2	2	1	0	0	0	0	0	4	.0
D	5	ROB RAMAGE	21	1	2	2	12-	16	0	0	0	0	23	.0
C	10	*TODD HLUSHKO	2	1	0	1	1	0	0	0	0	0	2	50.0
G	33	DOMINIC ROUSSEL	60	0	1	1	0	4	0	0	0	0	0	.0
D	40	*ARIS BRIMANIS	1	0	0	0	1-	0	0	0	0	0	1	.0
L	43	CLAUDE VILGRAIN	2	0	0	0	1-	0	0	0	0	0	0	.0
D	6	DAN KORDIC	4	0	0	0	0	5	0	0	0	0	0	.0
G	35	*FREDERIC CHABOT	5	0	0	0	0	0	0	0	0	0	0	.0
G	30	TOMMY SODERSTROM	34	0	0	0	0	0	0	0	0	0	0	.0

PITTSBURGH PENGUINS

POS	NO	PLAYER	GP	G	A	PTS	+/-	PIM	PP	SH	GW	GT	S	PCTG
R	68	JAROMIR JAGR	80	32	67	99	15	61	9	0	6	2	298	10.7
C	10	RON FRANCIS	82	27	66	93	3-	62	8	0	2	1	216	12.5
L	25	KEVIN STEVENS	83	41	47	88	24-	155	21	0	4	0	184	14.4
D	55	LARRY MURPHY	84	17	56	73	10	44	7	0	4	0	236	7.2
R	7	JOE MULLEN	84	38	32	70	9	41	6	2	9	0	231	16.5
C	82	MARTIN STRAKA	84	30	34	64	24	24	2	0	6	1	160	23.1
R	17	TOMAS SANDSTROM	78	23	35	58	7-	83	4	0	3	1	193	11.9
R	24	DOUG BROWN	77	18	37	55	19	18	2	0	1	0	152	11.8
C	15	SHAWN MCEACHERN	76	20	22	42	14	34	0	5	1	0	159	12.6
R	22	RICK TOCCHET	51	14	26	40	15-	134	5	1	2	1	150	9.3
C	66	MARIO LEMIEUX	22	18	20	37	2-	32	7	0	4	0	92	18.5
D	4	GREG HAWGOOD	64	6	28	34	9	36	4	0	2	0	112	5.4
D	5	ULF SAMUELSSON	80	5	24	29	23	199	1	0	0	1	106	4.7
C	19	BRYAN TROTTIER	41	4	11	15	12-	36	0	0	0	0	45	8.9
D	32	PETER TAGLIANETTI	60	2	12	14	5	142	0	0	0	0	57	3.5
D	28	KJELL SAMUELSSON	59	5	8	13	18	118	1	0	0	0	57	8.8
R	29	*MARKUS NASLUND	71	4	7	11	3-	27	1	0	0	0	80	5.0

POS	NO	PLAYER	GP	G	A	PTS	+/-	PIM	PP	SH	GW	GT	S	PCTG
D	34	GREG BROWN	36	3	8	11	1	28	1	0	0	0	37	8.1
L	33	JIM MCKENZIE	71	2	5	8	7-	146	0	0	1	0	33	9.1
D	3	GRANT JENNINGS	61	2	4	6	10-	126	0	1	1	0	49	4.1
R	44	*ED PATTERSON	27	3	1	4	5-	10	0	0	0	0	15	20.0
D	6	MIKE RAMSEY	65	2	2	4	4-	22	0	0	0	0	31	6.5
D	36	*PAT NEATON	9	1	1	2	3	12	1	0	0	0	11	9.1
C	12	LARRY DEPALMA	7	1	0	1	1	5	0	0	0	0	2	50.0
G	31	KEN WREGGET	42	0	1	1	0	8	0	0	0	0	0	.0
G	35	TOM BARRASSO	44	0	1	1	0	42	0	0	0	0	0	.0
G	30	ROBERTO ROMANO	2	0	0	0	0	0	0	0	0	0	0	.0
G	1	ROB DOPSON	2	0	0	0	0	0	0	0	0	0	0	.0
D	4	*GREG ANDRUSAK	3	0	0	0	1-	2	0	0	0	0	4	.0
R	37	*JUSTIN DUBERMAN	4	0	0	0	0	0	0	0	0	0	2	.0
L	14	*LADISLAV KARABIN	9	0	0	0	0	2	0	0	0	0	3	.0
D	2	*CHRIS TAMER	12	0	0	0	0	9	0	0	0	0	10	.0

QUEBEC NORDIQUES

POS	NO	PLAYER	GP	G	A	PTS	+/-	PIM	PP	SH	GW	GT	S	PCTG
C	19	JOE SAKIC	84	28	64	92	8-	18	10	1	9	1	279	10.0
C	13	MATS SUNDIN	84	32	53	85	1	60	6	2	4	0	226	14.2
L	31	VALEI KAMENSKY	76	28	37	65	12	42	6	0	1	0	170	16.5
C	9	MIKE RICCI	83	30	21	51	8-	113	13	3	6	1	138	21.7
R	48	SCOTT YOUNG	76	26	25	51	4-	14	6	1	1	0	236	11.0
C	22	RON SUTTER	73	15	25	40	2	90	5	0	2	0	108	13.9
C	38	*IAIN FRASER	60	17	20	37	5-	23	2	0	2	0	109	15.6
R	51	ANDREI KOVALENKO	58	16	17	33	5-	46	5	0	4	0	92	17.4
L	25	MARTIN RUCINSKY	60	9	23	32	4	58	4	0	1	0	96	9.4
C	28	BOB BASSEN	83	13	15	28	17-	99	1	1	0	1	129	10.1
C	47	CLAUDE LAPOINTE	59	11	17	28	2	70	1	1	1	0	73	15.1
D	5	ALEXEI GUSAROV	76	5	20	25	3	38	0	1	0	0	84	6.0
D	7	CURTIS LESCHYSHYN	72	5	17	22	2-	65	3	0	2	0	97	5.2
D	55	GARTH BUTCHER	77	4	15	19	7-	143	0	2	1	0	66	6.1
D	59	*DAVE KARPA	60	5	12	17	0	148	2	0	0	0	48	10.4
D	29	STEVEN FINN	80	4	13	17	9-	159	0	0	1	0	74	5.4
D	6	CRAIG WOLANIN	63	6	10	16	16	80	0	0	0	0	78	7.7
D	45	*MIKE MCKEE	48	3	12	15	5	41	2	0	0	0	60	5.0
L	17	CHRIS LINDBERG	37	6	8	14	1-	12	0	0	0	0	42	14.3
D	2	TOMMY SJODIN	29	1	11	12	4	22	1	0	0	0	54	1.9
D	27	BRAD WERENKA	26	0	11	11	3	22	0	0	0	0	28	.0
L	12	*CHRIS SIMON	37	4	4	8	2-	132	0	0	1	0	39	10.3
D	52	ADAM FOOTE	45	2	6	8	3	67	0	0	0	0	42	4.8

POS	NO	PLAYER	GP	G	A	PTS	+/-	PIM	PP	SH	GW	GT	S	PCTG
C	33	*REGGIE SAVAGE	17	3	4	7	3	16	1	0	0	0	25	12.0
R	23	PAUL MACDERMID	44	2	3	5	3-	35	0	0	0	0	16	12.5
R	11	OWEN NOLAN	6	2	2	4	2	8	0	0	0	0	15	13.3
L	15	TONY TWIST	49	0	4	4	1-	101	0	0	0	0	15	.0
G	35	STEPHANE FISET	50	0	3	3	0	8	0	0	0	0	0	.0
R	14	*DWAYNE NORRIS	4	1	1	2	1	4	0	0	0	0	7	14.3
L	55	*RENE CORBET	9	1	1	2	1	0	0	0	0	0	14	7.1
R	54	*ED WARD	7	1	0	1	0	5	0	0	0	0	3	33.3
D	4	MIKE HURLBUT	1	0	0	0	1-	0	0	0	0	0	1	.0
D	44	*AARON MILLER	1	0	0	0	1-	0	0	0	0	0	0	.0
L	24	*PAXTON SCHULTE	1	0	0	0	0	2	0	0	0	0	0	.0
G	1	*GARTH SNOW	5	0	0	0	0	2	0	0	0	0	0	.0
D	73	ALAIN COTE	6	0	0	0	2-	4	0	0	0	0	4	.0
D	42	*JON KLEMM	7	0	0	0	1-	4	0	0	0	0	11	.0
G	32	JACQUES CLOUTIER	14	0	0	0	0	2	0	0	0	0	0	.0
G	41	*JOCELYN THIBAULT	29	0	0	0	0	2	0	0	0	0	0	.0

SAN JOSE SHARKS

POS	NO	PLAYER	GP	G	A	PTS	+/-	PIM	PP	SH	GW	GT	S	PCTG
R	22	ULF DAHLEN	78	25	44	69	1-	10	15	0	5	1	190	13.2
R	24	SERGEI MAKAROV	80	30	38	68	11	78	10	0	5	0	155	19.4
C	27	TODD ELIK	79	25	41	66	3-	95	9	0	4	1	185	13.5
D	6	SANDIS OZONLINSH	81	26	38	64	16	24	4	0	3	0	157	16.6
C	7	IGOR LARIONOV	60	18	38	56	20	40	3	2	2	1	72	25.0
R	17	PAT FALLOON	83	22	31	53	3-	18	6	0	1	0	193	11.4
L	10	JOHAN GARPENLOV	80	18	35	53	9	28	7	0	3	0	125	14.4
L	14	RAY WHITNEY	61	14	26	40	2	14	1	0	0	1	82	17.1
D	8	JEFF NORTON	64	7	33	40	16	36	1	0	0	0	92	7.6
R	37	ROB GAUDREAU	84	15	20	35	10-	28	6	0	4	0	151	9.9
L	12	BOB ERREY	64	12	18	30	11-	126	5	0	2	0	89	13.5
L	11	GAETAN DUCHESNE	84	12	18	30	8	28	0	1	3	0	121	9.9
D	41	TOM PEDERSON	74	6	19	25	3	31	3	0	1	1	185	3.2
C	9	V. BUTSAYEV	59	12	11	23	0	68	2	0	3	0	85	14.1
R	36	JEFF ODGERS	81	13	8	21	13-	222	7	0	0	1	73	17.8
C	13	JAMIE BAKER	65	12	5	17	2	38	0	0	2	0	68	17.6
D	40	*MIKE RATHJE	47	1	9	10	9-	59	1	0	0	0	30	3.3
C	33	DALE CRAIGWELL	58	3	6	9	13-	16	0	1	0	0	35	8.6
D	4	JAY MORE	49	1	6	7	5	63	0	0	0	0	38	2.6
C	50	*JAROSLAV OTEVREL	9	3	2	5	5-	2	1	0	0	0	11	27.3
D	38	*MICHAL SYKORA	22	1	4	5	4-	14	0	0	0	0	22	4.5
C	20	KIP MILLER	11	2	2	4	1-	6	0	0	0	0	21	9.5

POS	NO	PLAYER	GP	G	A	PTS	+/-	PIM	PP	SH	GW	GT	S	PCTG
D	26	*VLASTIMIL KROUPA	27	1	3	4	6-	20	0	0	0	0	16	6.3
D	44	SHAWN CRONIN	34	0	2	2	2	76	0	0	0	0	14	.0
G	32	ARTURS IRBE	84	0	2	2	0	16	0	0	0	0	0	.0
C	9	GARY EMMONS	3	1	0	1	4-	0	1	0	0	0	6	16.7
C	43	JEFF MCLEAN	6	1	0	1	1	0	0	0	0	0	5	20.0
L	27	DAVE CAPUANO	4	0	1	1	5-	0	0	0	0	0	5	.0
R	23	*ANDREI NAZAROV	1	0	0	0	0	0	0	0	0	0	0	.0
R	15	DAVID BRUCE	2	0	0	0	2-	0	0	0	0	0	4	.0
G	29	JIM WAITE	15	0	0	0	0	6	0	0	0	0	0	.0

ST. LOUIS BLUES

POS	NO	PLAYER	GP	G	A	PTS	+/-	PIM	PP	SH	GW	GT	S	PCTG
L	19	BRENDAN SHANAHAN	81	52	50	102	9-	211	15	7	8	1	397	13.1
R	16	BRETT HULL	81	57	40	97	3-	38	25	3	6	1	392	14.5
C	15	CRAIG JANNEY	69	16	68	84	14-	24	8	0	7	0	95	16.8
R	14	KEVIN MILLER	75	23	25	48	6	83	6	3	5	0	154	14.9
D	28	STEVE DUCHESNE	36	12	19	31	1	14	8	0	1	0	115	10.4
L	25	VITALI PROKHOROV	55	15	10	25	6-	20	3	0	1	0	85	17.6
C	36	PHILIPPE BOZON	80	9	16	25	4	42	0	1	1	0	118	7.6
D	7	ALEXEI KASATONOV	63	4	20	24	3-	62	1	0	1	0	87	4.6
D	6	PHIL HOUSLEY	26	7	15	22	5-	12	4	0	1	1	60	11.7
L	12	*VITALI KARAMNOV	59	9	12	21	3-	51	2	0	1	0	66	13.6
C	93	PETR NEDVED	19	6	14	20	2	8	2	0	0	1	63	9.5
C	10	*JIM MONTGOMERY	67	6	14	20	1-	44	0	0	1	0	93	6.5
C	38	IGOR KOROLEV	73	6	10	16	12-	40	0	0	1	0	93	6.5
C	26	PETER STASTNY	17	5	11	16	2-	4	2	2	1	1	30	16.7
D	34	MURRAY BARON	77	5	9	14	14-	123	0	0	0	0	73	6.8
C	18	TONY HRKAC	36	6	5	11	11-	8	1	1	1	0	43	14.0
D	4	RICK ZOMBO	74	2	8	10	15-	85	0	0	0	0	53	3.8
D	32	DOUG CROSSMAN	50	2	7	9	1	10	1	0	0	0	30	6.7
D	20	TOM TILLEY	48	1	7	8	3	32	0	0	0	0	41	2.4
R	39	KELLY CHASE	68	2	5	7	5-	278	0	0	0	0	57	3.5
L	23	DAVE MACKEY	30	2	3	5	4-	56	0	0	0	0	21	9.5
D	41	*DANIEL LAPERRIERE	20	1	3	4	1-	8	1	0	0	0	20	5.0
L	17	BASIL MCRAE	40	1	2	3	7-	103	0	0	0	0	23	4.3
G	31	CURTIS JOSEPH	71	0	3	3	0	4	0	0	0	0	0	.0
R	9	*DENNY FELSNER	6	1	0	1	1-	2	0	0	0	0	6	16.7
R	27	*DENIS CHASSE	3	0	1	1	1	15	0	0	0	0	5	.0
C	37	*KEVIN MIEHM	14	0	1	1	3-	4	0	0	0	0	5	.0
G	29	JIM HRIVNAK	23	0	1	1	0	2	0	0	0	0	0	.0
L	21	*DAVID ROBERTS	1	0	0	0	0	2	0	0	0	0	1	.0

POS	NO	PLAYER	GP	G	A	PTS	+/-	PIM	PP	SH	GW	GT	S	PCTG
C	22	*IAN LAPERRIERE	1	0	0	0	0	0	0	0	0	0	1	.0
D	44	*TERRY HOLLINGER	2	0	0	0	1	0	0	0	0	0	0	.0
D	43	*JEFF BATTERS	6	0	0	0	1	7	0	0	0	0	1	.0

TAMPA BAY LIGHTNING

POS	NO	PLAYER	GP	G	A	PTS	+/-	PIM	PP	SH	GW	GT	S	PCTG
C	19	BRIAN BRADLEY	78	24	40	64	8-	56	6	0	2	0	180	13.3
R	85	PETR KLIMA	75	28	27	55	15-	76	10	0	2	0	167	16.8
C	9	DENIS SAVARD	74	18	28	46	1-	106	2	1	2	0	181	9.9
R	24	DANTON COLE	81	20	23	43	7	32	8	1	4	0	149	13.4
C	77	*CHRIS GRATTON	84	13	29	42	25-	123	5	1	2	1	161	8.1
R	14	JOHN TUCKER	66	17	23	40	9	28	2	0	6	1	126	13.5
D	22	SHAWN CHAMBERS	66	11	23	34	6-	23	6	1	1	0	142	7.7
D	23	CHRIS JOSEPH	76	11	20	31	21-	136	8	0	0	0	179	6.1
R	15	PAT ELYNUIK	67	13	15	28	21-	64	4	1	1	0	111	11.7
L	34	MIKAEL ANDERSSON	76	13	12	25	8	23	1	1	2	1	136	9.6
D	44	ROMAN HAMRLIK	64	3	18	21	14-	135	0	0	0	0	158	1.9
C	10	ADAM CREIGHTON	53	10	10	20	7-	37	2	0	1	0	77	13.0
D	25	MARC BERGEVIN	83	1	15	16	5-	87	0	0	1	0	76	1.3
C	28	MARC BUREAU	75	8	7	15	9-	30	0	1	1	0	110	7.3
L	17	GERARD GALLANT	51	4	9	13	6-	74	1	0	2	0	45	8.9
L	7	ROB ZAMUNER	59	6	6	12	9-	42	0	0	1	0	109	5.5
D	20	RUDY POESCHEK	71	3	6	9	3	118	0	0	1	1	46	6.5
C	11	BILL MCDOUGALL	22	3	3	6	4-	8	1	0	0	1	26	11.5
D	26	*CHRIS LIPUMA	27	0	4	4	1	77	0	0	0	0	20	.0
L	8	*JASON RUFF	6	1	2	3	2	2	0	0	0	0	14	7.1
C	49	*BRENT GRETZKY	10	1	2	3	0	2	0	0	0	0	14	7.1
R	12	*JIM CUMMINS	26	1	2	3	1-	84	0	0	0	0	20	5.0
D	39	ENRICO CICCONE	57	1	2	3	4-	226	0	0	0	0	33	3.0
G	93	DAREN PUPPA	63	0	1	1	0	2	0	0	0	0	0	.0
C	16	JASON LAFRENIERE	1	0	0	0	1-	0	0	0	0	0	2	.0
G	30	J.C. BERGERON	3	0	0	0	0	0	0	0	0	0	0	.0
D	3	*ERICK CHARRON	4	0	0	0	0	2	0	0	0	0	1	.0
D	4	*CORY CROSS	5	0	0	0	3-	6	0	0	0	0	5	.0
D	5	NORMAND ROCHEFORT	6	0	0	0	1-	10	0	0	0	0	4	.0
G	1	WENDELL YOUNG	9	0	0	0	0	4	0	0	0	0	0	.0

TORONTO MAPLE LEAFS

POS	NO	PLAYER	GP	G	A	PTS	+/-	PIM	PP	SH	GW	GT	S	PCTG
C	93	DOUG GILMOUR	83	27	84	111	25	105	10	1	3	2	167	16.2
L	14	DAVE ANDREYCHUK	83	53	46	99	22	98	21	5	8	0	333	15.9
L	17	WENDEL CLARK	64	46	30	76	10	115	21	0	8	0	275	16.7
R	11	MIKE GARTNER	81	34	30	64	20	62	11	5	4	0	275	12.4
D	4	DAVE ELLETT	68	7	36	43	6	42	5	0	1	1	146	4.8
D	15	DMITRI MIRONOV	76	9	27	36	5	78	3	0	0	2	147	6.1
R	16	NIKOLAI BORSCHEVSKY	45	14	20	34	6	10	7	0	1	0	105	13.3
C	19	JOHN CULLEN	53	13	17	30	2-	67	2	0	4	1	80	16.3
R	12	ROB PEARSON	67	12	18	30	6-	189	1	0	4	0	119	10.1
D	34	JAMIE MACOUN	82	3	27	30	5-	115	1	0	1	0	122	2.5
D	23	TODD GILL	45	4	24	28	8	44	2	0	1	0	74	5.4
L	21	MARK OSBORNE	73	9	15	24	2	145	1	1	2	0	103	8.7
L	10	BILL BERG	83	8	11	19	3-	93	0	0	1	0	99	8.1
C	32	MIKE EASTWOOD	54	8	10	18	2	28	1	0	2	0	41	19.5
C	41	PETER ZEZEL	8	8	16	5	19	0	0	0	0	0	47	17.0
L	18	KENT MANDERVILLE	67	7	9	16	5	63	0	0	1	0	81	8.6
D	3	BOB ROUSE	63	5	11	16	8	101	1	1	0	0	77	6.5
R	11	MARK GREIG	44	6	7	16	5-	41	0	0	0	0	55	10.9
C	26	MIKE KRUSHELNYSKI	54	5	6	11	5-	28	1	0	1	0	71	7.0
D	2	SYLVAIN LEFEBVRE	84	2	9	11	33	79	0	0	0	1	96	2.1
D	55	DRAKE BEREHOWSKY	49	2	8	10	3-	63	2	0	2	0	29	6.9
L	22	KEN BAUMGARTNER	64	4	4	8	6-	185	0	0	0	0	34	11.8
C	44	*YANIC PERREAULT	13	3	3	6	1	0	2	0	0	0	24	12.5
L	8	CHRIS GOVEDARIS	12	2	2	4	4	14	0	0	0	1	16	12.5
G	29	FELIX POTVIN	66	0	4	4	0	4	0	0	0	0	0	.0
D	7	*DAVID SACCO	4	1	1	2	2-	4	1	0	0	0	4	25.0
C	40	KEN MCRAE	9	1	1	2	1	36	0	0	0	0	11	9.1
C	20	*ALEXEI KUDASHOV	25	1	0	1	3-	4	0	0	0	0	24	4.2
D	33	*MATT MARTIN	12	0	1	1	0	6	0	0	0	0	6	.0
D	38	*CHRIS SNELL	2	0	0	0	1-	2	0	0	0	0	4	.0
R	24	*PATRIK AUGUSTA	2	0	0	0	0	0	0	0	0	0	3	.0
L	41	*ERIC LACROIX	3	0	0	0	0	2	0	0	0	0	3	.0
L	36	FRANK BIALOWAS	3	0	0	0	0	12	0	0	0	0	1	.0
D	28	*DAVID HARLOCK	6	0	0	0	2-	0	0	0	0	0	2	.0
G	35	PAT JABLONSKI	15	0	0	0	0	0	0	0	0	0	0	.0
G	1	*DAMIAN RHODES	22	0	0	0	0	2	0	0	0	0	0	.0

VANCOUVER CANUCKS

POS	NO	PLAYER	GP	G	A	PTS	+/-	PIM	PP	SH	GW	GT	S	PCTG
R	10	PAVEL BURE	76	60	47	107	1	86	25	4	9	0	374	16.0
L	14	GEOFF COURTNALL	82	26	44	70	15	123	12	1	2	0	264	9.8
C	7	CLIFF RONNING	76	25	43	68	7	42	10	0	4	1	197	12.7
D	22	JEFF BROWN	74	14	52	66	11-	56	7	0	3	1	237	5.9
R	16	TREVOR LINDEN	84	32	29	61	6	73	10	2	3	0	234	13.7
L	32	MURRAY CRAVEN	78	15	40	55	5	30	2	1	3	0	115	13.0
D	21	JYRKI LUMME	83	13	42	55	3	50	1	3	3	0	161	8.1
D	24	JIRI SLEGR	78	5	33	38	0	86	1	0	0	0	160	3.1
L	8	GREG ADAMS	68	13	24	37	1-	20	5	1	2	0	139	9.4
D	44	DAVE BABYCH	73	4	28	32	0	52	0	0	2	0	96	4.2
L	29	GINO ODJICK	76	16	13	29	13	271	4	0	5	0	121	13.2
L	23	MARTIN GELINAS	64	14	14	28	8-	34	3	0	1	2	107	13.1
C	17	JIMMY CARSON	59	11	17	28	15-	24	3	0	1	0	129	8.5
L	27	SERGIO MOMESSO	68	14	13	27	2-	149	4	0	1	0	112	12.5
D	5	DANA MURZYN	80	6	14	20	4	109	0	1	0	0	79	7.6
D	28	BRIAN GLYNN	64	2	13	15	19-	53	1	0	0	0	71	2.8
R	20	JOSE CHARBONNEAU	30	7	7	14	3-	49	1	0	0	0	28	25.0
D	3	BRET HEDICAN	69	0	12	12	7-	64	0	0	0	0	88	.0
D	4	GERALD DIDUCK	55	1	10	11	2	72	0	0	0	0	50	2.0
D	6	ADRIEN PLAVSIC	47	1	9	10	5-	6	0	0	1	0	41	2.4
C	15	JOHN MCINTYRE	62	3	6	9	9-	38	0	0	0	0	30	10.0
C	25	*NATHAN LAFAYETTE	49	3	4	7	7-	18	0	0	0	0	34	8.8
R	19	TIM HUNTER	56	3	4	7	7-	171	0	1	1	0	41	7.3
R	36	*DANE JACKSON	12	5	1	6	3	9	0	0	0	0	18	27.8
R	25	*DAN KESA	19	2	4	6	3-	18	1	0	1	0	18	11.1
D	2	*YEVGENY NAMESTNIKOV	17	0	5	5	2-	10	0	0	0	0	11	.0
C	23	NEIL EISENHUT	13	1	3	4	0	21	0	0	0	0	13	7.7
G	1	KIRK MCLEAN	52	0	4	4	0	2	0	0	0	0	0	.0
L	18	*SHAWN ANTOSKI	55	1	2	3	11-	190	0	0	1	0	25	4.0
C	25	STEPHANE MORIN	5	1	1	2	0	6	0	0	0	0	6	16.7
C	33	*MIKE PECA	4	0	0	0	1-	2	0	0	0	0	5	.0
G	35	KAY WHITMORE	32	0	0	0	0	6	0	0	0	0	0	.0

WASHINGTON CAPITALS

POS	NO	PLAYER	GP	G	A	PTS	+/-	PIM	PP	SH	GW	GT	S	PCTG
C	90	JOE JUNEAU	74	19	66	85	11	41	6	0	2	1	164	11.6
C	17	MIKE RIDLEY	81	26	44	70	15	24	10	2	4	3	144	18.1
C	8	DIMITRI KHRISTICH	83	29	29	58	2-	73	10	0	4	1	195	14.9
D	3	SYLVAIN COTE	84	16	35	51	30	66	3	2	2	0	212	7.5
C	20	MICHAL PIVONKA	82	14	36	50	2	38	5	0	4	0	138	10.1

POS	NO	PLAYER	GP	G	A	PTS	+/-	PIM	PP	SH	GW	GT	S	PCTG
R	12	PETER BONDRA	69	24	19	43	22	40	4	0	2	0	200	12.0
L	18	RANDY BURRIDGE	78	25	17	42	1-	73	8	1	5	0	150	16.7
D	6	CALLE JOHANSSON	84	9	33	42	3	59	4	0	1	0	141	6.4
D	4	KEVIN HATCHER	72	16	24	40	13-	108	6	0	3	0	217	7.4
L	10	KELLY MILLER	84	14	25	39	8	32	0	1	3	0	138	10.1
C	32	DALE HUNTER	52	9	29	38	4-	131	1	0	1	0	61	14.8
R	26	KEITH JONES	68	18	19	35	4	149	5	0	1	0	97	16.5
L	21	TODD KRYGIER	66	12	18	30	4-	60	0	1	3	0	146	8.2
C	14	*PAT PEAKE	49	11	18	29	1	39	3	0	1	1	91	12.1
C	22	STEVE KONOWALCHUK	62	12	14	26	9	33	0	0	0	0	63	19.0
C	9	DAVE POULIN	63	6	19	25	1-	52	0	1	0	0	64	9.4
D	29	JOE REEKIE	85	1	16	17	15	156	0	0	0	0	98	1.0
D	28	*JOHN SLANEY	47	7	9	16	3	27	3	0	1	0	70	.10.0
L	27	CRAIG BERUBE	84	7	7	14	4-	305	0	0	0	0	48	14.6
R	11	TIM BERGLAND	54	6	5	11	15-	10	0	0	0	0	65	9.2
D	36	SHAWN ANDERSON	50	0	9	9	1-	12	0	0	0	0	31	.0
D	2	JIM JOHNSON	61	0	7	7	7-	63	0	0	0	0	49	.0
C	23	*KEVIN KAMINSKI	13	0	5	5	2	87	0	0	0	0	9	.0
D	25	JASON WOOLLEY	10	1	2	3	2	4	0	0	0	0	15	6.7
D	40	*TODD NELSON	2	1	0	1	1	2	1	0	1	0	1	100.0
D	38	BRIAN CURRAN	26	1	0	1	2-	61	0	0	0	0	11	9.1
C	41	*JASON ALLISON	2	0	1	1	1	0	0	0	0	0	5	.0
G	33	DON BEAUPRE	53	0	1	1	0	16	0	0	0	0	0	.0
G	35	*BYRON DAFOE	5	0	0	0	0	0	0	0	0	0	0	.0
G	37	*OLAF KOLZIG	7	0	0	0	0	0	0	0	0	0	0	.0
G	31	RICK TABARACCI	32	0	0	0	0	6	0	0	0	0	0	.0

WINNIPEG JETS

POS	NO	PLAYER	GP	G	A	PTS	+/-	PIM	PP	SH	GW	GT	S	PCTG
L	7	KEITH TKACHUK	84	41	40	81	12-	255	22	3	3	1	218	18.8
C	19	NELSON EMERSON	83	33	41	74	38-	80	4	5	6	1	282	11.7
C	10	ALEXEI ZHAMNOV	61	26	45	71	20-	62	7	0	1	1	196	13.3
L	34	DARRIN SHANNON	77	21	37	58	28-	87	9	0	2	0	124	16.9
R	13	TEEMU SELANNE	51	25	29	54	23-	22	11	0	2	0	191	13.1
C	25	THOMAS STEEN	76	19	32	51	38-	32	6	0	1	1	137	13.9
C	18	DALLAS DRAKE	62	13	27	40	1-	49	1	2	3	0	112	11.6
D	4	STEPHANE QUINTAL	81	8	18	26	25-	119	1	1	1	0	154	5.2
D	27	TEPPO NUMMINEN	57	5	18	23	23-	28	4	0	1	0	89	5.6
D	3	DAVE MANSON	70	4	17	21	24-	191	1	0	0	0	180	2.2
R	20	TIE DOMI	81	8	11	19	8-	347	0	0	1	0	98	8.2
C	38	LUCIANO BORSATO	75	5	13	18	11-	28	1	1	2	0	65	7.7

POS	NO	PLAYER	GP	G	A	PTS	+/-	PIM	PP	SH	GW	GT	S	PCTG
D	5	IGOR ULANOV	74	0	17	17	11-	165	0	0	0	0	46	.0
D	6	WAYNE MCBEAN	50	3	13	16	34-	40	2	0	0	0	114	2.6
C	15	RANDY GILHEN	60	7	7	14	12-	50	0	0	0	0	95	7.4
L	21	RUSS ROMANIUK	24	4	8	12	11-	6	3	0	0	0	36	11.1
C	36	MIKE EAGLES	73	4	8	12	20-	96	0	1	0	0	53	7.5
L	17	KRIS KING	83	4	8	12	22-	205	0	0	1	0	86	4.7
D	26	DEAN KENNEDY	76	2	8	10	22-	164	0	0	1	0	38	5.3
R	37	JOHN LEBLANC	17	6	2	8	2-	2	1	1	1	0	29	20.7
C	11	*DAVE TOMLINSON	31	1	3	4	12-	24	0	0	0	0	29	3.4
D	24	DARRYL SHANNON	20	0	4	4	6-	18	0	0	0	0	14	.0
D	55	*ARTO BLOMSTEN	18	0	2	2	6-	6	0	0	0	0	15	.0
L	60	*MICHAL GROSEK	3	1	0	1	1-	0	0	0	0	0	4	25.0
D	42	OLEG MIKULCHIK	4	0	1	1	2-	17	0	0	0	0	3	.0
G	29	TIM CHEVELDAE	44	0	1	1	0	2	0	0	0	0	0	.0
D	39	*MARK VISHEAU	1	0	0	0	0	0	0	0	0	0	1	.0
L	23	ANDY BRICKLEY	2	0	0	0	2-	0	0	0	0	0	0	.0
C	50	*CRAIG FISHER	4	0	0	0	1-	2	0	0	0	0	0	.0
R	28	KEVIN MCCLELLAND	6	0	0	0	0	19	0	0	0	0	1	.0
C	12	ROB MURRAY	6	0	0	0	0	2	0	0	0	0	1	.0
C	14	*HARIJS VITOLINSH	8	0	0	0	0	4	0	0	0	0	7	.0
G	30	STEPH BEAUREGARD	13	0	0	0	0	0	0	0	0	0	0	.0
C	18	BRYAN ERICKSON	16	0	0	0	7-	0	0	0	0	0	8	.0
G	1	*MICHAEL O'NEILL	17	0	0	0	0	0	0	0	0	0	0	.0

1993-94 Record of Goaltenders

All goals against a team in any game are charged to the goaltender of the game for purposes of awarding the Bill Jennings Trophy.

Won-Lost-Tied Record is based upon which goaltender was playing when the winning or tying goal was scored.

Empty-Net Goals are not counted in personal averages but are included in the team total.

(GPI) Games Played In
(EN) Empty Net Goals
(SA) Shots Against

(MINS) Minutes Played
(SO) Shutouts
(SV%) Save Percentage

(AVG) 60 Minute Average
(GA) Goals Against

RNK	NO.	GOALTENDER	GPI	MINS	AVG	W	L	T	EN	SO	GA	SA	SV%	G	A	PIM
1	39	DOMINIK HASEK	58	3358	1.95	30	20	6	3	7	109	1552	.930	0	3	6
40	31	GRANT FUHR	32	1726	3.68	13	12	3	0	2	106	907	.883	0	4	16
		BUF TOTALS	84	5097	2.57	43	32	9	3	9	218	2462	.911			
2	30	*MARTIN BRODEUR	47	2625	2.40	27	11	8	0	3	105	1238	.915	0	0	2
10	31	CHRIS TERRERI	44	2340	2.72	20	11	4	2	2	106	1141	.907	0	2	4
	1	PETER SIDORKIEWIC	3	130	2.77	0	3	0	1	0	6	55	.891	0	0	0
		N.J. TOTALS	84	5104	2.59	47	25	12	3	5	220	2437	.910			
4	34	JOHN VANBIESBROUC	57	3440	2.53	21	25	11	4	1	145	1912	.924	0	0	38
11	30	MARK FITZPATRICK	28	1603	2.73	12	8	6	3	1	73	844	.914	0	2	4
	33	ELDON REDDICK	2	80	6.00	0	1	0	0	0	8	45	.822	0	0	0
		FLA TOTALS	84	5144	2.72	33	34	17	7	2	233	2808	.94			
5	35	MIKE RICHTER	68	3710	2.57	42	12	6	1	5	159	1758	.910	0	2	
22	30	GLENN HEALY	29	1368	3.03	10	12	2	2	2	69	567	.878	0	2	2
		NYR TOTALS	84	5089	2.72	52	24	8	3	7	231	2328	.901			
	50	*CHRISTIAN SOUCY	1	3	.00	0	0	0	0	0	0	0	.000	0	0	0
8	30	ED BELFOUR	70	3998	2.67	37	24	6	0	7	178	1892	.906	0	4	61
	31	JEFF HACKETT	22	1084	3.43	2	12	3	0	0	62	566	.890	0	1	2
		CHI TOTALS	84	5099	2.82	39	36	9	0	7	240	2458	.902			
6	1	*DAMIAN RHODES	22	1213	2.62	9	7	3	0	0	53	541	.902	0	0	2
19	29	FELIX POTVIN	66	3883	2.89	34	22	9	3	3	187	2010	.907	0	4	4
		TOR TOTALS	84	5115	2.85	43	19	12	3	3	143	1554	.905			
3	33	PATRICK ROY	68	3867	2.50	35	17	11	4	7	161	1/56	.918	0	1	30
	40	*LES KUNTAR	6	302	3.18	2	2	0	1	0	16	130	.877	0	0	2
26	1	RON TUGNUTT	8	378	3.81	2	3	1	0	0	24	182	.860	0	0	0
	37	ANDRE RACICOT	11	500	4.44	2	6	2	0	0	37	246	.850	0	0	0
		MTL TOTALS	84	5122	2.90	40	29	14	5	7	248	2533	.902			

RNK	NO.	GOALTENDER	GPI	MINS	AVG	W	L	T	EN	SO	GA	SA	SV%	G	A	PIM
	1	WENDELL YOUNG	9	480	2.50	2	3	1	1	1	20	211	.905	0	0	4
9	93	DAREN PUPPA	63	3653	2.71	22	33	6	4	4	165	1647	.899	0	1	2
	30	J.D. BERGERON	3	134	3.13	1	1	1	0	0	7	69	.899	0	0	0
	35	PAT JABLONSKI	15	834	3.88	5	6	3	0	0	54	374	.856	0	0	0
		T.B. TOTALS	84	5116	2.94	30	43	11	5	5	251	2296	.891			
18	30	JON CASEY	57	31/2	2.88	30	15	9	1	4	153	1289	.881	0	2	14
	39	JOHN BLUE	18	944	22.99	5	8	3	1	0	47	407	.885	0	0	7
30	37	VINCENT RIENDEAU	18	976	3.07	7	6	1	0	1	50	415	.880	01	0	
		BOS TOTALS	84	5116	2.96	42	29	13	2	5	252	2113	.881			
	35	MIKHAIL SHTALENKO	10	543	2.65	3	4	1	1	0	24	265	.909	0	0	0
13	31	GUY HEBERT	52	2991	2.83	20	27	3	5	2	141	1513	.907	0	0	2
26	1	RON TUGNUTT	28	1520	3.00	10	15	1	4	1	76	828	.908	0	0	2
		ANA TOTALS	84	5079	2.97	33	46	5	10	3	251	2616	.904			
	1	*ANDREI TREFILOV	11	623	2.50	3	4	2	1	2	26	305	.915	0	0	4
12	30	MIKE VERNON	48	2798	2.81	26	17	5	4	3	131	1209	.892	0	0	14
27	67	*TREVOR KIDD	31	1614	3.16	13	7	6	0	0	85	752	.887	0	4	4
	35	JEFF REESE	1	13	4.62	0	0	0	0	0	1	5	.800	0	0	0
	31	*JASON MUZZATTI	1	60	8.00	0	1	0	0	0	8	35	.771	0	0	0
		CGY TOTALS	84	5124	3.00	42	29	13	5	5	256	2311	.889			
16	29	*JAMIE MCLENNAN	22	1287	2.84	8	7	6	0	0	61	639	.905	0	1	6
23	82	RON HEXTALL	65	3581	3.08	27	26	6	3	5	184	1801	.898	0	3	52
	35	TOM DRAPER	7	227	4.23	1	3	0	0	0	16	118	.864	0	0	0
		NYI TOTALS	84	5119	3.09	46	46	12	3	5	264	2561	.897			
15	33	DON BEAUPRE	53	2853	2.84	24	16	8	3	2	135	1122	.880	0	1	16
24	31	RICK TABARACCI	32	1770	3.08	13	14	2	0	2	91	817	.889	0	0	6
	35	*BYRON DAFOE	5	230	3.39	2	2	0	0	0	13	101	.871	0	0	0
	37	*OLAF KOLZIG	7	224	5.36	0	3	0	1	0	20	128	.844	0	0	0
		WSH TOTALS	84	5099	3.09	39	35	10	4	4	263	2172	.879			
7	34	DARCY WAKALUK	36	2000	2.64	18	9	6	0	3	88	978	.910	0	2	34
28	35	ANDY MOOG	55	3121	3.27	24	20	7	7	2	170	1604	.894	0	1	16
		DAL TOTALS	84	5132	3.10	42	29	13	7	5	165	1589	.898			
14	32	ARTURS IRBE	74	4412	2.84	30	28	16	4	3	109	2064	.899	0	2	16
	29	JIM WAITE	15	697	4.30	3	7	0	2	0	50	319	.843	0	0	6
		S.J TOTALS	84	5125	3.10	33	35	16	6	3	265	2389	.889			
37	35	BOB ESSENSA	13	778	2.62	4	7	2	3	1	34	337	.899	02	0	
17	30	*CHRIS OSGOOD	41	2206	2.86	23	8	5	0	2	105	999	.895	0	0	2
38	2-	TIM CHEVELDAE	30	1572	3.47	16	9	1	3	1	91	727	.875	0	1	0
30	37	VINCENT RIENDEAU	8	345	4.00	2	4	0	1	0	23	131	.824	0	0	0
	31	PETER ING	3	170	5.29	1	2	0	0	0	15	102	.853	0	0	0
		DET TOTALS	84	5094	333.24	46	30	8	7	4	275	2303	.881			
20	1	KIRK MCLEAN	52	3128	2.99	23	26	3	5	3	156	1430	.891	0	4	2
36	35	KAY WHITMORE	32	1921	3.53	18	14	0	2	0	113	848	.867	0	06	
		VAN TOTALS	84	5107	3.32	40	33	11	1	1	283	2946	.904			

RNK	NO.	GOALTENDER	GPI	MINS	AVG	W	L	T	EN	SO	GA	SA	SV%	G	A	PIM
25	31	CURTIS JOSEPH	71	4127	3.10	36	23	11	0	1	213	2382	.911	0	3	4
	29	JIM HRIVNAK	23	970	4.27	4	10	0	1	0	69	563	.877	0	1	2
		STL TOTALS	84	5107	3.32	40	33	11	1	1	283	2946	.904			
30		ROBERTO ROMANO	2	025	1.44	1	0	1	0	0	3	56	.946	0	0	0
32	35	TOM BARRASSO	44	2482	3036	22	15	5	2	2	139	1304	.893	0	4	42
33	31	KEN WREGGET	42	2456	3.37	21	12	7	0	1	138	1291	.893	0	1	8
	1	ROB DOPSON	2	45	4.00	0	0	0	0	0	3	23	.870	0	0	0
		PIT TOTALS	84	5118	3.34	44	27	13	2	3	285	2676	.893			
	35	*MIKE LENARDUZZI	1	21	2.86	0	0	0	0	0	1	12	.917	0	0	0
21	1	SEAN BURKE	47	2750	2.99	17	24	5	7	2	137	1458	.906	0	0	16
	35	JEFF REESE	19	4086	3.09	5	9	3	4	1	56	514	.893	0	1	0
	40	FRANK PIETRANGELO	19	984	3.60	5	11	1	1	0	59	473	.875	0	0	2
	31	MARIO GOSSELIN	7	239	5.27	0	4	0	2	0	21	107	.804	0	0	0
		HFD TOTALS	84	5099	3.39	27	48	9	14	3	288	2588	.889			
	32	JACQUES CLOUTIER	14	475	3.03	3	2	1	1	0	24	232	.897	0	0	2
29	41	*JOCELYN THIBAULT	29	1504	3.31	8	13	3	3	0	83	748	.892	0	0	2
34	35	STEPHANE FISET	50	2798	3.39	20	25	4	7	2	158	1434	.890	0	3	8
	1	*GARTH SNOW	5	279	3.44	3	2	0	0	0	16	127	.874	0	0	2
		QUE TOTALS	84	5080	3.45	34	42	8	11	2	292	2572	.886			
	1	WAYNE COWLEY	1	57	3.16	0	1	0	0	0	3	35	.914	0	0	0
35	30	BILL RANFORD	71	4070	3.48	22	34	11	8	1	236	2325	.898	0	2	2
	31	*FRED BRATHWAITE	19	982	3.54	3	10	3	0	0	58	523	.889	0	0	0
		EDM TOTALS	84	5121	3.57	25	45	14	8	1	305	2891	.895			
31	33	DOMINIC ROUSSEL	60	3285	3.34	29	20	5	3	1	183	1762	.896	0	1	4
41	30	TOMMY SODERSTROM	34	1736	4.01	6	18	4	7	2	116	851	.864	0	0	0
	35	*FREDERIC CHABOT	4	80	4.29	0	1	1	0	0	5	40	.875	0	0	0
		PHI TOTALS	84	5102	3.69	35	39	10	10	3	314	2663	.882			
	1	RICK KNICKLE	4	174	3.10	1	2	0	2	0	9	71	.873	0	0	0
	35	ROBB STAUBER	22	1144	3.41	4	11	5	2	1	65	706	.908	0	0	18
39	32	KELLY HRUDEY	64	3713	3.68	22	31	7	9	1	228	2219	.897	0	1	6
	41	*DAVID GOVERDE	1	60	7.00	0	1	0	0	0	7	37	.811	0	0	0
		L.A. TOTALS	84	5124	3.77	27	45	12	13	2	322	3046	.894			
37	35	BOB ESSENSA	56	3136	3.85	19	30	6	5	1	201	1714	.883	0	0	6
38	29	TIM CHEVELDAE	14	788	3.96	5	8	1	0	1	52	485	.893	0	0	2
	1	*MICHAEL O'NEILL	17	738	4.15	0	9	1	1	0	51	382	.866	0	0	0
	30	STEPH BEAUREGARD	13	418	4.88	0	4	1	0	0	34	211	.839	0	0	0
		WPG TOTALS	84	5098	4.05	24	51	9	6	2	344	2798	.877			
42	60	*DARRIN MADELEY	32	1583	4.36	3	18	5	3	0	115	868	.868	0	0	0
43	1	CRAIG BILLINGTON	63	3319	4.59	11	41	4	6	0	254	1801	.859	0	0	8
	35	MARK LAFOREST	5	182	5.60	0	2	0	0	0	18	96	.823	0	0	0
	32	DANIEL BERTHIAUME	1	1	20.00	0	0	0	0	0	2	2	.000	0	0	0
		OTT TOTALS	84	5105	4.67	14	61	9	9	0	397	2776	.857			

GOALTENDING LEADERS
(Min. 27 GPI)

GOALS AGAINST AVERAGE

GOALTENDER	TEAM	GPI	MINS	GA	AVG
DOMINIK HASEK	BUFFALO	58	3358	109	1.95
MARTIN BRODEUR	NEW JERSEY	47	2625	105	2.40
PATRICK ROY	MONTREAL	68	3867	161	2.50
JOHN VANBIESBROUCK	FLORIDA	57	3440	145	2.53
MIKE RICHTER	NY RANGERS	68	3710	159	2.57

WINS

GOALTENDER	TEAM	GPI	MINS	W	L	T
MIKE RICHTER	NY RANGERS	68	3710	42	12	6
ED BELFOUR	CHICAGO	70	3998	2.67	37	24	6
CURTIS JOSEPH	ST LOUIS	71	4127	36	23	11
PATRICK ROY	MONTREAL	68	3867	2.50	35	17	11
FELIX POTVIN	TORONTO	66	3883	2.89	34	22	9

SAVE PERCENTAGE

GOALTENDER	TEAM	GPI	MINS	GA	SA	SPCTG	W	L	T
DOMINIK HASEK	BUFFALO	58	3358	109	.930	30	20	6	
JOHN VANBIESBROUCK	FLORIDA	57	3440	145	.924	21	25	11	
PATRICK ROY	MONTREAL	68	3867	161	2.50	.918	35	17	11
MARTIN BRODEUR	NEW JERSEY	47	2625	105	.915	27	11	8	
MARK FITZPATRICK	FLORIDA	28	1603	2.73	.913	12	8	6	

SHUTOUTS

GOALTENDER	TEAM	GPI	MINS	SO	W	L	T
DOMINIK HASEK	BUFFALO	58	3358	7	30	20	6
PATRICK ROY	MONTREAL	68	3867	7	35	17	11
ED BeLFOUR	CHICAGO	70	3998	7	37	24	6
RON HEXTALL	NY ISLANDERS	65	3581	5	27	26	6
MIKE RICHTER	NY RANGERS	68	3710	5	42	12	6
JOHN CASEY	BOSTON	57	3192	4	30	15	9
DAREN PUPPA	TAMPA BAY	63	3653	4	22	33	6

ROOKIE GOALTENDING LEADERS

GOALS AGAINST AVERAGE

GOALTENDER (R)	TEAM	GPI	MINS	GA	AVG
MARTIN BRODEUR	NEW JERSEY	47	2625	105	2.40
CHRIS OSGOOD	DETROIT	41	2206	105	2.86
TREVOR KIDD	CALGARY	31	1614	85	3.16
JOCELYN THIBAULT	QUEBEC	29	1504	83	3.31
DARRIN MADELEY	OTTAWA	32	1583	115	4.36

SAVE PERCENTAGE

GOALTENDER (R)	TEAM	GPI	MINS	GA	SA	SPCTG	W	L	T
MARTIN BRODEUR	NEW JERSEY	47	2625	105	1238	.915	27	11	8
CHRIS OSGOOD	DETROIT	41	2206	105	999	.895	23	8	5
JOCELYN THIBAULT	QUEBEC	29	1504	83	768	.892	8	13	3
TREVOR KIDD	CALGARY	31	1614	85	752	.887	13	7	6
DARRIN MADELEY	OTTAWA	32	1583	115	868	.867	3	18	5

1994-95 NHL Schedule

* DENOTES AFTERNOON GAME

Sat Oct 1

CHICAGO	AT	PITTSBURGH
WINNIPEG	AT	OTTAWA
BOSTON	AT	MONTREAL
BUFFALO	AT	QUEBEC
TAMPA BAY	AT	NY ISLANDERS
NY RANGERS	AT	NEW JERSEY
HARTFORD	AT	PHILADELPHIA
WASHINGTON	AT	TORONTO
ST LOUIS	AT	DETROIT
ANAHEIM	AT	DALLAS
VANCOUVER	AT	CALGARY
LOS ANGELES	AT	SAN JOSE

Sun Oct 2

ST LOUIS	AT	CHICAGO
VANCOUVER	AT	EDMONTON

Mon Oct 3

BOSTON	AT	OTTAWA
PITTSBURGH	AT	NY RANGERS

Tue Oct 4

QUEBEC	AT	TAMPA BAY
PHILADELPHIA	AT	FLORIDA
HARTFORD	AT	TORONTO
CALGARY	AT	DALLAS

Wed Oct 5

BUFFALO	AT	PITTSBURGH
WASHINGTON	AT	OTTAWA
MONTREAL	AT	WINNIPEG
ANAHEIM	AT	EDMONTON
SAN JOSE	AT	VANCOUVER
DETROIT	AT	LOS ANGELES

Thu Oct 6

QUEBEC	AT	BOSTON

PHILADELPHIA	AT	NY RANGERS
NEW JERSEY	AT	CHICAGO
ST LOUIS	AT	FLORIDA

Fri Oct 7

MONTREAL	AT	BUFFALO
OTTAWA	AT	NY ISLANDERS
PITTSBURGH	AT	WASHINGTON
ST LOUIS	AT	TAMPA BAY
EDMONTON	AT	WINNIPEG
ANAHEIM	AT	VANCOUVER
DETROIT	AT	SAN JOSE

Sat Oct 8

TORONTO	AT	BOSTON
QUEBEC	AT	HARTFORD
BUFFALO	AT	MONTREAL
OTTAWA	AT	NEW JERSEY
TAMPA BAY	AT	PHILADELPHIA
NY ISLANDERS	AT	WASHINGTON
* NY RANGERS	AT	FLORIDA
CHICAGO	AT	DALLAS
CALGARY	AT	LOS ANGELES

Sun Oct 9

EDMONTON	AT	CHICAGO
VANCOUVER	AT	SAN JOSE
CALGARY	AT	ANAHEIM

Mon Oct 10

* FLORIDA	AT	BOSTON
TORONTO	AT	BUFFALO

Tue Oct 11

PITTSBURGH	AT	QUEBEC
TAMPA BAY	AT	NY RANGERS
OTTAWA	AT	TORONTO

CHICAGO	AT	ST LOUIS
WINNIPEG	AT	DALLAS
SAN JOSE	AT	LOS ANGELES

Wed Oct 12

FLORIDA	AT	HARTFORD
WASHINGTON	AT	PITTSBURGH
NY ISLANDERS	AT	MONTREAL
PHILADELPHIA	AT	NEW JERSEY
BUFFALO	AT	DETROIT
CALGARY	AT	EDMONTON
BOSTON	AT	SAN JOSE
VANCOUVER	AT	ANAHEIM

Thu Oct 13

QUEBEC	AT	TORONTO
WINNIPEG	AT	CHICAGO
NY RANGERS	AT	ST LOUIS
VANCOUVER	AT	LOS ANGELES

Fri Oct 14

HARTFORD	AT	BUFFALO
MONTREAL	AT	WASHINGTON
FLORIDA	AT	DETROIT
PHILADELPHIA	AT	WINNIPEG
SAN JOSE	AT	CALGARY
BOSTON	AT	ANAHEIM

Sat Oct 15

NY RANGERS	AT	HARTFORD
MONTREAL	AT	PITTSBURGH
CHICAGO	AT	QUEBEC
DETROIT	AT	NY ISLANDERS
BUFFALO	AT	WASHINGTON
NEW JERSEY	AT	TAMPA BAY
ST LOUIS	AT	TORONTO
OTTAWA	AT	DALLAS
EDMONTON	AT	VANCOUVER

BOSTON	AT	LOS ANGELES

Sun Oct 16

NEW JERSEY	AT	FLORIDA
TAMPA BAY	AT	ST LOUIS
SAN JOSE	AT	WINNIPEG
PHILADELPHIA	AT	CALGARY

Mon Oct 17

CHICAGO	AT	MONTREAL
DALLAS	AT	DETROIT
PHILADELPHIA	AT	VANCOUVER
EDMONTON	AT	ANAHEIM

Tue Oct 18

NY RANGERS	AT	QUEBEC
LOS ANGELES	AT	NY ISLANDERS
PITTSBURGH	AT	TAMPA BAY
SAN JOSE	AT	ST LOUIS
WINNIPEG	AT	CALGARY

Wed Oct 19

OTTAWA	AT	HARTFORD
WASHINGTON	AT	NEW JERSEY
TORONTO	AT	FLORIDA
MONTREAL	AT	DETROIT
DALLAS	AT	WINNIPEG
ANAHEIM	AT	EDMONTON
BOSTON	AT	VANCOUVER

Thu Oct 20

LOS ANGELES	AT	NY RANGERS
QUEBEC	AT	PHILADELPHIA
TORONTO	AT	TAMPA BAY
SAN JOSE	AT	CHICAGO
ANAHEIM	AT	CALGARY

Fri Oct 21

FLORIDA	AT	BUFFALO
HARTFORD	AT	WASHINGTON
PITTSBURGH	AT	DETROIT
VANCOUVER	AT	DALLAS
BOSTON	AT	EDMONTON

Sat Oct 22

WASHINGTON	AT	HARTFORD
LOS ANGELES	AT	PITTSBURGH
NY RANGERS	AT	MONTREAL
DETROIT	AT	QUEBEC
FLORIDA	AT	NY ISLANDERS
* SAN JOSE	AT	NEW JERSEY
* OTTAWA	AT	PHILADELPHIA

TORONTO	AT	ST LOUIS
CHICAGO	AT	WINNIPEG
BOSTON	AT	CALGARY

Sun Oct 23

QUEBEC	AT	BUFFALO
* TAMPA BAY	AT	OTTAWA
SAN JOSE	AT	NY RANGERS
LOS ANGELES	AT	CHICAGO
VANCOUVER	AT	ST LOUIS
* EDMONTON	AT	DALLAS
ANAHEIM	AT	WINNIPEG

Mon Oct 24

NEW JERSEY	AT	MONTREAL
CALGARY	AT	TORONTO

Tue Oct 25

DALLAS	AT	PITTSBURGH
EDMONTON	AT	QUEBEC
VANCOUVER	AT	NY ISLANDERS
LOS ANGELES	AT	FLORIDA
ANAHEIM	AT	DETROIT
WASHINGTON	AT	ST LOUIS

Wed Oct 26

PITTSBURGH	AT	OTTAWA
EDMONTON	AT	MONTREAL
DALLAS	AT	NY RANGERS
CALGARY	AT	NEW JERSEY
LOS ANGELES	AT	TAMPA BAY

Thu Oct 27

MONTREAL	AT	BOSTON
QUEBEC	AT	HARTFORD
VANCOUVER	AT	PHILADELPHIA
BUFFALO	AT	FLORIDA
ANAHEIM	AT	CHICAGO
WASHINGTON	AT	WINNIPEG

Fri Oct 28

CALGARY	AT	NY RANGERS
EDMONTON	AT	TORONTO
LOS ANGELES	AT	DETROIT

Sat Oct 29

BUFFALO	AT	BOSTON
WINNIPEG	AT	HARTFORD
DETROIT	AT	OTTAWA
PITTSBURGH	AT	MONTREAL
DALLAS	AT	QUEBEC

CALGARY	AT	NY ISLANDERS
VANCOUVER	AT	NEW JERSEY
TORONTO	AT	PHILADELPHIA
ST LOUIS	AT	SAN JOSE

Sun Oct 30

VANCOUVER	AT	NY RANGERS
WINNIPEG	AT	NEW JERSEY
TAMPA BAY	AT	CHICAGO
WASHINGTON	AT	EDMONTON
ST LOUIS	AT	ANAHEIM

Tue Nov 1

OTTAWA	AT	PITTSBURGH
TAMPA BAY	AT	QUEBEC
HARTFORD	AT	DETROIT
NY ISLANDERS	AT	DALLAS
WASHINGTON	AT	CALGARY
NEW JERSEY	AT	SAN JOSE
NY RANGERS	AT	LOS ANGELES

Wed Nov 2

CHICAGO	AT	BUFFALO
PHILADELPHIA	AT	OTTAWA
TAMPA BAY	AT	MONTREAL
NY ISLANDERS	AT	ST LOUIS
TORONTO	AT	WINNIPEG
FLORIDA	AT	EDMONTON
WASHINGTON	AT	VANCOUVER
NY RANGERS	AT	ANAHEIM

Thu Nov 3

PITTSBURGH	AT	BOSTON

Fri Nov 4

PHILADELPHIA	AT	BUFFALO
TORONTO	AT	DETROIT
WINNIPEG	AT	DALLAS
EDMONTON	AT	CALGARY
LOS ANGELES	AT	VANCOUVER
NEW JERSEY	AT	ANAHEIM

Sat Nov 5

CHICAGO	AT	BOSTON
HARTFORD	AT	PITTSBURGH
MONTREAL	AT	OTTAWA
BUFFALO	AT	PHILADELPHIA
QUEBEC	AT	WASHINGTON
NY ISLANDERS	AT	TAMPA BAY
DETROIT	AT	TORONTO
WINNIPEG	AT	ST LOUIS
FLORIDA	AT	VANCOUVER

NY RANGERS	AT	SAN JOSE

Sun Nov 6

DALLAS	AT	CHICAGO
FLORIDA	AT	CALGARY
NEW JERSEY	AT	LOS ANGELES

Mon Nov 7

BOSTON	AT	OTTAWA
DALLAS	AT	NY ISLANDERS
SAN JOSE	AT	VANCOUVER

Tue Nov 8

MONTREAL	AT	HARTFORD
NEW JERSEY	AT	PITTSBURGH
TAMPA BAY	AT	BUFFALO
PHILADELPHIA	AT	QUEBEC
EDMONTON	AT	WASHINGTON
WINNIPEG	AT	DETROIT
ST LOUIS	AT	CALGARY
VANCOUVER	AT	SAN JOSE
ANAHEIM	AT	LOS ANGELES

Wed Nov 9

HARTFORD	AT	NY RANGERS
NY ISLANDERS	AT	FLORIDA
TAMPA BAY	AT	TORONTO

Thu Nov 10

QUEBEC	AT	BOSTON
OTTAWA	AT	BUFFALO
MONTREAL	AT	NEW JERSEY
WASHINGTON	AT	PHILADELPHIA
TORONTO	AT	CHICAGO
PITTSBURGH	AT	DALLAS
ST LOUIS	AT	WINNIPEG
ANAHEIM	AT	SAN JOSE
CALGARY	AT	LOS ANGELES

Fri Nov 11

NY ISLANDERS	AT	NY RANGERS
EDMONTON	AT	FLORIDA
VANCOUVER	AT	ANAHEIM

Sat Nov 12

* OTTAWA	AT	QUEBEC
HARTFORD	AT	NY ISLANDERS
* BOSTON	AT	NEW JERSEY
PHILADELPHIA	AT	WASHINGTON
EDMONTON	AT	TAMPA BAY
MONTREAL	AT	TORONTO
PITTSBURGH	AT	ST LOUIS

DETROIT	AT	DALLAS
CHICAGO	AT	WINNIPEG
BUFFALO	AT	SAN JOSE
VANCOUVER	AT	LOS ANGELES

Sun Nov 13

HARTFORD	AT	OTTAWA
* NEW JERSEY	AT	QUEBEC
WASHINGTON	AT	NY RANGERS
DALLAS	AT	PHILADELPHIA
BOSTON	AT	FLORIDA
ST LOUIS	AT	CHICAGO
CALGARY	AT	ANAHEIM

Mon Nov 14

EDMONTON	AT	WINNIPEG

Tue Nov 15

DALLAS	AT	WASHINGTON
CALGARY	AT	SAN JOSE
CHICAGO	AT	LOS ANGELES
BUFFALO	AT	ANAHEIM

Wed Nov 16

ST LOUIS	AT	HARTFORD
PITTSBURGH	AT	OTTAWA
NY ISLANDERS	AT	MONTREAL
DALLAS	AT	NEW JERSEY
DETROIT	AT	TAMPA BAY
WINNIPEG	AT	TORONTO
VANCOUVER	AT	EDMONTON

Thu Nov 17

ST LOUIS	AT	BOSTON
OTTAWA	AT	PITTSBURGH
MONTREAL	AT	QUEBEC
NY RANGERS	AT	PHILADELPHIA
DETROIT	AT	FLORIDA
ANAHEIM	AT	VANCOUVER
BUFFALO	AT	LOS ANGELES

Fri Nov 18

NY ISLANDERS	AT	NEW JERSEY
TORONTO	AT	WASHINGTON
WINNIPEG	AT	TAMPA BAY
SAN JOSE	AT	DALLAS
CALGARY	AT	EDMONTON

Sat Nov 19

WASHINGTON	AT	BOSTON
NY ISLANDERS	AT	HARTFORD
NY RANGERS	AT	OTTAWA

QUEBEC	AT	MONTREAL
PITTSBURGH	AT	PHILADELPHIA
NEW JERSEY	AT	TAMPA BAY
WINNIPEG	AT	FLORIDA
ST LOUIS	AT	TORONTO
CALGARY	AT	VANCOUVER

Sun Nov 20

DETROIT	AT	PHILADELPHIA
SAN JOSE	AT	EDMONTON
CHICAGO	AT	ANAHEIM

Mon Nov 21

PITTSBURGH	AT	BOSTON
HARTFORD	AT	MONTREAL
FLORIDA	AT	QUEBEC
VANCOUVER	AT	TORONTO
BUFFALO	AT	DALLAS

Tue Nov 22

LOS ANGELES	AT	CALGARY
CHICAGO	AT	SAN JOSE

Wed Nov 23

PHILADELPHIA	AT	HARTFORD
NY RANGERS	AT	PITTSBURGH
BOSTON	AT	BUFFALO
NEW JERSEY	AT	OTTAWA
FLORIDA	AT	MONTREAL
TAMPA BAY	AT	NY ISLANDERS
VANCOUVER	AT	WASHINGTON
ST LOUIS	AT	DETROIT
QUEBEC	AT	DALLAS
TORONTO	AT	WINNIPEG
LOS ANGELES	AT	EDMONTON
SAN JOSE	AT	ANAHEIM

Thu Nov 24

QUEBEC	AT	ST LOUIS
CHICAGO	AT	CALGARY

Fri Nov 25

* ANAHEIM	AT	BOSTON
VANCOUVER	AT	BUFFALO
* NEW JERSEY	AT	PHILADELPHIA
PITTSBURGH	AT	WASHINGTON
NY RANGERS	AT	WINNIPEG
CHICAGO	AT	EDMONTON

Sat Nov 26

* ANAHEIM	AT	HARTFORD
SAN JOSE	AT	PITTSBURGH

FLORIDA	AT	OTTAWA
LOS ANGELES	AT	MONTREAL
WASHINGTON	AT	QUEBEC
TORONTO	AT	NY ISLANDERS
* TAMPA BAY	AT	PHILADELPHIA
* NEW JERSEY	AT	DETROIT
ST LOUIS	AT	DALLAS
CALGARY	AT	EDMONTON

Sun Nov 27
* VANCOUVER	AT	BOSTON
TAMPA BAY	AT	HARTFORD
NY ISLANDERS	AT	BUFFALO
FLORIDA	AT	NY RANGERS

Mon Nov 28
LOS ANGELES	AT	OTTAWA
WASHINGTON	AT	MONTREAL
SAN JOSE	AT	DETROIT
WINNIPEG	AT	ST LOUIS
TORONTO	AT	DALLAS

Tue Nov 29
NY RANGERS	AT	HARTFORD
ANAHEIM	AT	PITTSBURGH
LOS ANGELES	AT	QUEBEC
BOSTON	AT	NY ISLANDERS

Wed Nov 30
WASHINGTON	AT	OTTAWA
BUFFALO	AT	NY RANGERS
FLORIDA	AT	TAMPA BAY
ANAHEIM	AT	TORONTO
PHILADELPHIA	AT	DETROIT
MONTREAL	AT	ST LOUIS
WINNIPEG	AT	EDMONTON

Thu Dec 1
HARTFORD	AT	BOSTON
WASHINGTON	AT	PITTSBURGH
QUEBEC	AT	NEW JERSEY
NY ISLANDERS	AT	PHILADELPHIA
SAN JOSE	AT	FLORIDA
MONTREAL	AT	CHICAGO

Fri Dec 2
LOS ANGELES	AT	BUFFALO
ANAHEIM	AT	NY RANGERS
SAN JOSE	AT	TAMPA BAY
CALGARY	AT	DETROIT
DALLAS	AT	VANCOUVER

Sat Dec 3
BOSTON	AT	PITTSBURGH
PHILADELPHIA	AT	OTTAWA
DETROIT	AT	MONTREAL
HARTFORD	AT	QUEBEC
BUFFALO	AT	NY ISLANDERS
* EDMONTON	AT	NEW JERSEY
TAMPA BAY	AT	WASHINGTON
CHICAGO	AT	FLORIDA
LOS ANGELES	AT	TORONTO
WINNIPEG	AT	VANCOUVER

Sun Dec 4
BOSTON	AT	HARTFORD
CALGARY	AT	OTTAWA
EDMONTON	AT	NY RANGERS
ANAHEIM	AT	CHICAGO
NEW JERSEY	AT	ST LOUIS

Mon Dec 5
TAMPA BAY	AT	FLORIDA
SAN JOSE	AT	DALLAS

Tue Dec 6
NY RANGERS	AT	PITTSBURGH
CALGARY	AT	QUEBEC
EDMONTON	AT	NY ISLANDERS
BOSTON	AT	DETROIT
TORONTO	AT	VANCOUVER

Wed Dec 7
DETROIT	AT	HARTFORD
PITTSBURGH	AT	BUFFALO
CALGARY	AT	MONTREAL
OTTAWA	AT	TAMPA BAY
ST LOUIS	AT	DALLAS
NEW JERSEY	AT	WINNIPEG
TORONTO	AT	SAN JOSE
WASHINGTON	AT	ANAHEIM

Thu Dec 8
EDMONTON	AT	BOSTON
NY ISLANDERS	AT	NY RANGERS
MONTREAL	AT	PHILADELPHIA
OTTAWA	AT	FLORIDA
VANCOUVER	AT	CHICAGO
WASHINGTON	AT	LOS ANGELES

Fri Dec 9
HARTFORD	AT	BUFFALO
DETROIT	AT	NEW JERSEY
QUEBEC	AT	TAMPA BAY

CHICAGO	AT	DALLAS
ANAHEIM	AT	SAN JOSE

Sat Dec 10
CALGARY	AT	BOSTON
EDMONTON	AT	HARTFORD
BUFFALO	AT	PITTSBURGH
PHILADELPHIA	AT	MONTREAL
OTTAWA	AT	NY ISLANDERS
QUEBEC	AT	FLORIDA
DALLAS	AT	ST LOUIS
VANCOUVER	AT	WINNIPEG
WASHINGTON	AT	SAN JOSE
TORONTO	AT	LOS ANGELES

Sun Dec 11
NEW JERSEY	AT	PHILADELPHIA
FLORIDA	AT	CHICAGO
DETROIT	AT	ST LOUIS
TORONTO	AT	ANAHEIM

Mon Dec 12
CALGARY	AT	HARTFORD
LOS ANGELES	AT	VANCOUVER

Tue Dec 13
NEW JERSEY	AT	OTTAWA
FLORIDA	AT	QUEBEC
NY RANGERS (Portland)	AT	NY ISLANDERS
WINNIPEG	AT	WASHINGTON
DALLAS	AT	DETROIT
TORONTO	AT	EDMONTON
PITTSBURGH	AT	ANAHEIM

Wed Dec 14
OTTAWA	AT	HARTFORD
BOSTON	AT	MONTREAL
BUFFALO	AT	TAMPA BAY
NY RANGERS	AT	VANCOUVER
DALLAS	AT	CHICAGO
NY ISLANDERS	AT	SAN JOSE

Thu Dec 15
FLORIDA	AT	NEW JERSEY
WINNIPEG	AT	PHILADELPHIA
QUEBEC	AT	DETROIT
TORONTO	AT	CALGARY
PITTSBURGH	AT	LOS ANGELES

Fri Dec 16
MONTREAL	AT	BUFFALO

BOSTON	AT	WASHINGTON
CHICAGO	AT	TAMPA BAY
ST LOUIS	AT	VANCOUVER
SAN JOSE	AT	ANAHEIM

Sat Dec 17

BUFFALO	AT	BOSTON
WASHINGTON	AT	HARTFORD
OTTAWA	AT	MONTREAL
* PHILADELPHIA	AT	QUEBEC
FLORIDA	AT	TORONTO
* WINNIPEG	AT	DETROIT
NEW JERSEY	AT	DALLAS
NY RANGERS	AT	EDMONTON
PITTSBURGH	AT	SAN JOSE
NY ISLANDERS	AT	LOS ANGELES

Sun Dec 18

* TAMPA BAY	AT	QUEBEC
DETROIT	AT	WINNIPEG
NY RANGERS	AT	CALGARY
PHILADELPHIA	AT	CHICAGO
ST LOUIS	AT	EDMONTON
NY ISLANDERS	AT	ANAHEIM

Mon Dec 19

BUFFALO	AT	OTTAWA
TAMPA BAY	AT	MONTREAL
DALLAS	AT	TORONTO

Tue Dec 20

DETROIT	AT	PITTSBURGH
HARTFORD	AT	NEW JERSEY
WASHINGTON	AT	FLORIDA
NY ISLANDERS	AT	CHICAGO
ST LOUIS	AT	CALGARY
EDMONTON	AT	SAN JOSE

Wed Dec 21

DALLAS	AT	HARTFORD
TAMPA BAY	AT	OTTAWA
QUEBEC	AT	PHILADELPHIA
BUFFALO	AT	MONTREAL
BOSTON	AT	NY RANGERS
CHICAGO	AT	TORONTO
ANAHEIM	AT	WINNIPEG
VANCOUVER	AT	SAN JOSE
(Portland)		

Thu Dec 22

DALLAS	AT	BOSTON
PITTSBURGH	AT	FLORIDA

ANAHEIM	AT	CALGARY
EDMONTON	AT	LOS ANGELES

Fri Dec 23

HARTFORD	AT	BUFFALO
QUEBEC	AT	NY ISLANDERS
MONTREAL	AT	NY RANGERS
OTTAWA	AT	NEW JERSEY
PHILADELPHIA	AT	WASHINGTON
PITTSBURGH	AT	TAMPA BAY
CHICAGO	AT	DETROIT
VANCOUVER	AT	ST LOUIS

Mon Dec 26

HARTFORD	AT	BOSTON
WASHINGTON	AT	NY ISLANDERS
OTTAWA	AT	NY RANGERS
BUFFALO	AT	NEW JERSEY
PHILADELPHIA	AT	TAMPA BAY
DETROIT	AT	CHICAGO
ST LOUIS	AT	DALLAS
LOS ANGELES	AT	ANAHEIM

Tue Dec 27

NEW JERSEY	AT	BUFFALO
TORONTO	AT	QUEBEC
NY RANGERS	AT	WASHINGTON
PHILADELPHIA	AT	FLORIDA
CHICAGO	AT	ST LOUIS
CALGARY	AT	WINNIPEG
SAN JOSE	AT	EDMONTON
MONTREAL	AT	VANCOUVER

Wed Dec 28

PITTSBURGH	AT	HARTFORD
NY ISLANDERS	AT	OTTAWA
DALLAS	AT	DETROIT
ANAHEIM	AT	LOS ANGELES

Thu Dec 29

BUFFALO	AT	PITTSBURGH
HARTFORD	AT	QUEBEC
FLORIDA	AT	WASHINGTON
DALLAS	AT	TORONTO
SAN JOSE	AT	ST LOUIS
BOSTON	AT	WINNIPEG
CALGARY	AT	VANCOUVER

Fri Dec 30

PHILADELPHIA	AT	NY ISLANDERS
FLORIDA	AT	NEW JERSEY
NY RANGERS	AT	TAMPA BAY

MONTREAL	AT	EDMONTON
CHICAGO	AT	ANAHEIM

Sat Dec 31

NY ISLANDERS	AT	PITTSBURGH
PHILADELPHIA	AT	BUFFALO
HARTFORD	AT	OTTAWA
BOSTON	AT	TORONTO
SAN JOSE	AT	DETROIT
DALLAS	AT	ST LOUIS
* LOS ANGELES	AT	WINNIPEG
MONTREAL	AT	CALGARY
NEW JERSEY	AT	WASHINGTON
QUEBEC	AT	VANCOUVER

Sun Jan 1

* NY RANGERS	AT	FLORIDA
SAN JOSE	AT	CHICAGO

Mon Jan 2

* TAMPA BAY	AT	BOSTON
OTTAWA	AT	TORONTO
(Hamilton)		
LOS ANGELES	AT	DALLAS
* ST LOUIS	AT	WASHINGTON
EDMONTON	AT	WINNIPEG
(Saskatoon)		
* MONTREAL	AT	ANAHEIM

Tue Jan 3

CHICAGO	AT	NY ISLANDERS
ST LOUIS	AT	NY RANGERS
VANCOUVER	AT	FLORIDA
CALGARY	AT	DETROIT

Wed Jan 4

LOS ANGELES	AT	HARTFORD
PITTSBURGH	AT	NEW JERSEY
VANCOUVER	AT	TAMPA BAY
MONTREAL	AT	SAN JOSE

Thu Jan 5

PHILADELPHIA	AT	BOSTON
FLORIDA	AT	PITTSBURGH
MONTREAL	AT	QUEBEC
(Phoenix)		
NY RANGERS	AT	NY ISLANDERS
CALGARY	AT	CHICAGO
OTTAWA	AT	WINNIPEG

Fri Jan 6

VANCOUVER	AT	HARTFORD

ANAHEIM	AT	BUFFALO
LOS ANGELES	AT	WASHINGTON
DALLAS	AT	TAMPA BAY
CHICAGO	AT	DETROIT

Sat Jan 7

DETROIT	AT	BOSTON
BUFFALO	AT	HARTFORD
PHILADELPHIA	AT	PITTSBURGH
(San Antonio)		
TORONTO	AT	OTTAWA
WASHINGTON	AT	NY ISLANDERS
ANAHEIM	AT	NEW JERSEY
NY RANGERS	AT	TAMPA BAY
FLORIDA	AT	ST LOUIS
WINNIPEG	AT	DALLAS
QUEBEC	AT	EDMONTON
* CALGARY	AT	SAN JOSE

Sun Jan 8

LOS ANGELES	AT	CHICAGO
WINNIPEG	AT	ST LOUIS
QUEBEC	AT	CALGARY

Mon Jan 9

NY ISLANDERS	AT	BUFFALO
(Minnesota)		
OTTAWA	AT	MONTREAL
FLORIDA	AT	NY RANGERS
PITTSBURGH	AT	NEW JERSEY
(Denver)		
ANAHEIM	AT	PHILADELPHIA
DALLAS	AT	EDMONTON

Tue Jan 10

WINNIPEG	AT	TORONTO
LOS ANGELES	AT	ST LOUIS
TAMPA BAY	AT	CALGARY

Wed Jan 11

WASHINGTON	AT	BUFFALO
BOSTON	AT	OTTAWA
FLORIDA	AT	NY ISLANDERS
PITTSBURGH	AT	NY RANGERS
PHILADELPHIA	AT	NEW JERSEY
ANAHEIM	AT	DETROIT
TAMPA BAY	AT	EDMONTON
CHICAGO	AT	VANCOUVER
DALLAS	AT	SAN JOSE

Thu Jan 12

WINNIPEG	AT	BOSTON

MONTREAL	AT	QUEBEC
FLORIDA	AT	PHILADELPHIA
ANAHEIM	AT	TORONTO
CHICAGO	AT	CALGARY
ST LOUIS	AT	LOS ANGELES

Fri Jan 13

HARTFORD	AT	PITTSBURGH
NY ISLANDERS	AT	NEW JERSEY
WINNIPEG	AT	DETROIT
BUFFALO	AT	CALGARY
TAMPA BAY	AT	VANCOUVER

Sat Jan 14

NY ISLANDERS	AT	PITTSBURGH
FLORIDA	AT	MONTREAL
BOSTON	AT	QUEBEC
OTTAWA	AT	PHILADELPHIA
NY RANGERS	AT	WASHINGTON
DETROIT	AT	TORONTO
EDMONTON	AT	VANCOUVER
ST LOUIS	AT	SAN JOSE
DALLAS	AT	LOS ANGELES

Sun Jan 15

ANAHEIM	AT	OTTAWA
NEW JERSEY	AT	NY RANGERS
HARTFORD	AT	CHICAGO
TAMPA BAY	AT	WINNIPEG
BUFFALO	AT	EDMONTON

Mon Jan 16

* WASHINGTON	AT	BOSTON
* PHILADELPHIA	AT	NY ISLANDERS
HARTFORD	AT	DALLAS
LOS ANGELES	AT	CALGARY
VANCOUVER	AT	SAN JOSE

Tue Jan 17

ANAHEIM	AT	QUEBEC
DETROIT	AT	NY RANGERS
NEW JERSEY	AT	FLORIDA
CHICAGO	AT	TORONTO
ST LOUIS	AT	WINNIPEG
LOS ANGELES	AT	EDMONTON

Wed Jan 18

PITTSBURGH	AT	BOSTON
ANAHEIM	AT	MONTREAL
QUEBEC	AT	NY ISLANDERS
WASHINGTON	AT	PHILADELPHIA
NEW JERSEY	AT	TAMPA BAY

TORONTO	AT	DETROIT
DALLAS	AT	HARTFORD
(Denver)		
WINNIPEG	AT	CALGARY
BUFFALO	AT	VANCOUVER

Sat Jan 21

ALL-STAR GAME	AT	SAN JOSE

Mon Jan 23

PHILADELPHIA	AT	PITTSBURGH
OTTAWA	AT	BUFFALO
HARTFORD	AT	MONTREAL
QUEBEC	AT	NY RANGERS
TAMPA BAY	AT	FLORIDA
EDMONTON	AT	CALGARY
LOS ANGELES	AT	SAN JOSE

Tue Jan 24

WASHINGTON	AT	QUEBEC
ST LOUIS	AT	NY ISLANDERS
VANCOUVER	AT	DETROIT
DALLAS	AT	LOS ANGELES

Wed Jan 25

OTTAWA	AT	HARTFORD
NEW JERSEY	AT	BUFFALO
BOSTON	AT	NY RANGERS
CALGARY	AT	TAMPA BAY
VANCOUVER	AT	TORONTO
EDMONTON	AT	CHICAGO
WINNIPEG	AT	SAN JOSE
DALLAS	AT	ANAHEIM

Thu Jan 26

NEW JERSEY	AT	BOSTON
WASHINGTON	AT	NY ISLANDERS
HARTFORD	AT	PHILADELPHIA
CALGARY	AT	FLORIDA
EDMONTON	AT	ST LOUIS
SAN JOSE	AT	LOS ANGELES

Fri Jan 27

VANCOUVER	AT	PITTSBURGH
QUEBEC	AT	BUFFALO
TAMPA BAY	AT	NY RANGERS
OTTAWA	AT	WASHINGTON
TORONTO	AT	CHICAGO
WINNIPEG	AT	ANAHEIM

Sat Jan 28

* FLORIDA	AT	HARTFORD

TORONTO	AT	PITTSBURGH
BUFFALO	AT	OTTAWA
* NEW JERSEY	AT	MONTREAL
NY RANGERS	AT	QUEBEC
TAMPA BAY	AT	NY ISLANDERS
* BOSTON	AT	PHILADELPHIA
* EDMONTON	AT	DETROIT
CALGARY	AT	ST LOUIS
* DALLAS	AT	SAN JOSE
WINNIPEG	AT	LOS ANGELES

Sun Jan 29

* PHILADELPHIA	AT	MONTREAL
* CHICAGO	AT	WASHINGTON

Mon Jan 30

FLORIDA	AT	BOSTON
NY ISLANDERS	AT	NY RANGERS
SAN JOSE	AT	TORONTO
DETROIT	AT	EDMONTON
HARTFORD	AT	VANCOUVER

Tue Jan 31

WASHINGTON	AT	NEW JERSEY
CHICAGO	AT	PHILADELPHIA
NY ISLANDERS	AT	FLORIDA
ANAHEIM	AT	ST LOUIS
WINNIPEG	AT	LOS ANGELES
(Phoenix)		

Wed Feb 1

SAN JOSE	AT	OTTAWA
MONTREAL	AT	TAMPA BAY
DETROIT	AT	CALGARY
HARTFORD	AT	EDMONTON
TORONTO	AT	VANCOUVER

Thu Feb 2

OTTAWA	AT	BOSTON
CHICAGO	AT	NY RANGERS
BUFFALO	AT	NEW JERSEY
NY ISLANDERS	AT	PHILADELPHIA
QUEBEC	AT	WASHINGTON
MONTREAL	AT	FLORIDA
LOS ANGELES	AT	ST LOUIS
TAMPA BAY	AT	DALLAS
PITTSBURGH	AT	WINNIPEG

Fri Feb 3

HARTFORD	AT	CALGARY
TORONTO	AT	EDMONTON
DETROIT	AT	ANAHEIM

Sat Feb 4

* NY ISLANDERS	AT	BOSTON
TAMPA BAY	AT	PITTSBURGH
NY RANGERS	AT	OTTAWA
VANCOUVER	AT	MONTREAL
* SAN JOSE	AT	QUEBEC
* CHICAGO	AT	NEW JERSEY
* BUFFALO	AT	PHILADELPHIA
FLORIDA	AT	WASHINGTON
DALLAS	AT	ST LOUIS
HARTFORD	AT	WINNIPEG
TORONTO	AT	CALGARY
DETROIT	AT	LOS ANGELES

Sun Feb 5

* NEW JERSEY	AT	QUEBEC
DALLAS	AT	FLORIDA
* EDMONTON	AT	ANAHEIM

Mon Feb 6

VANCOUVER	AT	OTTAWA
SAN JOSE	AT	MONTREAL
WINNIPEG	AT	NY RANGERS
TAMPA BAY	AT	DETROIT
(Hamilton)		
EDMONTON	AT	LOS ANGELES

Tue Feb 7

NY RANGERS	AT	BOSTON
FLORIDA	AT	PITTSBURGH
DALLAS	AT	BUFFALO
VANCOUVER	AT	QUEBEC
WINNIPEG	AT	NY ISLANDERS
PHILADELPHIA	AT	TORONTO

Wed Feb 8

SAN JOSE	AT	HARTFORD
MONTREAL	AT	OTTAWA
LOS ANGELES	AT	NEW JERSEY
WASHINGTON	AT	TAMPA BAY
CHICAGO	AT	EDMONTON
CALGARY	AT	ANAHEIM

Thu Feb 9

SAN JOSE	AT	BOSTON
QUEBEC	AT	PITTSBURGH
FLORIDA	AT	BUFFALO
NY RANGERS	AT	PHILADELPHIA
LOS ANGELES	AT	DETROIT
ST LOUIS	AT	ANAHEIM
(Las Vegas)		
CHICAGO	AT	VANCOUVER

Fri Feb 10

TORONTO	AT	NEW JERSEY
WASHINGTON	AT	PHILADELPHIA
(Halifax)		
HARTFORD	AT	TAMPA BAY
CALGARY	AT	DALLAS
WINNIPEG	AT	EDMONTON

Sat Feb 11

* LOS ANGELES	AT	BOSTON
MONTREAL	AT	PITTSBURGH
OTTAWA	AT	QUEBEC
* SAN JOSE	AT	NY ISLANDERS
NY RANGERS	AT	TAMPA BAY
HARTFORD	AT	FLORIDA
BUFFALO	AT	TORONTO
CALGARY	AT	ST LOUIS
DETROIT	AT	DALLAS
WINNIPEG	AT	VANCOUVER

Sun Feb 12

BOSTON	AT	BUFFALO
* NEW JERSEY	AT	WASHINGTON
(Halifax)		
PITTSBURGH	AT	FLORIDA
DETROIT	AT	ST LOUIS
* ANAHEIM	AT	EDMONTON

Mon Feb 13

HARTFORD	AT	MONTREAL
LOS ANGELES	AT	PHILADELPHIA
NY ISLANDERS	AT	TAMPA BAY
TORONTO	AT	DALLAS
ANAHEIM	AT	CALGARY

Tue Feb 14

EDMONTON	AT	PITTSBURGH

Wed Feb 15

MONTREAL	AT	HARTFORD
NY RANGERS	AT	BUFFALO
ST LOUIS	AT	NEW JERSEY
TAMPA BAY	AT	WASHINGTON
NY ISLANDERS	AT	FLORIDA
CHICAGO	AT	TORONTO
EDMONTON	AT	DETROIT
BOSTON	AT	DALLAS
CALGARY	AT	WINNIPEG
OTTAWA	AT	SAN JOSE
QUEBEC	AT	ANAHEIM

Thu Feb 16
MONTREAL   AT NY RANGERS
ST LOUIS   AT PHILADELPHIA
PITTSBURGH   AT CHICAGO
SAN JOSE   AT VANCOUVER
QUEBEC   AT LOS ANGELES

Fri Feb 17
NY ISLANDERS   AT NEW JERSEY
BOSTON   AT TAMPA BAY
BUFFALO   AT FLORIDA
WASHINGTON   AT DETROIT
DALLAS   AT WINNIPEG
OTTAWA   AT ANAHEIM

Sat Feb 18
* PITTSBURGH   AT HARTFORD
ST LOUIS   AT MONTREAL
NEW JERSEY   AT NY ISLANDERS
* EDMONTON   AT PHILADELPHIA
DETROIT   AT WASHINGTON
BUFFALO   AT TAMPA BAY
NY RANGERS   AT TORONTO
DALLAS   AT CALGARY
QUEBEC   AT SAN JOSE
OTTAWA   AT LOS ANGELES

Sun Feb 19
* HARTFORD   AT PITTSBURGH
BOSTON   AT FLORIDA
* WINNIPEG   AT CHICAGO
LOS ANGELES   AT ANAHEIM

Mon Feb 20
WINNIPEG   AT BUFFALO
* TORONTO   AT NY RANGERS
* MONTREAL   AT WASHINGTON
NY ISLANDERS   AT DETROIT
EDMONTON   AT ST LOUIS
DALLAS   AT CALGARY
QUEBEC   AT VANCOUVER
(Saskatoon)
* PHILADELPHIA AT SAN JOSE

Tue Feb 21
PITTSBURGH   AT NEW JERSEY
OTTAWA   AT CHICAGO
ANAHEIM   AT LOS ANGELES

Wed Feb 22
BOSTON   AT HARTFORD
NY ISLANDERS   AT BUFFALO

TAMPA BAY   AT DETROIT
TORONTO   AT ST LOUIS
VANCOUVER   AT WINNIPEG
SAN JOSE   AT CALGARY
(Phoenix)
DALLAS   AT EDMONTON
PHILADELPHIA   AT ANAHEIM

Thu Feb 23
QUEBEC   AT OTTAWA
TAMPA BAY   AT NEW JERSEY
MONTREAL   AT FLORIDA
WASHINGTON   AT CHICAGO
PHILADELPHIA   AT LOS ANGELES

Fri Feb 24
ST LOUIS   AT PITTSBURGH
HARTFORD   AT NY RANGERS
NY ISLANDERS   AT TORONTO
VANCOUVER   AT DALLAS
DETROIT   AT WINNIPEG
ANAHEIM   AT SAN JOSE

Sat Feb 25
BUFFALO   AT HARTFORD
FLORIDA   AT OTTAWA
TORONTO   AT MONTREAL
BOSTON   AT QUEBEC
PITTSBURGH   AT NY ISLANDERS
* WASHINGTON   AT NEW JERSEY
CHICAGO   AT ST LOUIS
PHILADELPHIA   AT EDMONTON
CALGARY   AT LOS ANGELES

Sun Feb 26
NY RANGERS   AT BUFFALO
* NEW JERSEY   AT WASHINGTON
DETROIT   AT CHICAGO
* TAMPA BAY   AT SAN JOSE
* VANCOUVER   AT ANAHEIM

Mon Feb 27
FLORIDA   AT MONTREAL
(Hamilton)
ST LOUIS   AT TORONTO

Tue Feb 28
QUEBEC   AT BOSTON
SAN JOSE   AT BUFFALO
CHICAGO   AT OTTAWA
HARTFORD   AT NY ISLANDERS
FLORIDA   AT NY RANGERS

EDMONTON   AT CALGARY
PITTSBURGH   AT VANCOUVER
TAMPA BAY   AT LOS ANGELES

Wed Mar 1
NEW JERSEY   AT HARTFORD
SAN JOSE   AT TORONTO
OTTAWA   AT DETROIT
MONTREAL   AT DALLAS
VANCOUVER   AT EDMONTON
TAMPA BAY   AT ANAHEIM

Thu Mar 2
NEW JERSEY   AT BOSTON
FLORIDA   AT PHILADELPHIA
NY ISLANDERS   AT WASHINGTON
BUFFALO   AT CHICAGO
QUEBEC   AT WINNIPEG
PITTSBURGH   AT CALGARY
LOS ANGELES   AT ST LOUIS
(Las Vegas)

Fri Mar 3
PHILADELPHIA   AT NY RANGERS
TORONTO   AT DETROIT
ANAHEIM   AT DALLAS
PITTSBURGH   AT EDMONTON

Sat Mar 4
* OTTAWA   AT BOSTON
* CHICAGO   AT HARTFORD
BUFFALO   AT QUEBEC
NY RANGERS   AT NY ISLANDERS
* FLORIDA   AT NEW JERSEY
SAN JOSE   AT WASHINGTON
CALGARY   AT TORONTO
* ST LOUIS   AT WINNIPEG
MONTREAL   AT LOS ANGELES

Sun Mar 5
BOSTON   AT HARTFORD
CALGARY   AT BUFFALO
NY ISLANDERS   AT OTTAWA
SAN JOSE   AT PHILADELPHIA
ANAHEIM   AT FLORIDA
* ST LOUIS   AT CHICAGO
* DETROIT   AT EDMONTON

Mon Mar 6
PITTSBURGH   AT QUEBEC
NEW JERSEY   AT NY RANGERS
ANAHEIM   AT TAMPA BAY

LOS ANGELES	AT	DALLAS
DETROIT	AT	VANCOUVER

Tue Mar 7

NEW JERSEY	AT	NY ISLANDERS
CALGARY	AT	WASHINGTON
WINNIPEG	AT	CHICAGO
OTTAWA	AT	ST LOUIS

Wed Mar 8

PHILADELPHIA	AT	HARTFORD
WASHINGTON	AT	MONTREAL
BUFFALO	AT	NY RANGERS
QUEBEC	AT	FLORIDA
DALLAS	AT	WINNIPEG
EDMONTON	AT	SAN JOSE

Thu Mar 9

QUEBEC	AT	PITTSBURGH
MONTREAL	AT	NY ISLANDERS
CALGARY	AT	PHILADELPHIA
BOSTON	AT	TAMPA BAY
(Minnesota)		
LOS ANGELES	AT	TORONTO
CHICAGO	AT	OTTAWA
(Phoenix)		
HARTFORD	AT	ST LOUIS
EDMONTON	AT	VANCOUVER
DETROIT	AT	ANAHEIM

Fri Mar 10

FLORIDA	AT	WASHINGTON
BUFFALO	AT	WINNIPEG
DETROIT	AT	SAN JOSE

Sat Mar 11

* CALGARY	AT	PITTSBURGH
NY RANGERS	AT	MONTREAL
NY ISLANDERS	AT	QUEBEC
PHILADELPHIA	AT	TAMPA BAY
NEW JERSEY	AT	TORONTO
LOS ANGELES	AT	WINNIPEG
OTTAWA	AT	VANCOUVER
ANAHEIM	AT	DALLAS
(San Antonio)		

Sun Mar 12

* BOSTON	AT	WASHINGTON
DETROIT	AT	FLORIDA
(Denver)		
* CALGARY	AT	CHICAGO
BUFFALO	AT	ST LOUIS

OTTAWA	AT	EDMONTON
* HARTFORD	AT	SAN JOSE

Mon Mar 13

WINNIPEG	AT	PITTSBURGH
NY RANGERS	AT	PHILADELPHIA
WASHINGTON	AT	TAMPA BAY
TORONTO	AT	DALLAS

Tue Mar 14

BUFFALO	AT	BOSTON
(Hamilton)		
QUEBEC	AT	NEW JERSEY
CHICAGO	AT	DETROIT
ST LOUIS	AT	EDMONTON
NY ISLANDERS	AT	VANCOUVER
HARTFORD	AT	LOS ANGELES

Wed Mar 15

WINNIPEG	AT	MONTREAL
NEW JERSEY	AT	NY RANGERS
WASHINGTON	AT	FLORIDA
PHILADELPHIA	AT	DALLAS
OTTAWA	AT	CALGARY
TORONTO	AT	SAN JOSE
HARTFORD	AT	ANAHEIM

Thu Mar 16

MONTREAL	AT	BOSTON
TAMPA BAY	AT	PITTSBURGH
DETROIT	AT	BUFFALO
WINNIPEG	AT	QUEBEC
VANCOUVER	AT	CHICAGO
ST LOUIS	AT	LOS ANGELES

Fri Mar 17

VANCOUVER	AT	DETROIT
SAN JOSE	AT	CALGARY
NY ISLANDERS	AT	EDMONTON
TORONTO	AT	ANAHEIM

Sat Mar 18

* BUFFALO	AT	BOSTON
HARTFORD	AT	CHICAGO
(Phoenix)		
* PITTSBURGH	AT	OTTAWA
DALLAS	AT	MONTREAL
* TAMPA BAY	AT	NEW JERSEY
NY RANGERS	AT	WASHINGTON
PHILADELPHIA	AT	FLORIDA
TORONTO	AT	LOS ANGELES

Sun Mar 19

* TAMPA BAY	AT	BUFFALO
DALLAS	AT	OTTAWA
* PITTSBURGH	AT	QUEBEC
BOSTON	AT	NEW JERSEY
* SAN JOSE	AT	WINNIPEG
NY ISLANDERS	AT	CALGARY
* ST LOUIS	AT	ANAHEIM

Mon Mar 20

MONTREAL	AT	PHILADELPHIA
TORONTO	AT	EDMONTON
(Saskatoon)		
FLORIDA	AT	LOS ANGELES

Tue Mar 21

PITTSBURGH	AT	BUFFALO
OTTAWA	AT	WASHINGTON
NY RANGERS	AT	DALLAS
DETROIT	AT	CALGARY
NEW JERSEY	AT	EDMONTON
ST LOUIS	AT	VANCOUVER
CHICAGO	AT	SAN JOSE
FLORIDA	AT	ANAHEIM

Wed Mar 22

QUEBEC	AT	HARTFORD
BOSTON	AT	MONTREAL
OTTAWA	AT	TAMPA BAY
DETROIT	AT	WINNIPEG

Thu Mar 23

PHILADELPHIA	AT	NY ISLANDERS
CALGARY	AT	NY RANGERS
(Phoenix)		
ANAHEIM	AT	ST LOUIS
EDMONTON	AT	DALLAS
NEW JERSEY	AT	VANCOUVER
FLORIDA	AT	SAN JOSE
CHICAGO	AT	LOS ANGELES

Fri Mar 24

MONTREAL	AT	PITTSBURGH
QUEBEC	AT	BUFFALO
BOSTON	AT	TAMPA BAY
WINNIPEG	AT	TORONTO
NEW JERSEY	AT	CALGARY

Sat Mar 25

* NY ISLANDERS	AT	HARTFORD
BUFFALO	AT	MONTREAL
OTTAWA	AT	QUEBEC

* ANAHEIM	AT	WASHINGTON
TORONTO	AT	WINNIPEG
DETROIT	AT	VANCOUVER
* SAN JOSE	AT	LOS ANGELES

Sun Mar 26

EDMONTON	AT	OTTAWA
* ANAHEIM	AT	NY ISLANDERS
PITTSBURGH	AT	PHILADELPHIA
* HARTFORD	AT	WASHINGTON
TAMPA BAY	AT	FLORIDA
* DALLAS	AT	CHICAGO
BOSTON	AT	ST LOUIS
VANCOUVER	AT	CALGARY
* LOS ANGELES	AT	SAN JOSE

Mon Mar 27

MONTREAL	AT	TAMPA BAY
EDMONTON	AT	TORONTO
CHICAGO	AT	DALLAS

Tue Mar 28

NY ISLANDERS	AT	BOSTON
PHILADELPHIA	AT	PITTSBURGH
ST LOUIS	AT	QUEBEC
NY RANGERS	AT	DETROIT
WINNIPEG	AT	SAN JOSE

Wed Mar 29

EDMONTON	AT	BUFFALO
ST LOUIS	AT	OTTAWA
WASHINGTON	AT	TAMPA BAY
HARTFORD	AT	FLORIDA
DALLAS	AT	TORONTO
DETROIT	AT	CHICAGO
LOS ANGELES	AT	VANCOUVER
WINNIPEG	AT	ANAHEIM

Thu Mar 30

BOSTON	AT	PITTSBURGH
MONTREAL	AT	NY ISLANDERS
QUEBEC	AT	NY RANGERS
NEW JERSEY	AT	PHILADELPHIA

Fri Mar 31

PHILADELPHIA	AT	WASHINGTON
HARTFORD	AT	TAMPA BAY
QUEBEC	AT	CHICAGO

Sat Apr 1

* NY RANGERS	AT	BOSTON
* BUFFALO	AT	NY ISLANDERS

MONTREAL	AT	NEW JERSEY
* DETROIT	AT	DALLAS
WINNIPEG	AT	LOS ANGELES

Sun Apr 2

* OTTAWA	AT	BUFFALO
* NY ISLANDERS	AT	QUEBEC
* BOSTON	AT	PHILADELPHIA
* FLORIDA	AT	TAMPA BAY
* PITTSBURGH	AT	TORONTO
* ST LOUIS	AT	DETROIT
* NY RANGERS	AT	CHICAGO
* WASHINGTON	AT	DALLAS
* CALGARY	AT	VANCOUVER
* SAN JOSE	AT	ANAHEIM

Mon Apr 3

MONTREAL	AT	OTTAWA
EDMONTON	AT	LOS ANGELES

Tue Apr 4

PHILADELPHIA	AT	BOSTON
ST LOUIS	AT	BUFFALO
PITTSBURGH	AT	NY ISLANDERS
HARTFORD	AT	NEW JERSEY
DALLAS	AT	VANCOUVER

Wed Apr 5

TORONTO	AT	HARTFORD
NEW JERSEY	AT	PITTSBURGH
QUEBEC	AT	MONTREAL
WASHINGTON	AT	NY RANGERS
OTTAWA	AT	FLORIDA
CHICAGO	AT	WINNIPEG
CALGARY	AT	SAN JOSE
EDMONTON	AT	ANAHEIM

Thu Apr 6

MONTREAL	AT	QUEBEC
BOSTON	AT	NY ISLANDERS
TAMPA BAY	AT	PHILADELPHIA
TORONTO	AT	CHICAGO
DETROIT	AT	ST LOUIS
VANCOUVER	AT	LOS ANGELES

Fri Apr 7

WASHINGTON	AT	BUFFALO
OTTAWA	AT	NY RANGERS
FLORIDA	AT	WINNIPEG
LOS ANGELES	AT	CALGARY
EDMONTON	AT	SAN JOSE
DALLAS	AT	ANAHEIM

Sat Apr 8

* TAMPA BAY	AT	BOSTON
* NEW JERSEY	AT	HARTFORD
QUEBEC	AT	OTTAWA
PITTSBURGH	AT	MONTREAL
BUFFALO	AT	WASHINGTON
DETROIT	AT	TORONTO
VANCOUVER	AT	CALGARY

Sun Apr 9

* TAMPA BAY	AT	HARTFORD
* NY RANGERS	AT	NEW JERSEY
* BOSTON	AT	CHICAGO
* PHILADELPHIA	AT	ST LOUIS
* FLORIDA	AT	DALLAS
* NY ISLANDERS	AT	WINNIPEG
SAN JOSE	AT	EDMONTON
* LOS ANGELES	AT	ANAHEIM

* DENOTES AFTERNOON GAME